# FIRST STEPS In Arabic Grammar

# الخطوات الأولى في القواعد العربية

By
**Yasien Mohamed and Muhammed Haron**

New Revised and Expanded Edition

**Fadel Abdallah**

 IQRA' International Educational Foundation

# Part of a Comprehensive and Systematic Program of Arabic Studies

**First Steps in Arabic Grammar**

A Textbook in the
Program of
Arabic Studies
Levels: Junior / Senior / General

New Revised and Expanded Edition

**Chief Program Editors**

Dr. Abidullah al-Ansari Ghazi
(Ph.D., History of Religion
Harvard University)

Tasneema Khatoon Ghazi
(Ph.D., Curriculum-Reading
University of Minnesota)

**Language Editing**

Fadel Abdallah
(M.A. Arabic & Islamic Studies,
University of Minnesota)

**Arabic Typesetting**

Randa Zaiter

Kamal Nazzal
(M.S. Civil Engineering, Moscow)

**Design**
Norlela Ahmed Yusoff

**Cover Design**
Aliuddin Khaja

**Production Coordinator**
Aliuddin Khaja

Printing February, 2007
Printed in China

Copyright © 2007, IQRA' International Educational Foundation. All Rights Reserved.

**Special note on copyright:**
This book is a part of IQRA's comprehensive and systematic program of Islamic Education.

No part of this book may be reproduced by any means including photocopying, electronic, mechanical, recording, or otherwise without the written consent of the publisher. In specific cases, permission is granted on written request to publish or translate IQRA's works. For information regarding permission, write to:
**IQRA' International Educational Foundation,
7450 Skokie Blvd., Skokie, IL 60077
Tel: 847-673-4072
Fax : 847-673-4095**

ISBN # 1-56316-016-1
Library of Congress Number 97-73903

# Table of Contents

IQRA's Note for Teachers and Students .................................................................. 3

Forward .................................................................. 4

Lesson 1: Parts of Speech: Noun, Verb, Particle .................................................................. 5

Lesson 2: The Noun: Masculine & Feminine .................................................................. 10

Lesson 3: The Adjective / The Adjectival Phrase .................................................................. 14

Lesson 4: The Feminine Noun / The Feminine Adjective .................................................................. 20

Lesson 5: Indefiniteness and Definiteness in Nouns and Adjectives .................................................................. 28

Lesson 6: The Sun and Moon Letters: Pronunciation and Writing with the Definite Article .................................................................. 34

Lesson 7: The Demonstrative Pronouns for Closeness and The Demonstrative Pronouns for Distance .................................................................. 40

Lesson 8: The Personal Subject Pronouns for: He / She / You (masculine) / You (feminine) / I .................................................................. 45

Lesson 9: The Suffix Possessive Pronouns for: His / Her / Your (masculine) / Your (feminine) / My .................................................................. 51

Lesson 10: The Nominal Sentence: Subject and Predicate .................................................................. 58

Lesson 11: The Interrogative (Question) Structures and Its Particles for: Is / Are...?/ What ...? / Who...? / How...? / Where...? .................................................................. 64

Lesson 12: The Interrogative (Question) Structures and Its Particles for: When...?/ How many ...? / What (action)...? / Why...? .................................................................. 72

Lesson 13: The Adverb (عِنْدَ) and Its Particulars .................................................................. 80

Lesson 14: The Prepositions: Their Meanings and Grammatical Function .................................................................. 85

Lesson 15: The Division of Nouns According to Numbers: Singular & Dual .................................................................. 92

Lesson 16: The Nominal Sentences: The Subject and Predicate with Dual Nouns ... 100

Lesson 17: The Types of Plurals: Masculine Sound Plural .................................................................. 108

Lesson 18: The Nominal Sentences: The Subject and Predicate with Masculine Sound Plurals .................................................................. 116

Lesson 19: The Types of Plurals: Feminine Sound Plural .................................................................. 125

**Lesson 20: The Adjectival Phrase with Feminine Sound Plurals for Humans and Non-Humans** .................................................................................. 134

**Lesson 21: The Types of Plurals: Broken Plural** ............................................ 139

**Lesson 22: The Conjunction Structures and Its Particles** ................................ 147

**Lesson 23: The *Idafah* Linguistic Structures ( تَرْكِيبُ الإِضَافَة )** ...................... 157

**Lesson 24: The Verb and Its Divisions: The Past (Perfect) Tense** ................. 163

**Lesson 25: The Present (Imperfect) Tense Verb** ............................................ 173

**Lesson 26: The Imperative (Command) Tense Verb** ..................................... 185

**Lesson 27: The Verb with Suffix (Attached) Pronouns** ................................. 196

**Revision Exercises: Section 1** ......................................................................... 204

**Revision Exercises: Section 2** ......................................................................... 210

**Revision Exercises: Section 3** ......................................................................... 216

**Revision Exercises: Section 4** ......................................................................... 222

**Appendices: Appendix 1: Greetings, Courtesy Expressions and Class Management Prompts** ............................................................................. 236

**Appendices: Appendix 2: Arabic Grammatical Terminology** ....................... 238

**Appendices: Appendix 3: Pronouns Paradigm: Subject Pronouns, Possessive Pronouns and Object Pronouns** ................................................... 240

**Appendices: Appendix 4: Prepositions and Adverbs of Time and Place** ...... 241

**Appendices: Appendix 5: Arabic Speaking States, Nationalities & Capital Cities** ... 243

**Appendices: Appendix 6: The Months of the Year According to Three Calendar Systems, Used in Arabic Countries, The Days of the Week, and the Four Seasons of the Year** ............................... 244

**Appendices: Appendix 7: Past Tense Verb Conjugation Chart** ..................... 246

**Appendices: Appendix 8: Present Indicative Verb Conjugation Chart** ......... 247

**Appendices: Appendix 9: Numerals: Cardinals, Ordinal, Multiples of Ten** .. 249

**Appendices: Appendix 10: English-Arabic Glossary** ..................................... 252

## IQRA' NOTE FOR TEACHERS AND STUDENTS

**First Steps in Arabic Grammar Part One,** is a grammar manual textbook, written and field tested by two South African professors of Arabic. It is written in simple language and the rules of grammar are gradually explained in a lucid language so that both young students and adult learners can understand and follow it without much difficulty. The present edition of this book is thoroughly revised by the scholar and educator of Arabic Language, Mr. Fadl Abdullah.

This book is part of IQRA's Program of Arabic Studies, but it can be followed as an independent textbook on Arabic grammar for junior high, high school, college students and adults. For the students who have studied IQRA' Arabic Reader series, this volume provides a natural transition to a formal introduction to Arabic grammar.

Though IQRA' has embarked a year ago on producing a second generation of expanded and improved IQRA' Arabic Reader series, First Steps in Arabic Grammar will continue to be a relevant supplementary volume for the Arabic program, since its lessons cover the basic grammatical rules of Arabic, which are permanent and universal, no matter what the new generation would look like.

This present volume will be followed, *in-sha'-Allah*, by **Second Steps in Arabic Grammar**, which will cover more advanced aspects of Arabic grammar.

Your encouragement, feed back, prayers, moral and financial support will always help us in continuing IQRA's pioneering and unique efforts in the field of education for generations to come.

The Chief Editors,
Skokie, IL
*Shawwal* 1427 / December 14th, 2006

# FOREWORD

The present book is a thoroughly revised and expanded new edition of **First Steps in Arabic Grammar**. Generally speaking, the language of this book is simple, and the rules of grammar are gradually explained in a lucid language that beginning students of Arabic language can understand without much difficulty. Though this is not a book for self-teaching, students who have acquired certain level of proficiency in Arabic can use it as a reference grammar book in conjunction with a higher level course in Arabic language. However, the usage of this book can yield best results if used with the help of and under the supervision of an instructor of Arabic language.

Thoroughly revised and expanded by IQRA' expert on Arabic language, Fadel Abdallah, this edition contains a more thorough and systemic covering of the topics than the original edition. Few more topics were added, the arrangement of the topics has been modified to make the presentation more cohesive and logical. .

This book is divided into relatively 27 short lessons that can be handled by an expert teacher in one to two contact hours in the classroom . Each lesson is introduced through model sentences, followed by explanation of the focal point of grammar, and then the rule is stated in a summary format, easy to remember. A section of each lesson highlights a selected vocabulary used in each lesson along with its English meanings. Further focused drills provide the learners with a practical way to reinforce the rules learned and acquire at a higher level of competency. The book ends with several sections of general drills along with easy to refer to reference lists in the form of appendices.

Those who have used the first for field-testing edition and found it useful, will be delighted to see the many improvements this new edition contains, both in content and format. Furthermore, it might be assuring for the users of this new edition that the editor and reviewer of this new edition is just a phone call or an e-mail way for further consultation on how best to use this book for best results and for any further general consultation on teaching and learning Arabic in general.

Fadel Abdallah, Head of Arabic Department
7450 Skokie Blvd. Skokie, IL 60077
*Shawwal* 1427 / October 2006
Phone: (847) 673-4072, Ext. 226; E-mail: fadel @iqra.org

# Lesson 1 — الدَّرْسُ الأَوَّلُ

## أَقْسَامُ الكَلِمَةِ : إِسْمٌ ، فِعْلٌ ، حَرْفٌ
### Parts of Speech: Noun, Verb, Particle

❖ Speech is divided into three main parts:

(1) **Noun**, (إِسْمٌ) in Arabic,

(2) **Verb** (فِعْلٌ) in Arabic,

(3) **Particle** (حَرْفٌ) in Arabic,

❖ The <u>noun</u> is any class or words denoting a thing, a person, a place or a quality, such as:

| | | | |
|---|---|---|---|
| Mary | = مَرْيَمُ | Adam | = آدَمُ |
| a pen | = قَلَمٌ | a book | = كِتَابٌ |
| Baghdadnew | = بَغْدَادُ | Iraq | = الْعِرَاقُ |
| new | = جَدِيدٌ | beautiful | = جَمِيلٌ |

❖ The verb is any class of words denoting an action related to a specific time in the past, present or future or requestiong an action (command verbs), such as:

| | | | |
|---|---|---|---|
| she drank | = شَرِبَتْ | he ate | = أَكَلَ |
| she plays | = تَلْعَبُ | he writes | = يَكْتُبُ |
| he will go | = سَيَذْهَبُ | I will study | = سَأَدْرُسُ |
| Listen! (imperative) | = اِسْمَعْ! | Say! (imperative) | = قُلْ! |

5

❖ The <u>particle</u> is usually a short, uninflected part of speech that does not convey an independent meaning in itself, but is used to show syntactical relationships with the two other parts of speech; such as the <u>definite article</u>, <u>prepositions</u>, <u>conjunctions</u> or <u>interrogative</u> particles:

| | | | | | |
|---|---|---|---|---|---|
| the | = | ال | in | = | فِي |
| to | = | إِلَى | from | = | مِنْ |
| and | = | وَ | or | = | أَوْ |
| How...? | = | كَيْفَ...؟ | Where...? | = | أَيْنَ...؟ |

❖ **Additional New Vocabulary**:

| | | | | |
|---|---|---|---|---|
| a father | أَبٌ | | a house | بَيْتٌ |
| he laughed | ضَحِكَ | | Who...? | مَنْ...؟ |
| then | ثُمَّ | | you | أَنْتَ |
| a boy | وَلَدٌ | | a lesson | دَرْسٌ |
| a man | رَجُلٌ | | easy | سَهْلٌ |
| on | عَلَى | | a desk | مَكْتَبٌ |
| a pupil | تِلْمِيذٌ | | he jumped | قَفَزَ |
| a friend | صَدِيقٌ | | What...? | مَا...؟ |
| he | هُوَ | | this | هَذَا |
| did you know | عَرَفْتَ | | dear | عَزِيزٌ |

❖ **Examples of Full Meaningful Sentences Containing the Three Different Parts of Speech:**

| | |
|---|---|
| He is a dear father. | ١- هُوَ أَبٌ عَزِيزٌ . = |
| This is a new book. | ٢- هَذَا كِتَابٌ جَدِيدٌ . = |
| Where is Baghdad? | ٣- أَيْنَ بَغْدَادُ ؟ = |
| Bahdad is in Iraq. | ٤- بَغْدَادُ في الْعِرَاقِ . = |
| Who is this man? | ٥- مَنْ هَذا الرَّجُلُ ؟ = |
| The pupil laughed. | ٦- ضَحِكَ التِّلْمِيذُ . = |
| The house is beautiful. | ٧- الْبَيْتُ جَمِيلٌ . = |
| How are you ? | ٨- كَيْفَ أَنْتَ ؟ = |
| The book is on the desk. | ٩- الْكِتَابُ عَلَى الْمَكْتَبِ . = |
| He ate then he drank. | ١٠- أَكَلَ ثُمَّ شَرِبَ . = |
| Where is the man from? | ١١- مِنْ أَيْنَ الرَّجُلُ ؟ = |

\* \* \*

Remember! / تَذَكَّرْ- تَذَكَّرِي!

1. The parts of speech are three: **Noun**, **Verb**, and **Particle**.
2. Pronouns and adjectives fall under the category of nouns.
3. Particles do not denote a thing, a person, a place, or a quality.

2. Like English too, Arabic nouns are divided into: Masculine (مُذَكَّر) and Feminine (مُؤَنَّث).

3. Also like English, nouns may be either definite or indefinite.

4. It is characteristic of indefinite nouns in Arabic to receive a "*Tanween*" over the last letter of the noun.

5. Pronouns like (هُوَ) and (هَذَا) are definite in nature; therefore they do not receive the "*Tanween*".

* * *

## تَدْرِيبَاتٌ / Exercises

**1.** Pronounce the following nouns; give their English meanings, and then classify them into two groups: one for <u>humans</u>, and the other for <u>non humans</u> by writing them under the correct column:

١- بَيْتٌ   ٢- رَجُلٌ   ٣- تِلْمِيذٌ

٤- أَبٌ   ٥- بَابٌ   ٦- دَرْسٌ

٧- مُعَلِّمٌ   ٨- كِتَابٌ   ٩- جِدَارٌ

١٠- مَكْتَبٌ   ١١- وَلَدٌ   ١٢- تِلْمِيذٌ

١٣- قَلَمٌ   ١٤- أَخٌ   ١٥- شَارِعٌ

١٦- هُوَ   ١٧- هَذَا   ١٨- مِفْتَاحٌ

١٩- جَدٌّ   ٢٠- صَدِيقٌ   ٢١- وَلَدٌ

| Non-Humans | Humans |
|---|---|
|  |  |

* * *

**2. Pronounce the following non-vocalized nouns and provide the missing vowels:**

هو   ولد   كتاب   مكتب   هذا   جدار

تلميذ   رجل   شارع   إبن   أب   صديق

* * *

**3. Translate the following sentences into Arabic (Orally and written):**

1. He is a pupil. = .................................................

2. This is a book. = .................................................

3. He is a teacher. = .................................................

4. This is a desk. = .................................................

5. This is a house. = .................................................

* * *

**4. Translate the following sentences into English orally:**

................................................. ← ١ - هَذَا قَلَمٌ .

................................................. ← ٢ - هُوَ وَلَدٌ .

................................................. ← ٣ - هُوَ مُعَلِّمٌ .

................................................. ← ٤ - هَذَا تِلْمِيذٌ .

................................................. ← ٥ - هُوَ رَجُلٌ .

................................................. ← ٦ - هَذَا مَكْتَبٌ .

* * *

**Lesson 2** ━━━━━━━━━━━━━━━━━━━━━━━━━━━━━━ الدَّرْسُ الثَّانِي

## الإِسْمُ : الْمُذَكَّرُ وَالْمُؤَنَّثُ
### The Noun: Masculine & Feminine

❖ In Arabic there are only two genders:

   (a) **Masculine** / مُذَكَّرٌ        (b) **Feminine** / مُؤَنَّثٌ

❖ In this lesson, we shall deal only with the nouns that are masculine:

| Its Meaning / مَعْنَاهَا | The Word / الكَلِمَةُ |
|---|---|
| a boy | وَلَدٌ |
| a book | كِتَابٌ |

❖ **Explanatory Notes:**

1. Both nouns above are <u>masculine</u>; وَلَدٌ refers to a <u>person</u>, and كِتَابٌ refers to a thing. Thus, in Arabic the Masculine noun can either refer to a person or to a non-person (i.e. to an object or thing.)
2. Both nouns are <u>indefinite</u>; وَلَدٌ means "a boy", and كِتَابٌ means "a book".
3. Their indefiniteness is indicated by the "*Tanween* of *Dammah*" ( ٌ ), that is, the sign on the last letter of each word.

❖ **Additional New Vocabulary**:

| For Non-Humans / لِغَيْرِ الْعَاقِلِ | For Persons / لِلْعَاقِلِ |
|---|---|
| a house   بَيْتٌ | a father   أَبٌ |
| a door   بَابٌ | a grandfather   جَدٌّ |

| | | | |
|---|---|---|---|
| a brother | أَخٌ | a wall | جِدَارٌ |
| a son | إِبْنٌ | a street | شَارِعٌ |
| a boy | وَلَدٌ | a lesson | دَرْسٌ |
| a man | رَجُلٌ | a pen | قَلَمٌ |
| a teacher | مُعَلِّمٌ | a desk | مَكْتَبٌ |
| a pupil | تِلْمِيذٌ | a key | مِفْتَاحٌ |
| a friend | صَدِيقٌ | this | هَذَا |
| he / this | هُوَ / هَذَا | | |

\* \* \*

❖ **Full Meaningful Sentences Using the Above Vocabulary**:

| For Persons / لِلْعَاقِلِ | For Non-Humans / لِغَيْرِ الْعَاقِلِ |
|---|---|
| هُوَ وَلَدٌ . = He is a boy. | هَذَا كِتَابٌ . = This is a book. |
| هُوَ أَبٌ . = He is a father. | هَذَا بَيْتٌ . = This is a house. |
| هُوَ جَدٌّ . = He is a grandfather. | هَذَا بَابٌ . = This is a door. |
| هُوَ أَخٌ . = He is a brother. | هَذَا جِدَارٌ . = This is a wall. |
| هُوَ رَجُلٌ . = He is a man. | هَذَا شَارِعٌ . = This is a street. |
| هُوَ مُعَلِّمٌ . = He is a teacher. | هَذَا دَرْسٌ . = This is a lesson. |
| هُوَ تِلْمِيذٌ . = He is a pupil. | هَذَا قَلَمٌ . = This is a pen. |
| هُوَ صَدِيقٌ . = He is a friend. | هَذَا مِفْتَاحٌ . = This is a key. |

### تَذَكَّرْ- تَذَكَّرِي! / Remember!

1. In Arabic, like English, nouns may refer to <u>humans</u> or to <u>non-humans</u>.

2. Like English too, Arabic nouns are divided into: <u>Masculine</u> (مُذَكَّر) and <u>Feminine</u> (مُؤَنَّث).

3. Also like English, nouns may be either <u>definite</u> or <u>indefinite</u>.

4. It is characteristic of indefinite nouns in Arabic to receive a "*Tanween*" over the last letter of the noun.

5. Pronouns like (هُوَ) and (هَذَا) are definite in nature; therefore they do not receive the "*Tanween*".

\* \* \*

### تَدْرِيبَاتُ / Exercises

**1.** Pronounce the following nouns; give their English meanings, and then classify them into two groups: one for <u>humans</u>, and the other for <u>non humans</u> by writing them under the correct column:

١- وَلَدٌ    ٢- مِفْتَاحٌ   ٣- صَدِيقٌ

٤- كِتَابٌ   ٥- أَبٌ    ٦- قَلَمٌ

٧- تِلْمِيذٌ   ٨- بَيْتٌ    ٩- جَدٌّ

١٠- دَرْسٌ   ١١- مُعَلِّمٌ   ١٢- بَابٌ

١٣- أَخٌ    ١٤- شَارِعٌ   ١٥- جِدَارٌ

١٦- هُوَ    ١٧- هَذَا

| Non-Humans | Humans |
|---|---|
|  |  |

12

**2. Pronounce the following non-vocalized nouns and provide the missing vowels:**

بيت   جد   مفتاح   قلم   كتاب   ولد

معلم   رجل   شارع   صديق   جدار   درس

\* \* \*

**3. Translate the following sentences into Arabic (Orally and written):**

1. He is a teacher. =  ............................................................

2. This is a wall. =  ............................................................

3. He is a boy. =  ............................................................

4. This is a book. =  ............................................................

5. This is a house. =  ............................................................

\* \* \*

**4. Translate the following sentences into English orally:**

١- هَذَا مَكْتَبٌ .  ⟵  ............................................................

٢- هُوَ تِلْميذٌ .  ⟵  ............................................................

٣- هُوَ مُعَلِّمٌ .  ⟵  ............................................................

٤- هَذَا شَارِعٌ .  ⟵  ............................................................

٥- هُوَ صَديقٌ .  ⟵  ............................................................

٦- هَذَا مِفْتَاحٌ .  ⟵  ............................................................

# Lesson 3 — الدَّرْسُ الثَّالِثُ

## اَلصِّفَةُ (النَّعْتُ) / التَّرْكِيبُ النَّعْتِيُّ
### The Adjective / The Adjectival Phrase

❖ The adjective is a noun with a descriptive quality. It describes a regular noun. It can either be masculine or feminine, and can be definite or indefinite.

❖ In this lesson, we shall deal with adjectives that are masculine and indefinite:

| The Adjective / الصِّفَةُ | Its Meaning / مَعْنَاهَا |
|---|---|
| صَغِيرٌ | small, little |
| كَبِيرٌ | big, large |
| جَدِيدٌ | new |
| قَدِيمٌ | old |
| جَمِيلٌ | beautiful |

\* \* \*

❖ **Explanatory Notes:**

1. Each of the five words above has a descriptive nature for a specific quality; therefore they are all adjectives.
2. They are all in masculine forms, which you will be able to distinguish once you learn their feminine counterparts, which will be introduced later.
3. They are all ending with the sign of the "*Tanween* of *Dammah*" which appears at the end of each of them.
4. Since adjectives tend to describe qualities, which in real life have their own opposites, adjectives very often exist in pairs which we call "Antonyms"; as can be seen from the examples above.
5. It will be a good practice to learn adjectives in pairs of opposite meanings for the purpose of comparing and contrasting.

\* \* \*

## ❖ The Adjectival Phrase:

1. In real language, the adjective does not exist in isolation; it must be connected to a regular noun that it serves to describe.
2. A combination of a noun and an adjective describing it is called either a "Noun-Adjective Phrase" or an "Adjectival Phrase."
3. Now, let's study the following "Noun-Adjective Phrases" as a prelude to learn the rules related to such structures:

| | | | |
|---|---|---|---|
| a big man = رَجُلٌ كَبِيرٌ -٢ | | a little boy = وَلَدٌ صَغِيرٌ -١ |
| an old book = كِتَابٌ قَدِيمٌ -٤ | | a new house = بَيْتٌ جَدِيدٌ -٣ |
| a big man = رَجُلٌ كَبِيرٌ -٦ | | a little boy = وَلَدٌ صَغِيرٌ -٥ |
| a long street = شَارِعٌ طَوِيلٌ -٨ | | a short lesson = دَرْسٌ قَصِيرٌ -٧ |

\* \* \*

## ❖ Explanatory Notes:

1. By examining the "Noun-Adjective Phrases" above, we find out that each consisted of a noun, which is being described, and is called, in Arabic, (مَوْصُوفٌ).
2. Then the noun is being followed by the adjective which describes a certain quality of the preceding noun; an adjective in Arabic is called (نَعْتٌ) or (صِفَةٌ).
3. The adjectives in Arabic not only must follow the nouns they describe, but they must agree with their nouns in regard to four things: Gender: masculine with masculine and feminine with feminine; Number: singular with singular, and plural with plural; Definiteness or Indefiniteness: if the noun is indefinite, then the adjective must be so; if the noun is definite, then the adjective must be so; Case ending: if the noun is nominative, accusative, or genitive, then the adjective must show the same case-ending. We will discuss these issues in future lessons.
4. As far as the examples given are concerned, we should notice that both the nouns and their adjectives are indefinite; therefore they both receive

the "*Tanween* of *Dammah*" which appears at the end of each of them. And they are all masculine in gender.

\* \* \*

❖ **Additional New Vocabulary:**

| happy | سَعيدٌ | | ugly | قَبيحٌ |
| clever | ذَكِيٌّ | | sad | حَزينٌ |
| narrow | ضَيِّقٌ | | good, nice | جَيِّدٌ |
| active, energetic | نَشيطٌ | | wide | عَريضٌ |
| difficult | صَعْبٌ | | easy | سَهْلٌ |
| play ground | مَلْعَبٌ | | scene | مَنْظَرٌ |

\* \* \*

❖ **Full Meaningful Sentences Using the New Vocabulary:**

| This is a new book. | = هَذا كِتابٌ جَديدٌ. | | He is a clever boy. | = هُوَ وَلَدٌ ذَكِيٌّ. |
| This is an old house. | = هَذا بَيْتٌ قَديمٌ. | | He is a happy father. | = هُوَ أَبٌ سَعيدٌ. |
| This is a big door. | = هَذا بابٌ كَبيرٌ. | | He is a good brother. | = هُوَ أَخٌ جَيِّدٌ. |
| This is a long wall. | = هَذا جِدارٌ طَويلٌ. | | He is a sad man. | = هُوَ رَجُلٌ حَزينٌ. |
| This is a narrow street. | = هَذا شارِعٌ ضَيِّقٌ. | | He is a clever pupil. | = هُوَ تِلميذٌ ذَكِيٌّ. |
| This is an easy lesson. | = هَذا دَرْسٌ سَهْلٌ. | | He is a good teacher. | = هُوَ مُعَلِّمٌ جَيِّدٌ. |
| This is a wide play ground. | = هَذا مَلْعَبٌ عَريضٌ | | He is a an active grandfather. | = هُوَ جَدٌّ نَشيطٌ. |
| This is an ugly scene. | = هَذا مَنْظَرٌ قَبيحٌ. | | He is an old friend. | = هُوَ صَديقٌ قَديمٌ. |

\* \* \*

## Remember! / تَذَكَّرْ- تَذَكَّرِي!

1. In Arabic, like English, <u>nouns</u> may have <u>adjectives</u> to describe one of their qualities.

2. Unlike English, Arabic adjectives follow the nouns they describe rather than preceding them.

3. The adjectives must agree with the nouns they describe in respect to <u>gender</u>, <u>number</u>, <u>definiteness or indefiniteness</u>, and <u>case-endings</u>.

4. The Arabic term for the <u>described noun</u> is (إِسْمٌ مَوْصُوفٌ) and the Arabic term for the <u>adjective</u> is (صِفَةٌ) or (نَعْتٌ).

\* \* \*

## Exercises / تَدْرِيبَاتٌ

**1. Give the Arabic equivalent of the following English adjectives:**

| English | Arabic | English | Arabic |
|---------|--------|---------|--------|
| beautiful |  | short |  |
| tall |  | happy |  |
| sad |  | wide |  |
| clever |  | good |  |
| small |  | narrow |  |
| ugly |  | big, large |  |
| sad |  | small, little |  |

**2. From among the Arabic Adjectives you have given above, select the most appropriate one to fill in the blanks of the following sentences:**

١- هُوَ رَجُلٌ ................ .     ٢- هَذا شَارِعٌ ................ .

٣- هُوَ صَدِيقٌ ................ .     ٤- هَذَا مَلْعَبٌ ................ .

٥- هُوَ تِلْمِيذٌ ................ .     ٦- هَذَا كِتَابٌ ................ .

٧- هُوَ مُعَلِّمٌ ................ .     ٨- هَذَا مَنْظَرٌ ................ .

٩- هُوَ أَخٌ ................ .     ١٠- هَذَا قَلَمٌ ................ .

١١- هُوَ أَبٌ ................ .     ١٢- هَذَا بَيْتٌ ................ .

١٣- هُوَ جَدٌّ ................ .     ١٤- هَذَا بَابٌ ................ .

\* \* \*

**3. Translate the following sentences into Arabic (Orally and written):**

1. He is a happy pupil. =   •......................................

2. This is a new book. =   •......................................

3. He is a good teacher. =   •......................................

4. This is an old desk. =   •......................................

5. This is a big house. =   •......................................

\* \* \*

**4. Translate the following sentences into English orally:**

١- هَذَا قَلَمٌ صَغِيرٌ .   ................................

٢- هُوَ وَلَدٌ جَمِيلٌ .   ................................

٣- هُوَ مُعَلِّمٌ .   ................................

٤- هَذَا تِلْمِيذٌ سَعِيدٌ .   ................................

٥- هُوَ رَجُلٌ ذَكِيٌّ .   ................................

4. Many of the adjectives you learned in this lesson stand as antonyms to others; classify the adjectives in the following shaded box into two columns of antonym pairs. The first is done for you as an example:

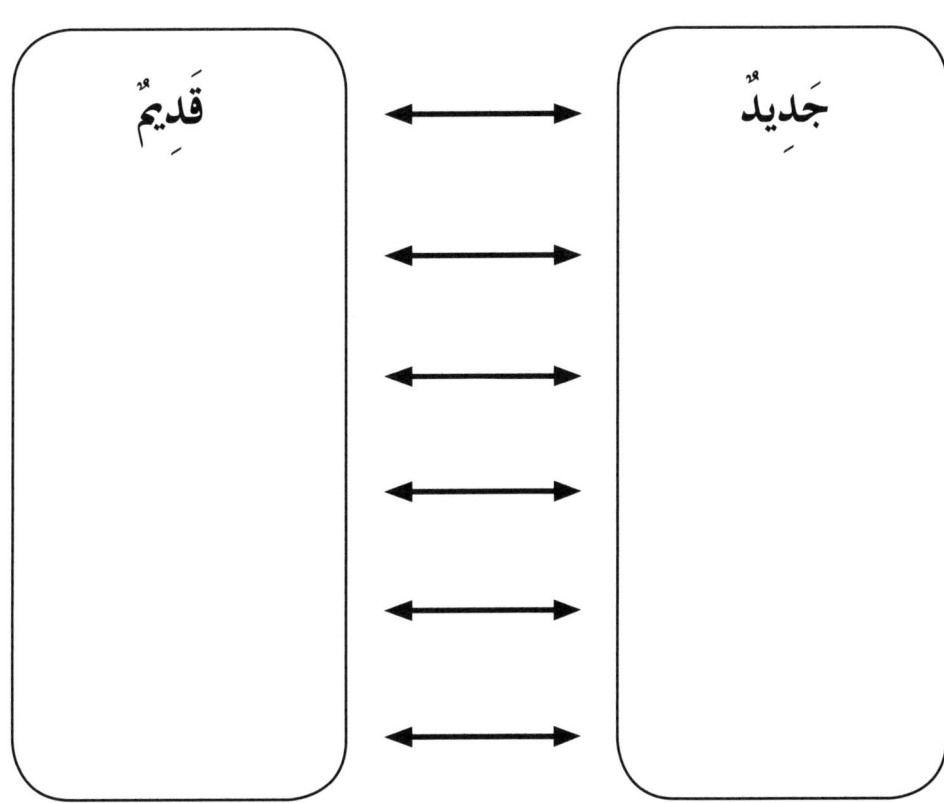

5. (True or False): State whether each of the following statements is true or false; if it is false, modify the statement to make it true:

(A) In Arabic the adjective comes before the noun like English.

(B) Adjectives can be used only to describe human beings.

(C) The Arabic term for the adjective is (صِفَةٌ).

(D) The Arabic term for the described noun is (نَعْتٌ).

(E) Adjectives do not need to agree with the nouns they describe in gender.

\* \* \*

# Lesson 4 — الدَّرْسُ الرَّابِعُ

## الإِسْمُ الْمُؤَنَّثُ / الصِّفَةُ الْمُؤَنَّثَةُ
### The Feminine Noun / The Feminine Adjective

❖ The feminine noun in Arabic, like the masculine, can either refer to a person (human being) or to non-human beings. Examples:

| الإِسْمُ الْمُؤَنَّثُ لِغَيْرِ الْعَاقِلِ | | الإِسْمُ الْمُؤَنَّثُ لِلْعَاقِلِ | |
|---|---|---|---|
| **Feminine Non-Human Nouns** | | **Feminine Human Nouns** | |
| a school | مَدْرَسَةٌ | a female teacher | مُعَلِّمَةٌ |
| a chalkboard | سَبُّورَةٌ | a female doctor | طَبِيبَةٌ |
| a car | سَيَّارَةٌ | a female pupil | تِلْمِيذَةٌ |
| a ruler | مِسْطَرَةٌ | a female friend | صَدِيقَةٌ |
| a food table | مَائِدَةٌ | a female cook | طَبَّاخَةٌ |
| a university | جَامِعَةٌ | a female professor | أُسْتَاذَةٌ |
| a window | نَافِذَةٌ | a female student | طَالِبَةٌ |
| a room | غُرْفَةٌ | a daughter | إِبْنَةٌ |

\* \* \*

❖ **Explanatory Notes:**

1. All the nouns in the right hand column refer to humans; moreover, they are all ending with a "*Taa Marbutah*" (ة / ـة).
2. All the nouns in the left hand column refer to non-humans; yet they also end with a "*Taa Marbutah*" (ة / ـة).

3. In light of this, we can say that the "*Taa Marbutah*" (ة / ـة) is the most dominant sign of feminine gender; however there are few exceptions to this general rule.

4. However, it is not necessary that every feminine noun in Arabic must end with a "*Taa Marbutah*".

5. Another dominant sign of feminine gender is the "*Alif Maqsurah*" (ى / ـى), as in the following:

| | | | |
|---|---|---|---|
| *Layla* (female proper name) | لَيْلَى | *Salma* (female proper name) | سَلْمَى |
| guidance, *Huda* (female proper name) | هُدَى | wish, *Muna* (female proper name) | مُنَى |
| glad tidings, *Bushra* (female proper name) | بُشْرَى | ease | يُسْرَى |
| oldest one | كُبْرَى | youngest one | صُغْرَى |

6. Yet another dominant sign of feminine gender is a non-radical "*long Alif-Hamzah*" at the end of nouns and adjectives; such as:

| | | | |
|---|---|---|---|
| sky | سَمَاءُ | desert | صَحْرَاءُ |
| white | بَيْضَاءُ | black | سَوْدَاءُ |
| green | خَضْرَاءُ | red | حَمْرَاءُ |
| blue | زَرْقَاءُ | yellow | صَفْرَاءُ |

7. Besides these three major categories, one can add another category from the body parts that occur in pairs; such as:

| | | | |
|---|---|---|---|
| an eye | عَيْنٌ | an ear | أُذُنٌ |
| a hand | يَدٌ | a leg | رِجْلٌ |
| an arm | ذِرَاعٌ | | |

21

1. Beyond these, we might encounter words that, despite not falling under one of the main categories mentioned above, they are feminine by their linguistic meanings or frame of reference; such as:

| | | | |
|---|---|---|---|
| a girl | بِنْتٌ | a mother | أُمٌّ |
| a mare | فَرَسٌ | a sister | أُخْتٌ |

2. And finally, the dictionary will determine the gender of certain words whose gender is not determined through one of the criteria mentioned above, as for example:

| | | | |
|---|---|---|---|
| sun | شَمْسٌ | soul | رُوحٌ |

\* \* \*

❖ **Examples of Adjectival Phrases with Feminine Nouns and Adjectives:**

| | | | |
|---|---|---|---|
| a big woman | ٢- إِمْرَأَةٌ كَبِيرَةٌ | a little girl | ١- بِنْتٌ صَغِيرَةٌ |
| a white mare | ٤- فَرَسٌ بَيْضَاءُ | a new school | ٣- مَدْرَسَةٌ جَدِيدَةٌ |
| a noble mother | ٦- أُمٌّ كَرِيمَةٌ | a younger sister | ٥- أُخْتٌ صُغْرَى |
| a red car | ٨- سَيَّارَةٌ حَمْرَاءُ | a short arm | ٧- ذِرَاعٌ قَصِيرَةٌ |

\* \* \*

❖ **Explanatory Notes:**

1. By examining the "Noun-Adjective Phrases" above, we find out that each consisted of a <u>feminine noun</u>, which is being described, and is called, in Arabic, (مَوْصُوفٌ).

2. Then the feminine noun is being followed by a feminine adjective which describes a certain quality of the preceding noun; an adjective in Arabic is called (نَعْتٌ) or (صِفَةٌ).

3. The adjective is agreeing with the noun it modifies in the feminine gender, the singular number, the indefiniteness, and thus the *Tanween*, and finally the case-ending, which is here nominative as indicated by the "*Tanween* of *Dammah*".

## ❖ Additional New Vocabulary:

| | | | |
|---|---|---|---|
| this (feminine) | هَذِهِ | she | هِيَ |
| skillful | مَاهِرَةٌ | dear one | عَزِيزَةٌ |
| a ship | سَفِينَةٌ | excellent | مُمْتَازَةٌ |
| polite, well-mannered | مُهَذَّبَةٌ | a library | مَكْتَبَةٌ |
| shining | سَاطِعَةٌ | a sheet of paper, a leaf | وَرَقَةٌ |

* * *

## ❖ Full Meaningful Sentences Using the New Vocabulary:

| | | | |
|---|---|---|---|
| This is a new library. | = هَذِهِ مَكْتَبَةٌ جَدِيدَةٌ. | She is a clever girl. | = هِيَ بِنْتٌ ذَكِيَّةٌ. |
| This is a white ship. | = هَذِهِ سَفِينَةٌ بَيْضَاءُ. | She is a noble mother. | = هِيَ أُمٌّ كَرِيمَةٌ. |
| This is a long arm. | = هَذِهِ ذِرَاعٌ طَوِيلَةٌ. | She is a happy sister. | = هِيَ أُخْتٌ سَعِيدَةٌ. |
| This is a shining sun. | = هَذِهِ شَمْسٌ سَاطِعَةٌ. | She is a sad woman. | = هِيَ امْرَأَةٌ حَزِينَةٌ. |
| This is a yellow leaf. | = هَذِهِ وَرَقَةٌ صَفْرَاءُ. | She is a polite pupil. | = هِيَ تِلْمِيذَةٌ مُهَذَّبَةٌ. |
| This is a long ear. | = هَذِهِ أُذُنٌ كَبِيرَةٌ. | She is a good teacher. | = هِيَ مُعَلِّمَةٌ جَيِّدَةٌ. |
| This is a small ruler. | = هَذِهِ مِسْطَرَةٌ صَغِيرَةٌ. | She is a skillful cook. | = هِيَ طَبَّاخَةٌ مَاهِرَةٌ. |
| *Salma* is beautiful. | = سَلْمَى جَمِيلَةٌ. | *Huda* is a friend. | = هُدَى صَدِيقَةٌ. |
| This is a short hand. | = هَذِهِ يَدٌ قَصِيرَةٌ. | *Layla* is excellent. | = لَيْلَى مُمْتَازَةٌ. |

* * *

## Remember! / !اتَذَكَّرْ – تَذَكَّري

1. The "*Taa Marbutah*" (ة / ـة) is the most dominant sign of feminine gender in nouns and adjectives.

2. However, it is not necessary that every feminine noun in Arabic must end with a "*Taa Marbutah*".

3. Another dominant sign of feminine gender is the "*Alif Maqsurah*" (ى / ـى).

4. Yet another dominant sign of feminine gender is a non-radical "*long Alif-Hamzah*" (اء) at the end of nouns and adjectives.

5. Besides these three major categories, one can add another category from the body parts that occur in pairs.

6. Beyond these, we might encounter words that, despite not falling under one of the main categories mentioned above, they are feminine by their linguistic meanings or frame of reference.

7. And finally, the dictionary will determine the gender of certain words whose gender is not determined through one of the criteria mentioned above.

8. The majority of nouns and adjectives which occur in real life in masculine-feminine pairs, we can form the feminine gender by adding a "*Taa Marbutah*" (ة / ـة) to the masculine form.

\* \* \*

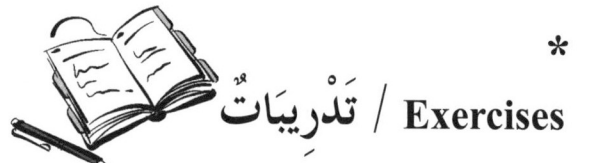 تَدْريباتٌ / Exercises

1. Give the English equivalent of the following feminine adjectival phrases:

١- بِنْتٌ صَغيرَةٌ = ..................    ٢- إمْرَأَةٌ كَبيرَةٌ = ..................

٣- مَدْرَسَةٌ جَديدَةٌ = ..................    ٤- فَرَسٌ سَوْداءُ = ..................

٥- أُخْتٌ كُبْرى = ..................    ٦- أُمٌّ عَزيزَةٌ = ..................

٧- ذِراعٌ طَويلَةٌ = ..................    ٨- سَيّارَةٌ بَيْضاءُ = ..................

24

**3. Give the Arabic equivalent of the following feminine adjectival phrases:**

1. a happy female pupil = ..................................................

2. an old ship = ..................................................

3. s short hand = ..................................................

4. a younger sister = ..................................................

5. a new car = ..................................................

6. a big library = ..................................................

7. a sincere mother = ..................................................

8. a beautiful sister = ..................................................

9. a noble soul = ..................................................

**3. The following box contains mixed masculine and feminine nouns and adjectives; isolate them into two categories, one for masculine ad the other for feminine:**

رَجُلٌ / جَدِيدَةٌ / لَيْلَى / هِيَ / هَذَا / إِمْرَأَةٌ / أَبٌ / أُمٌّ / زَرْقَاءُ / رِجْلٌ / عَيْنٌ / رُوحٌ / أَخٌ / هَذِهِ / هُوَ / سَهْلٌ / قَصِيرٌ / جَمِيلَةٌ / شَمْسٌ / صُغْرَى / كِتَابٌ

| Feminine | Masculine | Feminine | Masculine |
|---|---|---|---|
|  |  |  |  |

4. Fill in the blanks of the following sentences with an appropriate masculine or feminine adjective to make full meaningful sentences; then translate the resultant sentences into English:

١- هُوَ رَجُلٌ ............ .            ٢- هَذه مَدْرَسَةٌ ............ .

٣- هِيَ صَدِيقَةٌ ............ .         ٤- هُوَ أَبٌ ............ .

٥- هَذه سَفِينَةٌ ............ .         ٦- هَذَا كِتَابٌ ............ .

٧- هُوَ مُعَلِّمٌ ............ .          ٨- هَذه سَيَّارَةٌ ............ .

٩- هَذه مُعَلِّمَةٌ ............ .         ١٠- هِيَ تِلْمِيذَةٌ ............ .

١١- هَذه طَبَّاخَةٌ ............ .        ١٢- هُوَ وَلَدٌ ............ .

١٣- هِيَ امْرَأَةٌ ............ .         ١٤- هَذَا دَرْسٌ ............ .

\* \* \*

5. Translate the following sentences into Arabic (Orally and written):

1. She is a happy pupil. =  • ....................................................

2. This is a new table. =  • ....................................................

3. She is an excellent teacher. =  • ....................................................

4. This is an old library. =  • ....................................................

5. She is a good friend. =  • ....................................................

\* \* \*

4. Translate the following sentences into English orally:

١- هَذه مِسْطَرَةٌ صَغِيرَةٌ .             ............................................

٢- هِيَ بِنْتٌ جَمِيلَةٌ .                ............................................

٣- هِيَ مُعَلِّمَةٌ مُخْلِصَةٌ .             ............................................

٤- هَذه جَامِعَةٌ مَشْهُورَةٌ .            ............................................

٥- هِيَ تِلْمِيذَةٌ ذَكِيَّةٌ .              ............................................

4. Many of the adjectives you learned in this lesson stand as antonyms to others; classify the adjectives in the following shaded box into two columns of antonym pairs. The first is done for you as an example:

جَدِيدَةٌ / جَمِيلَةٌ / حَزِينَةٌ / سَعِيدَةٌ / سَهْلَةٌ / صَعْبَةٌ / صَغِيرَةٌ / ضَيِّقَةٌ / غَبِيَّةٌ / طَوِيلَةٌ / عَرِيضَةٌ / قَبِيحَةٌ / قَصِيرَةٌ / قَدِيمَةٌ / كَبِيرَةٌ / ذَكِيَّةٌ

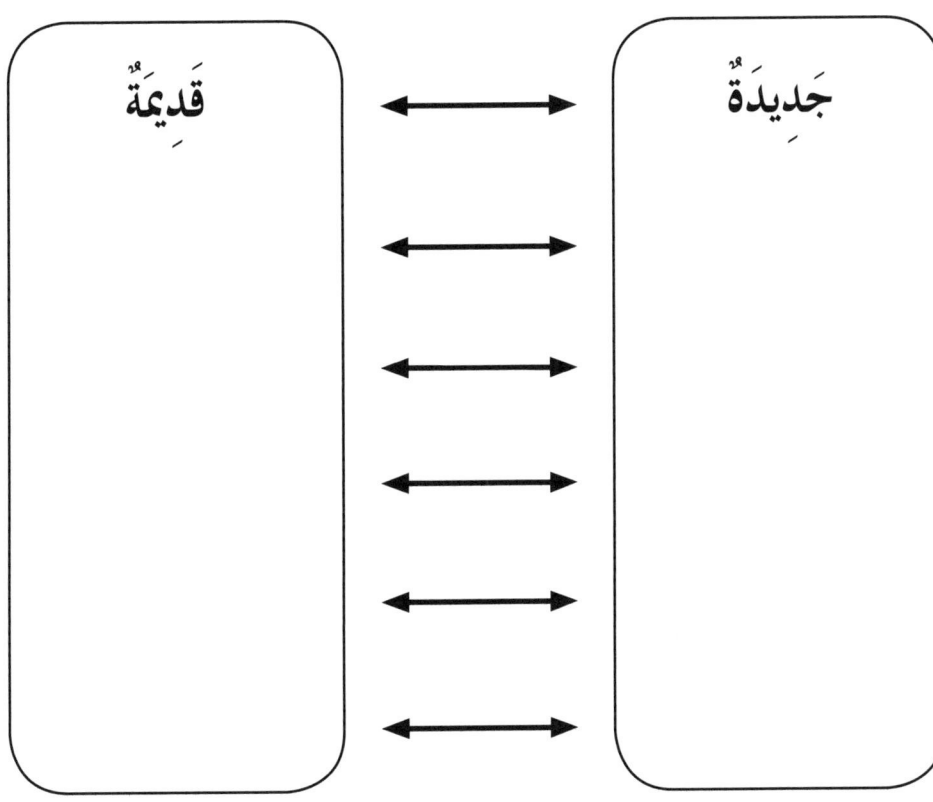

## Lesson 5 — الدَّرْسُ الْخَامِسُ

### التَّنْكِيرُ والتَّعْرِيفُ في الأَسْمَاءِ والصِّفَاتِ
### Indefiniteness and Definiteness in Nouns and Adjectives

- A great many of the nouns and adjectives introduced thus far appeared in the form of indefinite; and indefinite noun is called in Arabic (نَكِرَة).

- We can say that all regular nouns (with the exception of proper names) and adjectives must be indefinite if they receive a form of "*Tanween*" at the end; therefore in regular nouns and adjectives, the "*Tanween*" is the sign of indefiniteness, equivalent to the "*a*" or "*an*" in English in words such as: "*a book*" or "*an apple*".

- If we add the definite article "*the*" to a noun, then it becomes definite, and the "*a*" or "*an*" disappears; and the new structures appear as "*the book*" and "*the apple*" respectively.

- We have the same process in Arabic. The Arabic definite article is (اَل), called in Arabic (ال التَّعْرِيف), and it is written before the nouns and adjectives, attached to them and forming with these nouns and adjectives what physically looks as one word, when in fact we have two words that appear as one. The definite noun is called in Arabic (مَعْرِفة).

- Let's now examine the parallel sets of indefinite and definite nouns and adjectives:

| | مَعْرِفَةٌ Definite | | نَكِرَةٌ Indefinite |
|---|---|---|---|
| the lesson | الدَّرْسُ | a lesson | دَرْسٌ |
| the book | الْكِتَابُ | a book | كِتَابٌ |
| the letter | الرِّسَالَةُ | a letter | رِسَالَةٌ |

28

| | | | |
|---|---|---|---|
| the boy | الْوَلَدُ | a boy | وَلَدٌ |
| the school | الْمَدْرَسَةُ | a school | مَدْرَسَةٌ |
| the small | الصَّغِيرُ | a small | صَغِيرٌ |
| the beautiful | الْجَمِيلُ | a beautiful | جَمِيلٌ |
| the new | الْجَدِيدُ | a new | جَدِيدٌ |

\* \* \*

❖ **Explanatory Notes:**

1. All words in the right hand column are either nouns or adjectives. Because they do not have the definite article (ال), they all end with the "*Tanween*" sign ( ٌ ) which serves as the sign of indefiniteness.

2. In the parallel same words on the left, the Arabic definite article (ال) was added at the beginning of each noun or adjective, making each definite and resulting in the loss of the "*Tanween*" sign from its end.

\* \* \*

❖ **Examples of Indefinite and Definite Adjectival Phrases:**

| | | | |
|---|---|---|---|
| the little girl = | الْبِنْتُ الصَّغِيرَةُ | a little girl = | بِنْتٌ صَغِيرَةٌ | ١- |
| the new house = | الْبَيْتُ الْجَدِيدُ | a new house = | بَيْتٌ جَدِيدٌ | ٢- |
| the beautiful car = | السَّيَّارَةُ الْجَمِيلَةُ | a beautiful car = | سَيَّارَةٌ جَمِيلَةٌ | ٣- |
| the faithful friend = | الصَّدِيقُ الْمُخْلِصُ | a faithful friend = | صَدِيقٌ مُخْلِصٌ | ٤- |
| the skilful cook = | الطَّبَّاخَةُ الْمَاهِرَةُ | a skilful cook = | طَبَّاخَةٌ مَاهِرَةٌ | ٥- |
| the big door = | الْبَابُ الْكَبِيرُ | a big door = | بَابٌ كَبِيرٌ | ٦- |

\* \* \*

❖ **Explanatory Note:**

1. In "Noun-Adjective Phrases" if the noun is indefinite, then the adjective describing it must be indefinite too, and if the noun is definite, then the adjective describing it must be definite too.

\* \* \*

 Remember ! / تَذَكَّرْ- تَذَكَّرِي!

1. The indefinite noun is called in Arabic (نَكِرَة), and the definite noun is called (مَعْرِفَة).

2. All regular nouns (with the exception of proper names) and adjectives must be indefinite if they receive a form of "*Tanween*" at the end; therefore in regular nouns and adjectives, the "*Tanween*" is the sign of indefiniteness, equivalent to the "*a*" or "*an*" in English in words such as: "*a book*" or "*an apple*".

3. If we add the definite article "*the*" to a noun, then it becomes definite, and the "*a*" or "*an*" disappears.

4. We have the same process in Arabic. The Arabic definite article is (ال), called in Arabic (ال التَّعْرِيف), and it is written before the nouns and adjectives, attached to them and forming with these nouns and adjectives what physically looks as one word, when in fact we have two words that appear as one.

5. In "Noun-Adjective Phrases" if the noun is indefinite, then the adjective describing it must be indefinite too, and if the noun is definite, then the adjective describing it must be definite too.

\* \* \*

 Exercises / تَدْرِيبَاتٌ

1. Give the English equivalent of the following feminine adjectival phrases:

١- بِنْتٌ صَغِيرَةٌ = ....................   ٢- الْوَلَدُ الْكَبِيرُ = ....................

٣- الْمَدْرَسَةُ الْجَدِيدَةُ = ....................   ٥- أُمٌّ عَزِيزَةٌ = ....................

٥- تِلْميذٌ ذَكِيٌّ = ................     ٦- الدَّرْسُ السَّهْلُ = ................

٧- ذِراعٌ طَويلَةٌ = ................     ٨- السَّيّارَةُ الْبَيْضاءُ = ................

٩- الْمَلْعَبُ الْكَبيرُ = ................     ١٠- دَرْسٌ قَصيرٌ = ................

١١- شارِعٌ ضَيِّقٌ = ................     ١٢- السَّماءُ الزَّرْقاءُ = ................

١٣- الْمُعَلِّمَةُ النَّشيطَةُ = ................     ١٤- جامِعَةٌ مَشْهورَةٌ = ................

* * *

## 2. Give the Arabic equivalent of the following adjectival phrases:

1. a happy female pupil = ................

2. the old ship = ................

3. a short hand = ................

4. the younger sister = ................

5. a new car = ................

6. the big library = ................

7. a sincere mother = ................

8. the beautiful sister = ................

9. the noble soul = ................

10. a new school = ................

11. the polite girl = ................

12. a sad woman = ................

13. the dear daughter = ................

* * *

31

3. The following box contains a mixture of definite and indefinite nouns and adjectives, both masculine and feminine; isolate them into two categories, one for the indefinite and the other for the definite:

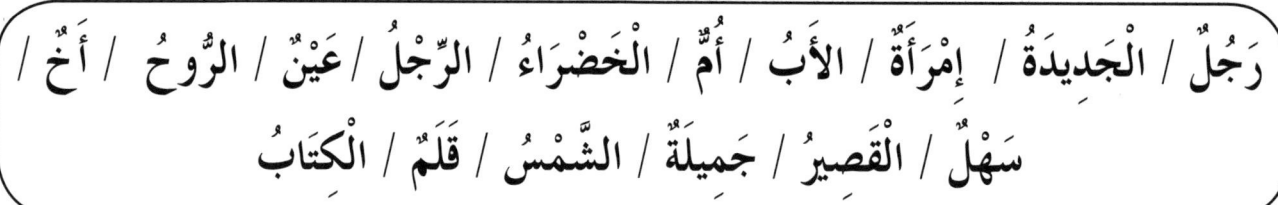

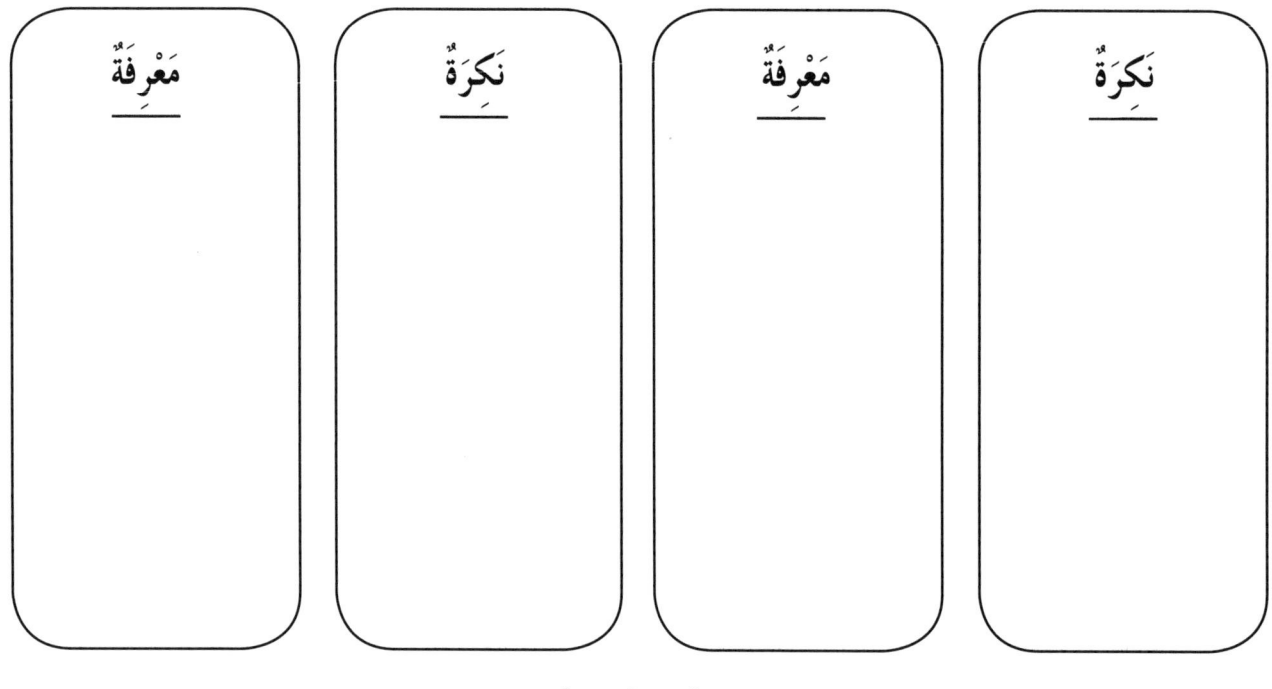

* * *

4. Fill in the blanks of the following sentences with an appropriate definite or indefinite adjective to make full meaningful sentences; then translate the resultant sentences into English:

١- هُوَ الرَّجُلُ ............... .  ٢- هَذِه مَدْرَسَةٌ ............... .

٣- هِيَ صَدِيقَةٌ ............... .  ٤- هُوَ الأَبُ ............... .

٥- هَذِه السَّفِينَةُ ............... .  ٦- هَذَا كِتَابٌ ............... .

٧- هُوَ مُعَلِّمٌ ............... .  ٨- هَذِه السَّيَّارَةُ ............... .

٩- هَذَا الأَخُ ............... .  ١٠- هِيَ تِلْمِيذَةٌ ............... .

١١- هَذِه طَبَّاخَةٌ ............... .  ١٢- هُوَ الوَلَدُ ............... .

## 5. Translate the following sentences into Arabic (Orally and written):

1. She is the happy pupil. = ................................................

2. This is the new table. = ................................................

3. She is the excellent teacher. = ................................................

4. This is the old library. = ................................................

5. He is the good friend. = ................................................

6. This is the big boy. = ................................................

7. He is the ugly scene. = ................................................

\* \* \*

## 6. Translate the following sentences into English orally:

١- هَذِهِ مِسْطَرَةٌ صَغِيرَةٌ . ................................................

٢- هِيَ الْبِنْتُ الْمُهَذَّبَةُ . ................................................

٣- هُوَ الْمُعَلِّمُ الْمُخْلِصُ . ................................................

٤- هَذِهِ جَامِعَةٌ مَشْهُورَةٌ . ................................................

٥- هِيَ التِّلْمِيذَةُ الذَّكِيَّةُ . ................................................

٦- هُوَ الصَّدِيقُ الْمُخْلِصُ . ................................................

٧- هَذِهِ أُسْتَاذَةٌ مَشْهُورَةٌ . ................................................

٨- هِيَ الْأُمُّ الْعَزِيزَةُ . ................................................

\* \* \*

**Lesson 6** — الدَّرْسُ السَّادِسُ

### الْحُرُوفُ الشَّمْسِيَّةُ والْقَمَرِيَّةُ : نُطْقُهَا وكِتَابَتُهَا
### The Sun and Moon Letters: Pronunciation and Writing with the Definite Article

- In Arabic, the alphabet is divided into two equal groups: one is called the "Moon Letters", (الْحُرُوفُ الْقَمَرِيَّةُ) in Arabic; being named so after the word for "Moon", which is (قَمَرٌ). The other group is called the "Sun Letters", (الْحُرُوفُ الشَّمْسِيَّةُ) in Arabic; being named so after the word for "Sun", which is (شَمْسٌ).

- We need to know this division because there is some difference in the pronunciation and writing of the letters of these two groups when the Arabic definite article (الْ) is introduced to them.

- Since this modification in pronunciation affects the "Sun Letters" only, then we will start by introducing them first:

| الْحُرُوفُ الشَّمْسِيَّةُ مَعَ (ال) / The Sun Letters with (ال) | الْحُرُوفُ الشَّمْسِيَّةُ بِدُونِ (ال) / The Sun Letters without (ال) |
|---|---|
| التِّينُ — the fig | ت   تِينٌ   fig |
| الثَّوَابُ — the reward | ث   ثَوَابٌ   reward |
| الدِّينُ — the religion | د   دِينٌ   religion |
| الذَّهَبُ — the gold | ذ   ذَهَبٌ   gold |
| الرَّحِيمُ — the merciful | ر   رَحِيمٌ   merciful |
| الزَّيْتُونُ — the olive trees | ز   زَيْتُونٌ   olive trees |

| | | | | | |
|---|---|---|---|---|---|
| the peace | السَّلامُ | | peace | سَلامٌ | س |
| the sun | الشَّمْسُ | | sun | شَمْسٌ | ش |
| the patience | الصَّبرُ | | patience | صَبرٌ | ص |
| the guest | الضَّيْفُ | | a guest | ضَيْفٌ | ض |
| the bird | الطَّيْرُ | | a bird | طَيْرٌ | ط |
| the noon | الظُّهْرُ | | noon | ظُهْرٌ | ظ |
| the kind | اللَّطِيفُ | | kind, gentle | لَطِيفٌ | ل |
| the star | النَّجْمُ | | a star | نَجْمٌ | ن |

\* \* \*

❖ **Explanatory Notes:**

1. When we pronounce a word starting with one of the "Sun Letters" to which we have added the definite article (ال), we notice that in pronunciation we do not pronounce the **Laam** (ل), part, though it is there in writing.

2. Furthermore, the first letter of the word, which is the "Sun Letter" itself, is written and pronounced with a "*Shaddah*" ( ّ ). Another way of saying this is that the **Laam** (ل) of the definite article is assimilated with the "Sun Letter" and consequently pronounced and written with a "*Shaddah*"

3. The rest of the Arabic letters not covered above are "Moon Letters", and with these no modification in either pronunciation or writing is introduced.

\* \* \*

❖ **Examples of Nouns and Adjectives Starting with Moon Letters:**

| | | | | | |
|---|---|---|---|---|---|
| the family | الأَهْلُ | | family | أَهْلٌ | أ |
| the sea | البَحْرُ | | a sea | بَحْرٌ | ب |

35

| | | | | | | |
|---|---|---|---|---|---|---|
| the camel | الْجَمَلُ | | a camel | جَمَلٌ | ج |
| the donkey | الْحِمَارُ | | a donkey | حِمَارٌ | ح |
| the bread | الْخُبْزُ | | bread | خُبْزٌ | خ |
| the Arab | الْعَرَبِيُّ | | an Arab | عَرَبِيٌّ | ع |
| the rich | الْغَنِيُّ | | rich | غَنِيٌّ | غ |
| the bounty | الْفَضْلُ | | bounty | فَضْلٌ | ف |
| the moon | الْقَمَرُ | | a moon | قَمَرٌ | ق |
| the book | الْكِتَابُ | | a book | كِتَابٌ | ك |
| the believer | الْمُؤْمِنُ | | a believer | مُؤْمِنٌ | م |
| the air | الْهَوَاءُ | | air | هَوَاءٌ | هـ |
| the promise | الْوَعْدُ | | promise | وَعْدٌ | و |
| the day | الْيَوْمُ | | a day | يَوْمٌ | ي |

\* \* \*

❖ **Explanatory Note:**

1. As you clearly see from the examples above, after adding the definite article (ال) to words starting with "Moon Letters", we still continue to fully pronounce the (ل) and the first letter of the original words continue to bear the vowel they had in the singular form, without a "*Shaddah*" or assimilation we observed with the "Sun Letters"

\* \* \*

❖ **Additional New Vocabulary:**

from / مِنْ / with / عِنْدَ / Where (is)…? / أَيْنَ…؟ / God اللهُ

in, at / فِي / **on** / عَلَى / **Friday** الْجُمُعَةُ

## Remember! / تَذَكَّرْ- تَذَكَّرِي!

1. When we pronounce a word starting with one of the "Sun Letters" to which we have added the definite article (ال), then, in pronunciation, we do not pronounce the **Laam** (ل), part, though it is there in writing.

2. Furthermore, the first letter of the word, which is the "Sun Letter" itself, is written and pronounced with a "Shaddah" ( ّ ). Another way of saying this is that the **Laam** (ل) of the definite article is assimilated with the "Sun Letter" and consequently pronounced and written with a "Shaddah"

3. With the "Moon Letters", there is no modification in either pronunciation or writing is introduced.

\* \* \*

## Exercises / تَدْرِيبَاتٌ

**1.** Add the definite article to the following indefinite nouns and adjectives and observe the rules of pronunciation with the "Sun Letters" while pronouncing them:

أَهْلٌ   بَحْرٌ   تِينْ   ثَوَابٌ   جَمَلٌ   حِمَارٌ

خُبْزٌ   دِينْ   ذَهَبٌ   رَحِيمٌ   زَيْتُونٌ   سَلَامٌ

شَمْسٌ   صَبْرٌ   ضَيْفٌ   طَيْرٌ   ظُهْرٌ   عَرَبِيٌّ

غَنِيٌّ   فَضْلٌ   قَمَرٌ   كِتَابٌ   لَطِيفٌ   مُؤْمِنٌ

نَجْمٌ   هَوَاءٌ   وَعْدٌ   يَوْمٌ

37

2. Classify the nouns and adjectives of the previous drill into the two categories of the "Moon Letters" and "Sun Letters" by writing them down in the appropriate column, with the definite article and full vocalization signs:

| الْحُرُوفُ الشَّمْسِيَّةُ | الْحُرُوفُ الْقَمَرِيَّةُ |
|---|---|
|  |  |
|  |  |
|  |  |
|  |  |
|  |  |
|  |  |
|  |  |
|  |  |
|  |  |
|  |  |
|  |  |

\* \* \*

3. Read the following sentences and then translate them into English orally:

١- أَيْنَ التِّينُ ؟

٢- اللهُ هُوَ الرَّحِيمُ .

٣- الثَّوَابُ عِنْدَ اللهِ .

٤- اللهُ هُوَ السَّلَامُ .

٥- هُوَ الرَّجُلُ الْغَنِيُّ .

٦- أَيْنَ الزَّيْتُونُ ؟

٧- الْقَمَرُ فِي السَّمَاءِ .

٨- الْفَضْلُ مِنَ اللهِ .

٩- الْيَوْمُ هُوَ الْجُمُعَةُ .

١٠- الْكِتَابُ الْجَدِيدُ فِي الْبَيْتِ .

**4. Translate the following English sentences into Arabic and provide full vocalization signs:**

1. God is the Kind.  = ..........................................

2. The bird is in the sky.  = ..........................................

3. Where is the bread?  = ..........................................

4. The family is in the house.  = ..........................................

5. The new book is on the table.  = ..........................................

6. Where is the big camel?  = ..........................................

7. The ship is in the sea.  = ..........................................

\* \* \*

**5. Fill in the blanks of the following sentences with an appropriate definite adjective to make full meaningful sentences; then translate the resultant sentences into English:**

١- هُوَ الرَّجُلُ .......... .   ٢- أَيْنَ الْمَدْرَسَةُ .......... ؟

٣- هِيَ الصَّدِيقَةُ .......... .   ٤- هُوَ الأَبُ .......... .

٥- هَذِه السَّفِينةُ .......... .   ٦- أَيْنَ الْكِتَابُ .......... ؟

٧- هُوَ الْمُعَلِّمُ .......... .   ٨- هَذِه السَّيَّارَةُ .......... .

٩- هَذَا الأَخُ .......... .   ١٠- الْبِنْتُ .......... أُخْتِي .

١١- هِيَ الطَّبَّاخَةُ .......... .   ١٢- أَيْنَ الْحِمَارُ .......... ؟

\* \* \*

39

# Lesson 7 — الدَّرْسُ السَّابِعُ

## أَسْمَاءُ الإِشَارَةِ لِلْقَرِيبِ : هَذَا / هَذِه
## وَأَسْمَاءُ الإِشَارَةِ لِلْبَعِيدِ : ذَلِكَ / تِلْكَ

**The Demonstrative Pronouns for Closeness & The Demonstrative Pronouns for Distant**

- We have already introduced the two demonstrative pronouns (هَذَا) and (هَذِه) as vocabulary; both of which are equivalent to the English "This"; but in Arabic, the first one is the <u>masculine form</u> and the second one is the feminine form.

- Each of these is called (إِسْمُ إِشَارَة), which literally means "*A Noun of Pointing*".

- Further more, these two are used to point to or refer to nouns that are relatively near or close by the speaker.

- Parallel and in contrast to these two, there is another pair of masculine-feminine demonstrative pronouns, which are used either to refer to nouns which we perceive as relatively distant or far away, or for the purpose of contrasting a previous reference to a following one. These two demonstrative pronouns are (ذَلِكَ) and (تِلْكَ); both of which are equivalent to the English "That" "; but in Arabic, the first one is the <u>masculine form</u> and the second one is the <u>feminine form</u>.

- Let's now study the following sets of parallel examples:

### 1

| The Feminine Demonstrative Pronoun إِسْمُ الإِشَارَةِ الْمُؤَنَّث (هَذِه) | The Masculine Demonstrative Pronoun إِسْمُ الإِشَارَةِ الْمُذَكَّرِ (هَذَا) |
|---|---|
| هَذِه بِنْتٌ .   This is a girl. | هَذَا وَلَدٌ .   This is a boy. |
| هَذِه مُعَلِّمَةٌ .   This is a (female) teacher. | هَذَا مُعَلِّمٌ .   This is a (male) teacher. |
| هَذِه سَبُّورَةٌ .   This is a chalkboard. | هَذَا فَصْلٌ .   This is a classroom. |

هَذِهِ سَاعَةٌ . — This is a watch (clock).     هَذَا دَفْتَرٌ . — This is a notebook.

هَذِهِ مَرْيَمُ . — This is Mary.     هَذَا آدَمُ . — This is Adam.

\* \* \*

## 2

### إِسْمُ الإِشَارَةِ الْمُؤَنَّث (تِلْكَ) — The Feminine Demonstrative Pronoun
### إِسْمُ الإِشَارَةِ الْمُذَكَّرِ (ذَلِكَ) — The Masculine Demonstrative Pronoun

تِلْكَ مَرْيَمُ . — That is Mary.     ذَلِكَ آدَمُ . — That is Adam.

تِلْكَ أُسْتَاذَةٌ . — That is a (female) professor.     ذَلِكَ أُسْتَاذٌ . — That is a (male) professor.

تِلْكَ وَرَقَةٌ . — That is a leaf.     ذَلِكَ قَلَمٌ . — That is a pen.

تِلْكَ نَافِذَةٌ . — That is a window.     ذَلِكَ بَابٌ . — That is a door.

تِلْكَ فَرَسٌ . — That is a mare.     ذَلِكَ حِصَانٌ . — That is a horse.

\* \* \*

## 3

### إِسْمُ الإِشَارَةِ الْمُؤَنَّث (هَذِه / تِلْكَ) — Feminine Demonstrative Pronoun
### إِسْمُ الإِشَارَةِ الْمُذَكَّرِ (هَذَا / ذَلِكَ) — Masculine Demonstrative Pronoun

هَذِهِ مَرْيَمُ وَتِلْكَ لَيْلَى .
This is a Mary and that is *Layla*.

هَذَا آدَمُ وَذَلِكَ عُمَرُ .
This is Adam and that is Omar.

هَذِهِ سَيَّارَةٌ وَتِلْكَ سَفِينَةٌ .
This is a car and that is a ship.

هَذَا كِتَابٌ وَذَلِكَ دَفْتَرٌ .
This is a book and that is a notebook.

هَذِهِ سَيَّارَةٌ جَدِيدَةٌ وَتِلْكَ سَيَّارَةٌ قَدِيمَةٌ .
This is a new car and that is an old car.

هَذَا بَيْتٌ صَغِيرٌ وَذَلِكَ بَيْتٌ كَبِيرٌ .
This is a small house and that is a big house.

هَذِهِ كَلِمَةٌ سَهْلَةٌ وَتِلْكَ كَلِمَةٌ صَعْبَةٌ .
This is an easy word and that is a difficult word.

هَذَا شَارِعٌ طَوِيلٌ وَذَلِكَ شَارِعٌ قَصِيرٌ .
This is a long street and that is a short street.

هَذِهِ صُورَةٌ جَمِيلَةٌ وَتِلْكَ صُورَةٌ قَبِيحَةٌ .
This is beautiful picture and that is an ugly picture.

هَذَا وَلَدٌ سَعِيدٌ وَذَلِكَ وَلَدٌ حَزِينٌ .
This is a happy boy and that is a sad boy.

### ❖ Explanatory Notes:

1. When we examine the sentences of group one above, we find that we used the masculine demonstrative pronoun (هَذَا) to point to or refer to masculine nouns in the sentences on the right hand, and we used the feminine demonstrative pronoun (هَذِه) to point to or refer to feminine nouns in the sentences on the left hand,

2. Furthermore, when we examine the sentences of group two above, we find that we used the masculine demonstrative pronoun (ذَلِك) to point to or refer to masculine nouns in the sentences on the right hand, and we used the feminine demonstrative pronoun (تِلْك) to point to or refer to feminine nouns in the sentences on the left hand,

3. But in the sentences of group three above, we used (هَذَا) and (ذَلِك) combined in the same sentence, and (هَذِه) and (تِلْك) combined in the same sentence; that is because there is an expressed or implied process of comparing and contrasting. In this case we use (هَذَا) and (هَذِه) in reference to the first noun mentioned, and we use (ذَلِك) and (تِلْك) in reference to second noun mentioned, even if both are close by or are far away.

*  *  *

### ❖ New Vocabulary:

| | | | | |
|---|---|---|---|---|
| that (feminine) | تِلْكَ | | that (masculine) | ذَلِكَ |
| a notebook | دَفْتَرٌ | | a classroom | فَصْلٌ |
| a horse | حِصَانٌ | | a watch, a clock | سَاعَةٌ |
| a picture | صُورَةٌ | | a word | كَلِمَةٌ |
| a merchant | تَاجِرٌ | | an airplane | طَائِرَةٌ |
| a female nurse | مُمَرِّضَةٌ | | a male doctor | طَبِيبٌ |
| obedient | مُطِيعٌ | | useful | مُفِيدٌ |
| | | | yes | نَعَمْ |

# تَذَكَّرْ - تَذَكَّرِي! / Remember!

1. The masculine demonstrative pronoun (هَذَا) is used to point to or refer to masculine nouns.

2. The feminine demonstrative pronoun (هَذِه) is used to point to or refer to feminine nouns. These two are translated into the English "This."

3. The masculine demonstrative pronoun (ذَلِكَ) is used to point to or refer to masculine nouns perceived as being relatively remote either in time or place.

4. The feminine demonstrative pronoun (تِلْكَ) is used to point to or refer to feminine nouns perceived as being relatively remote either in time or place. These two are translated into the English "That."

5. We can combine (هَذِه) / (هَذَا), and (تِلْكَ) / (ذَلِكَ) in the same sentence if there is an expressed or implied process of comparing and contrasting. In this case we use (هَذَا) / (هَذِه) in reference to the first noun mentioned, and we use (ذَلِكَ) / (تِلْكَ) in reference to second noun mentioned, even if both are close by or far away.

## تَدْرِيبَات / Exercises

**1.** Based on the gender of the noun being referred to, say and then write down the appropriate form of the demonstrative pronoun (هَذَا) or (هَذِه):

| | | | |
|---|---|---|---|
| ٢- ............... سَاعَةٌ جَمِيلَةٌ. | | ١- ............... فَصْلٌ كَبِيرٌ. | |
| ٤- ............... طَبِيبٌ مَشْهُورٌ. | | ٣- ............... مُمَرِّضَةٌ نَشِيطَةٌ. | |
| ٦- ............... طَائِرَةٌ كَبِيرَةٌ. | | ٥- ............... دَفْتَرٌ جَدِيدٌ. | |
| ٨- ............... دَرْسٌ مُفِيدٌ. | | ٧- ............... سَبُّورَةٌ خَضْرَاءُ. | |
| ١٠- ............... أُخْتٌ عَزِيزَةٌ. | | ٩- ............... حِصَانٌ جَمِيلٌ. | |
| ١٢- ............... مُعَلِّمٌ مُمْتَازٌ. | | ١١- ............... طَبَّاخَةٌ مَاهِرَةٌ. | |

2. Based on the gender of the noun being referred to, say and then write down the appropriate form of the demonstrative pronouns (هَذا), (هَذِهِ), (ذَلِكَ), (تِلْكَ) to compare and contrast two nouns in the same sentence :

١- ............ صُورَةٌ جَمِيلَةٌ وَتِلْكَ صُورَةٌ قَبِيحَةٌ .

٢- هَذا شارِعٌ طَوِيلٌ وَ ............ شارِعٌ قَصِيرٌ .

٣- ............ سَيَّارَةٌ جَدِيدَةٌ وَ ............ سَيَّارَةٌ قَدِيمَةٌ .

٤- ............ جَمَلٌ كَبِيرٌ وَ ............ جَمَلٌ صَغِيرٌ .

٥- هَذِهِ دَرَّاجَةٌ حَمْرَاءُ وَ ............ دَرَّاجَةٌ زَرْقَاءُ .

٦- هَذا دَرْسٌ سَهْلٌ وَ ............ دَرْسٌ صَعْبٌ .

٧- ............ سَفِينَةٌ صَغِيرَةٌ وَ ............ سَفِينَةٌ كَبِيرَةٌ .

٨- ............ أُخْتٌ صُغْرَى وَ ............ أُخْتٌ كُبْرَى .

٩- هَذا تِلْمِيذٌ نَشِيطٌ وَ ............ تِلْمِيذٌ كَسُولٌ .

١٠- ............ دَرْسٌ طَوِيلٌ وَ ............ دَرْسٌ قَصِيرٌ .

| |
|---|
| هَذا |
| هَذِهِ |
| ذَلِكَ |
| تِلْكَ |

3. Read the following sentences and then translate them into English orally:

١- هَذا تِينٌ جَيِّدٌ . ٢- هَذِهِ امْرَأَةٌ جَمِيلَةٌ .

٣- هَذا وَلَدٌ طَوِيلٌ وَذَلِكَ وَلَدٌ قَصِيرٌ . ٤- تِلْكَ غُرْفَةٌ صَغِيرَةٌ .

٥- ذَلِكَ رَجُلٌ غَنِيٌّ . ٦- هَذا مَلْعَبٌ كَبِيرٌ وَذَلِكَ مَلْعَبٌ صَغِيرٌ .

٧- تِلْكَ أُسْتاذَةٌ مُمْتازَةٌ . ٨- هَذا تاجِرٌ مَشْهُورٌ .

٩- هَذِهِ ساعَةٌ قَدِيمَةٌ وَتِلْكَ ساعَةٌ جَدِيدَةٌ . ١٠- هَذِهِ جامِعَةٌ مَشْهُورَةٌ .

\* \* \*

**Lesson 8** ━━━━━━━━━━━━━━━━━━━━━━━━━━━━━ الدَّرْسُ الثَّامِنُ

> ضَمائِرُ الرَّفْعِ الْمُنْفَصِلَةُ : هُوَ / هِيَ / أَنْتَ / أَنْتِ / أَنا
>
> **The Personal Subject Pronouns for:**
> **He / She / You (masculine) / You (feminine) / I**

❖ We have already introduced the two personal subject pronouns (هُوَ) for "**He**" and (هِيَ) for "**She**". In this lesson we treat the five singular personal pronouns as one integrated topic. The plural and dual forms will be dealt with at a later stage.

❖ The Arabic word for a personal pronoun is (ضَمِيرٌ), the plural of which is (ضَمَائِرُ). Let's now study the following sentences:

١- هُوَ آدَمُ وَهِيَ مَرْيَمُ .   =   He is Adam and she is *Maryam*.

٢- هُوَ طَبِيبٌ وَهِيَ طَبِيبَةٌ .   =   He is doctor and she is doctor.

٣- هُوَ قَصِيرٌ وَهِيَ طَوِيلَةٌ .   =   He is short and she is tall.

\* \* \*

١- هَلْ أَنْتَ عُمَرُ ؟   =   Are you *Omar*?

٢- هَلْ أَنْتِ لَيْلَى ؟   =   Are you *Layla*?

٣- أَنْتَ صَدِيقٌ مُخْلِصٌ .   =   You are a sincere friend.

٤- أَنْتِ أُخْتٌ عَزِيزَةٌ .   =   Are you dear sister.

\* \* \*

١- أَنَا فَضْل عَبد الله .   =   I am *Fadl Abdu-Allah*.

٢- أَنَا أُسْتَاذٌ جَدِيدٌ .   =   I am a new (male) professor.

٣- أَنَا أُسْتَاذَةٌ جَدِيدَةٌ .   =   I am a new (female) professor.

45

### ❖ Explanatory Notes:

- ❖ (هُوَ) and (هِيَ) are the two masculine-feminine pair for the 3rd person singular personal pronouns; a situation similar to English.

- ❖ However, when we come to the 2nd person, Arabic has two pronouns; one for masculine, which is (أَنْتَ), and one for feminine, which is (أَنْتِ); both of which are equivalent to the English "You"; but in Arabic, the first one is the <u>masculine form</u> and the second one is the <u>feminine form</u>.

- ❖ You might want to pay special attention to the fact that the difference between these two is in the vowel of the last letter (ت), which bears a <u>"Fathah" with the masculine form</u> and a <u>"Kasrah" with the feminine form</u>.

- ❖ As for the 1st person personal pronoun, in Arabic, like English, there is one form, used for both masculine and feminine, and that is (أَنَا).

- ❖ All personal subject pronouns function as <u>subjects in sentences</u>, and they are <u>invariable</u>, in the sense that they do not change their vowel signs.

- ❖ As you can clearly see from the examples above, personal subject pronouns can be used in connection with proper names, regular nouns and adjectives.

* * *

### ❖ Additional New Vocabulary:

| | | | |
|---|---|---|---|
| an engineer | مُهَنْدِسٌ | a worker | عَامِلٌ |
| a teacher, an instructor | مُدَرِّسٌ | a leader | زَعِيمٌ |
| humble | مُتَوَاضِعٌ | an author | مُؤَلِّفٌ |
| a Muslim | مُسْلِمٌ | a Christian | مَسِيحِيٌّ |
| a Jew | يَهُودِيٌّ | a poet | شَاعِرٌ |
| good, delicious | طَيِّبٌ | generous, noble | كَرِيمٌ |
| gentle, pleasant, kind | لَطِيفٌ | a baker | خَبَّازٌ |
| a peasant, a farmer | فَلَّاحٌ | poor | فَقِيرٌ |

46

## ❖ New Vocabulary Used in Full Meaningful Sentences:

| | |
|---|---|
| هُوَ وَلَدٌ مُطِيعٌ . | He is an obedient boy. |
| هِيَ بِنْتٌ مُطِيعَةٌ . | She is an obedient girl. |
| هُوَ عَرَبِيٌّ وهِيَ عَرَبِيَّةٌ . | He is an Arab and she is an Arab. |
| هَلْ أَنْتَ مُهَنْدِسٌ ؟ | Are you an engineer (masculine)? |
| هَلْ أَنْتِ مُهَنْدِسَةٌ ؟ | Are you an engineer (feminine)? |
| أَنَا مُدَرِّسٌ جَدِيدٌ . | I am a new (male) instructor. |
| أَنَا مُدَرِّسَةٌ جَدِيدَةٌ . | I am a new (female) instructor. |
| هِيَ مَسِيحِيَّةٌ وَهُوَ يَهُودِيٌّ | She is a Christian and he is a Jew. |
| أَنْتَ زَعِيمٌ مُتَوَاضِعٌ . | You are a humble leader. |
| هَلْ أَنْتَ مُسْلِمٌ ؟ | Are you a Muslim. (masculine)? |
| هَلْ أَنْتِ مُسْلِمَةٌ ؟ | Are you a Muslim. (feminine) ? |
| هُوَ شَاعِرٌ مَشْهُورٌ . | He is a famous poet. |
| أَنَا فَلَّاحٌ فَقِيرٌ . | I am a poor peasant (farmer). |
| هِيَ بِنْتٌ لَطِيفَةٌ . | She is a gentle (pleasant) girl. |
| أَنْتَ مُؤَلِّفٌ مَشْهُورٌ . | You (masculine) are a famous author. |
| هَلْ أَنْتِ مَسِيحِيَّةٌ ؟ | Are you (feminine) a Christian? |

\* \* \*

## تَذَكَّرْ- تَذَكَّري! / Remember!

1. The <u>masculine 3rd person personal pronoun</u> (هُوَ) is used refer to masculine subjects; equivalent to the English "He".

2. The <u>feminine 3rd person personal pronoun</u> (هِيَ) is used to refer to feminine subjects; equivalent to the English "She".

3. The <u>masculine 2nd person personal pronoun</u> (أَنْتَ) is used to refer to masculine subjects.

4. The <u>feminine 2nd person personal pronoun</u> (أَنْتِ) is used to refer to feminine subjects.

5. Note that, for the 2nd person, Arabic has two personal pronouns, one for each gender; this is unlike English where there is only one.

6. The 1st person personal pronoun is (أَنا); and this is used to refer both to masculine as well as feminine subjects, exactly like English.

## تَدْريبَاتٌ / Exercises

**1. Read the following sentences and identify the personal subject pronouns, and say verbally its English equivalent:**

١- هُوَ تِلْميذٌ مُهَذَّبٌ .

٢- هِيَ بِنْتٌ لَطيفَةٌ .

٣- هَلْ أَنْتِ مُمَرِّضَةٌ جَديدَةٌ ؟

٤- هَلْ أَنْتَ يَهوديٌّ ؟

٥- أَنا فضْلٌ وهُوَ خَليلٌ .

٦- هِيَ مُهَنْدِسَةٌ مُمْتازَةٌ .

٧- أَنْتَ مُؤَلِّفٌ جَيِّدٌ .

٨- هُوَ زَعيمٌ مُتَواضِعٌ ؟

٩- أَنا أُسْتاذٌ وهِيَ طَبيبَةٌ .

١٠- أَنْتِ مُعَلِّمَةٌ مُخْلِصَةٌ .

١١- هِيَ فَلَّاحَةٌ نَشيطَةٌ .

١٢- هَلْ أَنْتِ خَبَّازَةٌ ؟

\* \* \*

**2. Translate the following English sentences into Arabic and provide full vocalization signs:**

1. She is a clever girl. = ..................................

2. He is a sincere friend. = ..................................

3. Are you (masculine) a new student? = ..................................

4. I am an engineer and she is a teacher. = ..................................

5. Is he a humble leader? = ..................................

6. Are you (feminine) a Jew? = ..................................

7. You (masculine) are a good Christian. = ..................................

\* \* \*

**3. Read the following sentences and then translate them into English orally:**

١- هُوَ عَامِلٌ نَشِيطٌ .     ٢- أَنَا شَاعِرٌ عَرَبِيٌّ .

٣- هُوَ قَصِيرٌ وهِيَ طَوِيلَةٌ .     ٤- هَلْ أَنْتَ مُهَنْدِسٌ ؟

٥- هَلْ أَنْتِ مُمَرِّضَةٌ ؟     ٦- هَلْ هِيَ مُسْلِمَةٌ ؟

٧- هِيَ أُخْتٌ عَزِيزَةٌ .     ٨- هُوَ رَجُلٌ مُؤْمِنٌ .

٩- أَنْتَ زَعِيمٌ مُخْلِصٌ .     ١٠- أَنَا فَلَّاحٌ فَقِيرٌ .

\* \* \*

**4. Choose the correct subject pronoun from those in brackets to fill in the blanks in the following sentences:**

١- ............... تِلْمِيذَةٌ مُهَذَّبَةٌ . (هُوَ / هِيَ)

٢- هَلْ ............... مُدَرِّسٌ جَدِيدٌ ؟ (أَنْتِ / أَنْتَ)

٣- ............... شَاعِرٌ عَرَبِيٌّ . (أَنَا / هِيَ)

٤- ............... فَلَّاحَةٌ فَقِيرَةٌ . (هُوَ / أَنَا)

٥- ............ زَعيمٌ مُتَواضِعٌ . (هِيَ / أَنْتَ)

٦- ............ امْرَأَةٌ يَهودِيَّةٌ . (أَنْتَ / هِيَ)

٧- هَلْ ............ وَلَدٌ ذَكِيٌّ ؟ (هُوَ / أَنْتِ)

٨- ............ تاجِرٌ غَنِيٌّ . (أَنْتِ / هُوَ)

٩- هَلْ ............ يَهودِيَّةٌ ؟ (أَنا / أَنْتِ)

\* \* \*

**5. Choose the correct noun from those in brackets to fill in the blanks in the following sentences:**

١- أَنا ............ فَقيرٌ . (فَلّاحَةٌ / فَلّاحٌ / خَبّازَةٌ)

٢- هَلْ أَنْتَ ............ جَديدٌ ؟ (يَهودِيَّةٌ / مُدَرِّسٌ / مُدَرِّسَةٌ)

٣- هَلْ أَنْتِ ............ ؟ (حَزينَةٌ / حَزينٌ / سَعيدٌ)

٤- هُوَ ............ مَشْهورٌ . (مُتَواضِعَةٌ / شاعِرٌ / شاعِرَةٌ)

٥- هِيَ ............ مُسْلِمَةٌ . (عَرَبِيَّةٌ / عَرَبِيٌّ / يَهودِيٌّ)

\* \* \*

**6. Give <u>affirmative oral answers</u> to the following questions using (نَعَمْ) before the subject pronoun in the answer: (Note: if the question is in the 2<sup>nd</sup> person you need to use the 1<sup>st</sup> person pronoun in the answer!)**

١- هَلْ هُوَ مَسيحِيٌّ ؟

٢- هَلْ أَنْتِ طالِبَةٌ جَديدَةٌ ؟

٣- هَلْ هِيَ أُسْتاذَةٌ مَشْهورَةٌ ؟

٤- هَلْ أَنْتَ زَعيمٌ مُخْلِصٌ ؟

٥- هَلْ أَنْتِ مُمَرِّضَةٌ ؟

٦- هَلْ هُوَ مُهَنْدِسٌ مَشْهورٌ ؟

٧- هَلْ هِيَ يَهودِيَّةٌ ؟

٨- هَلْ أَنْتَ تاجِرٌ غَنِيٌّ ؟

50

# Lesson 9

الدَّرْسُ التَّاسِعُ

> الضَّمَائِرُ (الْمِلْكِيةُ) الْمُتَّصِلَةُ : ـهُ / ـهَا / ـكَ / ـكِ / ـِي
>
> **Suffix Possessive Pronouns:**
> **His / Her / Your (masculine) / Your (feminine) / My**

❖ Parallel to the personal subject pronouns introduced in the previous lesson, Arabic has a set of pronouns that are suffixed to the end of nouns to express the meaning of possessive relationship.

❖ These are called in English **possessive pronouns**, and are written in English separately from the nouns that come after them.

❖ In Arabic, the equivalent of the English possessive pronouns come after the nouns they are related to, and are actually written suffixed to the nouns and appearing as an integral part of them.

❖ Let's now study the following examples where the suffix possessive pronouns are underlined:

| | | |
|---|---|---|
| This is his book. | = | ١- هَذَا كِتَابُهُ . |
| This is her book. | = | ٢- هَذَا كِتَابُهَا . |
| This is your book. (Masculine) | = | ٣- هَذَا كِتَابُكَ . |
| This is your book. (Feminine) | = | ٤- هَذَا كِتَابُكِ . |
| This is my book. (Masculine + Feminine) | = | ٥- هَذَا كِتَابِي . |

\* \* \*

| | | |
|---|---|---|
| This is his car. | = | ١- هَذِه سَيَّارَتُهُ . |
| This is her car. | = | ٢- هَذِه سَيَّارَتُهَا . |
| This is your car. (Masculine) | = | ٣- هَذِه سَيَّارَتُكَ . |
| This is your car. (Feminine) | = | ٤- هَذِه سَيَّارَتُكِ . |
| This is my car. (Masculine + Feminine) | = | ٥- هَذِه سَيَّارَتِي . |

❖ **Explanatory Notes:**

1. When we examine the set of pronouns highlighted above, we will notice that these are short suffixes, consisting of one letter in four cases and two letters in one case.

2. They are all attached in writing to the end of the nouns with which they form the possessive relationship; that's why these are called in Arabic "**Suffix Pronouns**".

3. The suffix pronoun corresponding to (هُوَ) is (ـهُ). As long as the vowel of the preceding letter is a "*Fathah*" or a "*Dammah*", then the vowel of the pronoun is a "*Dammah*". If, however, the vowel of the preceding letter is either a "*Kasrah*" or a "*Yaa*", then the vowel of the suffix pronoun changes to a "*Kasrah*" too, to harmonize with the preceding sound and facilitate the pronunciation; thus it becomes: (فِي كِتَابِهِ), for example.

4. The suffix pronoun corresponding to (هِيَ) is (ـهَا).

5. For the 2nd person, Arabic has also two suffix pronouns; one for masculine, which is (ـكَ), corresponding to (أَنْتَ), and one for feminine, corresponding to (أَنْتِ), both of which are equivalent to the English "Your".

6. The suffix pronoun corresponding to (أَنَا) is (ـِي), corresponding to the English "My". This 1st person suffix pronoun is in fact the long vowel (ـِي), which requires the vowel of the preceding consonant to be always a "*Kasrah*".

7. If you examine the noun of the second group above, you will notice that the original noun (سَيَّارَةٌ) is feminine in gender, ending with a "*Taa Marbutah*". In this case the "*Taa Marbutah*" changes automatically in writing to a regular "*Taa*" to which we attach the suffix pronouns.

8. <u>Arabic suffix pronouns are added only to pure nouns, but not to adjectives.</u>

9. Also, once a noun receives a suffix pronoun, then it automatically becomes definite. Therefore, if we want to describe a noun with a suffix pronoun, then the adjective must have the definite article as the way to define it, since it does not receive the suffix pronouns. Examples:

١- هَذَا كِتَابِي الْجَدِيدُ .    This is my new book.

٢- هَلْ هَذِهِ سَيَّارَتُكَ الْجَدِيدَةُ ؟    Is this your new car?

## ❖ New Vocabulary Used in Full Meaningful Sentences:

|  |  |
|---|---|
| Her oven is clean. | فُرْنُهَا نَظِيفٌ . |
| Your cup is broken. | كُوبُكَ مَكْسُورٌ . |
| Your restaurant is excellent. | مَطْعَمُكَ مُمْتَازٌ . |
| My window is open. | نَافِذَتِي مَفْتُوحَةٌ . |
| Her refrigerator is new. | ثلاَّجَتُهَا جَدِيدَةٌ . |
| Is this your new cupboard? | هَلْ هَذِهِ خِزَانَتُكَ الْجَدِيدَةُ ؟ |
| Your pen is in his drawer. | قَلَمُكَ فِي دُرْجِهِ . |
| This is my new company. | هَذِهِ شَرِكَتِي الْجَدِيدَةُ . |
| Is your kettle in the cabinet? | هَلْ إِبْرِيقُكَ فِي الْخِزَانَةِ ؟ |
| Is your pot in the refrigerator? | هَلْ قِدْرُكَ فِي الثَّلاَّجَةِ ؟ |
| This is my plate and that is your plate. | هَذَا صَحْنِي وَذَلِكَ صَحْنُكَ . |
| This is his knife and that is her knife. | هَذَا سِكِّينُهُ وَذَلِكَ سِكِّينُهَا . |
| His fork is in his plate. | شَوْكَتُهُ فِي صَحْنِهِ . |

\* \* \*

**Remember!** / تَذَكَّرْ- تَذَكَّرِي!

1. The Arabic equivalents of the English "Possessive Pronouns" are short suffixes, consisting of one letter in four cases and two letters in one case.

2. They are all attached in writing to the end of the nouns with which they form the possessive relationship; that's why these are called in Arabic "Suffix Pronouns".

3. The suffix pronoun corresponding to (هُوَ) is (ـهُ); equivalent to the English (His). Its vowel changes from a "Dammah" to a "Kasrah" if the vowel of the preceding letter is a "Kasrah" **or a** "Yaa."

4. The suffix pronoun corresponding to (هِيَ) is (ـهَا); equivalent to the English (Her).

5. For the 2nd person, Arabic has also two suffix pronouns; one for masculine, which is (ـكَ), corresponding to (أَنْتَ), and one for feminine, corresponding to (أَنْتِ), both of which are equivalent to the English "Your".

6. The suffix pronoun corresponding to (أَنَا) is (ـِي), equivalent to the English "My". This 1st person suffix pronoun is, in fact, the long vowel (ـِي), which requires the vowel of the preceding consonant to be always a "Kasrah".

7. Nouns of feminine gender, ending with a "Taa Marbutah" change automatically in writing to a regular "Taa" to which we attach the suffix pronouns.

8. Arabic suffix pronouns are added only to pure nouns, but not to adjectives.

9. Once a noun receives a suffix pronoun, then it automatically becomes definite. Therefore, if we want to describe a noun that has a suffix pronoun, then that adjective must have the definite article as the way to define it, since it does receive the suffix pronouns.

## تَدْريباتٌ / Exercises

**1.** Read the following sentences and identify the possessive suffix pronouns, and say verbally their English equivalents:

١- دَفْتَري في حَقيبَتي .

٢- هَذِه سَيَّارَتُهُ الْقَديمَةُ .

٣- هَذَا صَحْنُكَ وَمِلعَقَتُكَ .

٤- شَوْكَتُهَا في صَحْنِها .

٥- هَلْ هَذِه شَرِكَتُكِ الْجَديدَةُ ؟

٦- سَاعَتُكَ جَميلَةٌ .

٧- فُرْنُهَا نَظيفٌ وَجَديدٌ .

٨- هَذَا قَلَمُكَ الأَحْمَرُ .

٩- هَلْ قِدْرُكِ في خِزَانَتِكِ ؟

١٠- هَلْ ثَلاَّجَتُكِ جَديدَةٌ ؟

١١- هَذَا بَيْتي الْجَديدُ .

١٢- هُوَ صَديقُهَا الْعَزيزُ .

\* \* \*

**2.** Translate the following English sentences into Arabic and provide full vocalization signs:

1. Is this your (masculine) notebook? = ..............................................

2. He is my dear friend. = ..............................................

3. This is your (feminine) spoon and fork. = ..............................................

4. Is he your (masculine) instructor? = ..............................................

5. This is his new car. = ..............................................

6. The book is in her drawer. = ..............................................

7. This is my new company. = ..............................................

\* \* \*

**3. Read the following sentences and then translate them into English orally:**

١- هَذَا صَدِيقِي الْعَرَبِيُّ .

٢- هَذِه سَيَّارَتُهُ الْقَدِيمَةُ .

٣- ثلاَّجَتُهَا جَدِيدَةٌ وَفُرْنُهَا قَدِيمٌ .

٤- هَلْ هَذِهِ أُخْتُكَ ؟

٥- هَلْ كُوبُكَ نَظِيفٌ ؟

٦- هَلْ هِيَ مُسْلِمَةٌ ؟

٧- هِيَ أُخْتٌ عَزِيزَةٌ .

٨- كِتَابُكِ فِي دُرْجِي .

٩- هَلْ دَفْتَرُكَ فِي حَقِيبَتِكَ ؟

١٠- هَلْ أَخِي صَدِيقُكَ ؟

* * *

**4. Restructure the following sentences by adding a <u>suffix pronoun</u> which corresponds to the <u>subject pronoun</u> provided in brackets; you might need to modify other parts of the sentence. The first is done as an example to follow:**

١- هَذِه سَيَّارَةٌ جَدِيدَةٌ . (أَنَا) ← هَذِهِ سَيَّارَتِي الْجَدِيدَةُ .

٢- هَلْ هَذَا مُدَرِّسٌ جَدِيدٌ ؟ (أَنْتَ) ← .................................... ؟

٣- هَلْ هُوَ صَدِيقٌ عَرَبِيٌّ ؟ (أَنْتِ) ← .................................... ؟

٤- هَلْ هِيَ أُمٌّ ؟ (هِيَ) ← .................................... ؟

٥- هَذَا أُسْتَاذٌ مُمْتَازٌ . (هُوَ) ← .................................... ؟

٦- هَذَا بَيْتٌ قَدِيمٌ . (أَنَا) ← .................................... ؟

**5. Choose the correct noun from those in brackets to fill in the blanks in the following sentences:**

١- هَلْ هَذِهِ خِزانَتُكَ .................... ؟ (جَديدَةٌ / الْجَديدَةُ / الْجَديدُ)

٢- هَلْ هُوَ صَديقُكَ .................... ؟ (الْيَهوديُّ / يَهوديٌّ / يَهوديَّةٌ)

٣- هَذا بَيْتُهُ .................... . (قَديمٌ / قَديمَةٌ / القَديمُ)

٤- هُوَ أُسْتاذُها .................... . (مَشْهورَةٌ / الْمَشْهورُ / مَشْهورٌ)

٥- هَذِهِ أُخْتي .................... . (صُغْرَى / صَغيرٌ / الصُّغْرَى)

٦- هِيَ صَديقَتُهُ .................... . (الْعَرَبيَّةُ / عَرَبيَّةٌ / عَرَبيٌّ)

٧- هَلْ هَذِهِ أُخْتُكَ .................... ؟ (كُبْرَى / كَبيرَةٌ / الْكُبْرَى)

\* \* \*

**5. Give full affirmative oral answers to the following questions using (نَعَمْ) at the beginning of the answer:** (Note: if the question implies the 2nd person, you need to use the 1st person pronoun in the answer, and if the question implies a 1st person, you need to use the 2nd person pronoun in the answer!)

١- هَلْ أُسْتاذُكَ مَسيحيٌّ ؟       ٢- هَلْ سَيّارَتُهُ جَديدَةٌ ؟

٣- هَلْ هَذِهِ مَدْرَسَتُكِ ؟        ٤- هَلْ جامِعَتُها مَشْهورَةٌ ؟

٥- هَلْ مَطْعَمي جَيِّدٌ ؟         ٦- هَلْ هُوَ صَديقُكَ ؟

٧- هَلْ هِيَ أُخْتُكَ ؟           ٨- هَلْ أَنْتَ تاجِرٌ غَنيٌّ ؟

٩- هَلْ دَرّاجَتُكَ حَمْراءُ ؟      ١٠- هَلْ هِيَ فَلّاحَةٌ فَقيرَةٌ ؟

١١- هَلْ دَرْسي سَهْلٌ ؟        ١٢- هَلْ أَنْتَ طالِبٌ جَديدٌ ؟

\* \* \*

# Lesson 10 — الدَّرْسُ الْعَاشِرُ

## الْجُمْلَةُ الإِسْمِيَّةُ : الْمُبْتَدَأُ والْخَبَرُ
### The Nominal Sentence: Subject and Predicate

❖ The nominal sentence in Arabic must start with a noun or a pronoun, and must, at least, have another noun or adjectival noun to provide information about the subject, to render the structure full and meaningful.

❖ Though nominal sentences in Arabic might not contain a verb at all, they correspond to English sentences where there is a verb to be (i.e. *is / are*) separating the first part of the sentence from the second part.

❖ In Arabic, the first part of such sentences is called (مُبْتَدَأٌ); English "Subject" and the second part is called (خَبَرٌ); English "Predicate."

❖ Let's now study the following examples of nominal sentences, containing subjects and predicates:

### أ

| | |
|---|---|
| ١- آدَمُ طَالِبٌ . = Adam is a student. | ٢- مَرْيَمُ مُدَرِّسَةٌ . = Maryam is a teacher. |
| ٣- هُوَ صَدِيقٌ . = He is a friend. | ٤- هِيَ أُخْتِي . = She is my sister. |
| ٥- أَنْتَ ذَكِيٌّ . = You are clever. | ٦- أَنْتِ مُخْلِصَةٌ . = You are sincere. |
| ٧- الشَّارِعُ وَسِخٌ . = The street is dirty. | ٨- الْغُرْفَةُ نَظِيفَةٌ . = The room is clean. |
| ٩- وَالِدُهُ تَاجِرٌ . = His father is a merchant. | ١٠- وَالِدَتُهَا طَبِيبَةٌ . = Her mother is a doctor. |

### ب

١- الأُسْتَاذُ الْجَدِيدُ مُمْتَازٌ . = The new professor is excellent.

٢- الطَّالِبَةُ الْعَرَبِيَّةُ ذَكِيَّةٌ . = The (female) Arab student is intelligent.

٣- هُوَ صَدِيقٌ عَزِيزٌ . = He is a dear friend.

٤- الْمَرْأَةُ أُسْتَاذَةٌ مَشْهُورَةٌ . = The woman is a famous professor.

\* \* \*

❖ **Explanatory Notes:**

1. When we examine the ten sentences in group (أ) above, we find that each consists of two words; the <u>first word</u> in each sentence is the <u>subject</u>, and the <u>second word</u> is the <u>predicate</u>. The <u>predicate</u> being a <u>noun</u> or <u>adjective</u> that provides information about the subject, thus rendering the whole structure as a full meaningful sentence.

2. In all these sentences, the <u>subject must be a definite noun</u>; a noun can be definite if it is a proper name, such as (آدَمُ) and (مَرْيَمُ) in the first two sentences; or a subject <u>pronoun</u>, such as (هُوَ) , (هِيَ), (أَنْتَ) and (أَنْتَ) in sentences 2 through 6; or a noun <u>with the definite article</u>, such as (الشَّارِعُ) and (الْغُرْفَةُ) in sentences 7 and 8; or a <u>noun with a suffix pronoun</u>, such as (ـهُ) an (ـهَا) in sentences 9 and 10.

3. In all these sentences, the <u>predicate</u> is either an <u>indefinite noun</u>, such as (طَالِبٌ) (مُدَرِّسَةٌ), (صَدِيقٌ), in sentences 1, 2, and 3 above; or a <u>noun with a suffix pronoun</u>, such as (أُخْتِي) in sentence 3; or and <u>adjectival noun</u> in the rest of the sentences. By adjectival noun, we mean a word that is an adjective, but is not directly related to another noun in a noun-adjective phrase.

4. An important note about such adjectival predicates is that <u>they have to agree with the subject in gender, but not in definiteness</u>. In fact, all predicates of nominal sentences agree with their subjects in gender, but not in definiteness.

5. Both the subjects and predicates of nominal sentences can be expanded by adding a direct adjective to each, such as the first two sentences of group (ب) above, where the phrases (الطَّالِبَةُ الْعَرَبِيَّةُ) and (الأُسْتَاذُ الْجَدِيدُ) are both noun-adjective phrases functioning as one unit subject; in this case the adjective

59

has to agree with the noun both in gender as well as in definiteness. The predicates of the above two sentences are respectively, (ذَكِيَّةٌ) and (مُمْتَازٌ); two adjectival nouns not directly forming a one unit adjectival phrases with the nouns preceding them.

6. The last two sentences of group (ب) above show us how the predicates of nominal sentences were expanded by making the predicate a noun-adjective phrase; respectively, (صَديقٌ عَزيزٌ) and (أُسْتَاذَةٌ مَشْهُورَةٌ).

\* \* \*

❖ **New Vocabulary:**

| | | | |
|---|---|---|---|
| miser, stingy | بَخيلٌ | dirty, unclean | وَسِخٌ |
| a river | نَهْرٌ | a village | قَرْيَةٌ |
| heavy | ثَقيلٌ | light (weight) | خَفيفٌ |
| weak | ضَعيفٌ | strong | قَويٌّ |
| an orchard | بُسْتَانٌ | a market | سُوقٌ |
| a family | عَائِلَةٌ | a garden | حَديقَةٌ |
| a box | صُنْدُوقٌ | a language | لُغَةٌ |
| a cow | بَقَرَةٌ | a dog | كَلْبٌ |

\* \* \*

❖ **New Vocabulary Used in Full Meaningful Nominal Sentences:**

| | |
|---|---|
| The street is dirty. | الشَّارِعُ وَسِخٌ . |
| He is a miser man. | هُوَ رَجُلٌ بَخيلٌ . |
| The village is small. | الْقَرْيَةُ صَغيرَةٌ . |

| | |
|---|---|
| This is a long river. | هَذَا نَهْرٌ طَوِيلٌ . |
| The box is light. | الصُّنْدُوقُ خَفِيفٌ . |
| That is a heavy box. | ذَلِكَ صُنْدُوقٌ ثَقِيلٌ . |
| He is a strong boy. | هُوَ وَلَدٌ قَوِيٌّ . |
| She is a weak girl. | هِيَ بِنْتٌ ضَعِيفَةٌ . |
| This is a big market. | هَذَا سُوقٌ كَبِيرٌ . |
| The orchard is beautiful. | الْبُسْتَانُ جَمِيلٌ . |
| This is a large garden. | هَذِهِ حَدِيقَةٌ وَاسِعَةٌ . |
| This is a happy family. | هَذِهِ عَائِلَةٌ سَعِيدَةٌ . |
| The Arabic language is easy. | اللُّغَةُ الْعَرَبِيَّةُ سَهْلَةٌ . |
| This is a small dog. | هَذَا كَلْبٌ صَغِيرٌ . |
| This is a big cow. | هَذِهِ بَقَرَةٌ كَبِيرَةٌ . |

\* \* \*

## Remember! / اِتَذَكَّرْ - تَذَكَّرِي!

1. The nominal sentences introduced in this lesson represent a very common type of sentences that have no verbs.
2. Rendering these sentences into English would require using a verb to be (i.e. *is* or *are*).
3. Such sentences consist of two parts: subject and predicate.
4. The subject must always be definite.
5. The predicate can be an indefinite adjectival noun.
6. But the predicate must always agree with the subject in gender, though not in definiteness.
7. Both the subject and the predicate may consist of a noun-adjective phrase.

## تَدْرِيبَاتٌ / Exercises

**1.** Read the following sentences and identify the subjects by underlining them once and the predicates by underlining them twice:

١- الْغُرْفَةُ نَظِيفَةٌ .　　　　٢- هُوَ مَدَرِّسٌ غَنِيٌّ .

٣- هَذَا تِلْمِيذٌ فَقِيرٌ .　　　　٤- الدَّرْسُ الأَوَّلُ سَهْلٌ .

٥- قَرْيَتِي صَغِيرَةٌ .　　　　٦- نَهْرُ الْمِسِسِيبِّي طَوِيلٌ .

٧- الْبُسْتَانُ جَمِيلٌ .　　　　٨- هَذَا صُنْدُوقٌ خَفِيفٌ .

٩- هِيَ عَائِلَةٌ سَعِيدَةٌ .　　　　١٠- عُمَرُ رَجُلٌ مَشْهُورٌ .

١١- هَذَا بَيْتٌ جَدِيدٌ .　　　　١٢- هُوَ صَدِيقٌ عَزِيزٌ .

\* \* \*

**2.** Translate the following English sentences into Arabic and provide full vocalization signs:

1. This is an easy language. = ...........................................

2. The street is dirty. = ...........................................

3. That's a happy family. = ...........................................

4. The market is big. = ...........................................

5. This is his new car. = ...........................................

6. The garden is spacious. = ...........................................

7. This is a heavy box. = ...........................................

8. This is a strong man. ...........................................

9. The small dog is weak. ...........................................

3. Read the following sentences and then translate them into English orally:

١- لَيْلَى بِنْتٌ مُهَذَّبَةٌ .   ٢- هَذِهِ بَقَرَةٌ كَبِيرَةٌ .

٣- الثَّلاَّجَةُ جَدِيدَةٌ .   ٤- أُخْتِي طَالِبَةٌ مُجْتَهِدَةٌ .

٥- كُوبُكَ نَظِيفٌ .   ٦- هَذِهِ سَيَّارَةٌ جَدِيدَةٌ .

٧- ذَلِكَ صُنْدُوقٌ ثَقِيلٌ .   ٨- هُوَ رَجُلٌ بَخِيلٌ .

٩- هِيَ طَالِبَةٌ عَرَبِيَّةٌ .   ١٠- هَذَا أَخِي الْعَزِيزُ .

* * *

4. The following linguistic structures contain both full meaningful sentences and adjectival phrases that are not full meaningful sentences. Your task is to identify the full meaningful sentences first by placing a period at the end of these, and by placing three suspension points at the end of those which are only noun-adjective phrases, and then translate each into English; follow the two given examples:

---
١- سَيَّارَتِي الْجَدِيدَةُ   ⇦   سَيَّارَتِي الْجَدِيدَةُ ...   ⇦   my new car...

٢- هَذَا مُدَرِّسٌ جَدِيدٌ .   ⇦   هَذَا مُدَرِّسٌ جَدِيدٌ   ⇦   This is a new teacher .

---

٣- هُوَ صَدِيقٌ عَرَبِيٌّ   ..............................

٤- دَرْسٌ صَعْبٌ   ..............................

٥- أُسْتَاذٌ مُمْتَازٌ   ..............................

٦- هَذَا بَيْتٌ قَدِيمٌ   ..............................

٧- الْغُرْفَةُ النَّظِيفَةُ   ..............................

٨- الْقَرْيَةُ صَغِيرَةٌ   ..............................

٩- هِيَ تِلْمِيذَةٌ ذَكِيَّةٌ   ..............................

* * *

**Lesson 11**

تَرَاكِيبُ الإِسْتِفْهَام وَأَدَوَاتُهُ : (١)
(هَلْ) و (مَا) و (مَنْ) و (كَيْفَ) و (أَيْنَ) ؟

The Interrogative (Question) Structures and Its Particles:

(هَلْ ...؟) = Is / Are...? / (مَا ...؟) = What...?

(كَيْفَ ...؟) = How ...? / (مَنْ ...؟) = Who ...?

(أَيْنَ ...؟) = Where ...?

❖ In this lesson, we introduce five commonly used interrogative particles and learn about their characteristics through using them in full meaningful contexts.

❖ Following, you will see examples of the usage of these question particles in full context; then you will see parallel to the question a typical answer:

| An Answer / جَوَابٌ | | A Question / سُؤَالٌ |
|---|---|---|
| نَعَمْ ، أَنَا طَالِبٌ .<br>Yes, I am a student. | هَلْ ؟<br>Is / Are? | هَلْ أَنْتَ طَالِبٌ ؟<br>Are you a student? |
| لَا ، هِيَ مُهَنْدِسَةٌ .<br>No, she is an engineer. | | هَلْ هِيَ أُسْتَاذَةٌ ؟<br>Is she a professor |
| نَعَمْ ، أَدْرُسُ الْعَرَبِيَّةَ .<br>Yes, I am studying Arabic. | | هَلْ تَدْرُسُ الْعَرَبِيَّةَ؟<br>Are you studying Arabic? |

\* \* \*

| | | |
|---|---|---|
| هَذَا كِتَابٌ جَدِيدٌ .<br>This is a new book. | مَا ؟<br>What? | مَا هَذَا ؟<br>What is this? |
| هَذِهِ رِسَالَةٌ عَاجِلَةٌ .<br>This is an express letter. | | مَا هَذِهِ ؟<br>What is this? |

64

| | | | |
|---|---|---|---|
| إِسْمِي آدَمُ. | My name is Adam. | مَا اسْمُكَ ؟ | What is your name? |
| أَنَا مُهَنْدِسَةٌ. | I am an engineer. | مَا مِهْنَتُكِ ؟ | What is your profession? |

**مَنْ ؟ Who?**

| | | | |
|---|---|---|---|
| هَذِهِ مَرْيَمُ. | This is Maryam. | مَنْ هَذِهِ ؟ | Who is this? |
| أَنَا عُمَرُ الشَّرِيفُ. | I am Omar Ash-Shareef. | مَنْ أَنْتَ ؟ | Who are you? |
| هِيَ صَدِيقَتِي لَيْلَى. | She is my friend Layla. | مَنْ هِيَ ؟ | Who is she? |

**كَيْفَ ؟ How?**

| | | | |
|---|---|---|---|
| بِخَيْرٍ، الْحَمْدُ لِلَّهِ! | Fine, praise be to God! | كَيْفَ حَالُكَ ؟ | How are you? |
| لاَ بَأْسَ، أَحْسَنُ. | Not bad, better. | كَيْفَ صِحَّةُ وَالِدِكَ ؟ | How is your father's health? |
| سَافَرْتُ بِالسَّيَّارَةِ. | I traveled by car. | كَيْفَ سَافَرْتَ ؟ | How did you travel? |

**أَيْنَ ؟ Where?**

| | | | |
|---|---|---|---|
| الْقَلَمُ عَلَى الْمَكْتَبِ. | The pen is on the desk! | أَيْنَ الْقَلَمُ ؟ | Where is the pen? |
| أُمِّي فِي السُّوقِ. | My mother is in the market. | أَيْنَ أُمُّكَ ؟ | Where is your mother? |
| دَرَسْتُ الْعَرَبِيَّةَ فِي الْجَامِعَةِ. | I studied Arabic at the university. | أَيْنَ دَرَسْتَ الْعَرَبِيَّةَ ؟ | Where did you study Arabic? |
| أَنَا قَادِمٌ مِنَ الْقَاهِرَةِ. | I am coming from Cairo. | مِنْ أَيْنَ أَنْتَ قَادِمٌ ؟ | Where are you coming from? |

❖ **Explanatory Notes:**

1. The Arabic interrogative particle (هَل ...؟) is equivalent to an English question starting with the verbs to be "Is / Are…?" Like English, the answer to such question must start with "Yes" or "No." As you can see from the examples above it can be followed by a <u>pronoun</u>, a <u>noun</u> or a <u>verb</u>.

2. The Arabic interrogative particle (مَا ...؟) is equivalent to the English "What…?", but it is restricted to ask about the nature of things that are not humans. Also, unlike English, it cannot be followed by a verb. It is commonly used followed by the demonstrative pronouns (هَذا / هَذِه), or to ask about someone's name or profession.

3. The Arabic interrogative particle (مَنْ ...؟), is equivalent to the English "Who…?" and it is exclusively used to ask about the identity of persons or human beings.

4. The Arabic interrogative particle (كَيْفَ ...؟), is equivalent to the English "How…?" Like English, it is most commonly used to ask about how someone is doing, or about someone's health or state of well being. Also, like English, it can <u>be followed by a verb if the intent is to ask about how a certain action was done.</u>

5. The Arabic interrogative particle (أَيْنَ ...؟), is equivalent to the English "Where…?" Like the English, it is used exclusively to ask about the <u>location of someone or something, or about the place where a certain action happened.</u> In this sense it can be <u>equally followed by a noun or a verb.</u>

6. Since (أَيْنَ ...؟) is a particle related to location, then it is commonly used in conjunction with two prepositions used to express the meanings of, "Where from…?" or "Where to…?" In such cases, the prepositions (مِنْ) and (إِلَى) are used before the interrogative particle (أَيْنَ ...؟). Examples:

مِنْ أَيْنَ أَنْتَ قَادِمٌ ؟          إِلَى أَيْنَ أَنْتَ ذَاهِبٌ ؟

<u>Where</u> are you coming <u>from</u>?    * * *    <u>Where</u> are you going <u>to</u>?

❖ **New Vocabulary:**

## Nouns / أَسْمَاء

| | | | |
|---|---|---|---|
| a question = سُؤَالٌ | an answer = جَوَابٌ |
| a letter = رِسَالَةٌ | express = عَاجِلَةٌ |
| name / your name = إِسْمٌ / اسْمُكَ | profession / your... = مِهْنَةٌ / مِهْنَتُكَ |
| condition / your... = حَالٌ / حَالُكَ | a magazine = مَجَلَّةٌ |
| a newspaper = جَرِيدَةٌ | a driver = سَائِقٌ |
| a shop = دُكَّانٌ | a hotel = فُنْدُقٌ |
| a barber = حَلَّاقٌ | a carpenter = نَجَّارٌ |
| an apartment = شَقَّةٌ | a key = مِفْتَاحٌ |
| health = صِحَّةٌ | father / your ... = وَالِدٌ / وَالِدُكَ |
| good, in good state = خَيْرٌ / بِخَيْرٍ | going (noun) = ذَاهِبٌ |
| coming (noun) = قَادِمٌ | Cairo = القَاهِرَة |

## Verbs / أَفْعَال

| | | | |
|---|---|---|---|
| you study = تَدْرُسُ | I study = أَدْرُسُ |
| you studied = دَرَسْتَ | I studied = دَرَسْتُ |
| you traveled = سَافَرْتَ | I traveled = سَافَرْتُ |

67

## حُرُوف / Particles

Is ? Are...? = ؟ ... هَلْ          Who...? = ؟ ... مَنْ

What...? = ؟ ... مَا            How...? = ؟ ... كَيْفَ

Where...? = ؟ ... أَيْنَ

\* \* \*

## تَذَكَّرْ- تَذَكَّرِي! / Remember!

1. Arabic, like English, has a set of "Interrogative Particles"; each with its specific meaning which determines its usage.

2. Like English too, the place of the "Interrogative Particle" is at the beginning of the question linguistic structure.

3. "Interrogative Particles" can be followed by a proper name, noun, pronoun or a verb if the question is related to action.

4. (هَلْ ...؟) means "Is / Are...?" The answer to a question with this particle must start with (نَعَمْ) or (لَا); Arabic for "Yes" or "No."

5. (مَا ...؟) means "What...?" and it is used to ask about the nature of things that are non-human.

6. (مَنْ ...؟) means "Who...?" and it is used to ask about the identity of human beings.

7. (كَيْفَ ...؟) means "How...?" Like English, it is used to ask about the condition or state of well being of some one; also it can be followed by a verb to ask about how a certain action took place.

8. (أَيْنَ ...؟), like the English "Where...?" is used to ask about the location or place of something or someone. It also appears in conjunction with the two prepositions (مِنْ) or (إِلَى) if the situation involves a destination of coming from or going to.

# تَدْرِيبَاتٌ / Exercises

**1. Read the following questions; answer them verbally first, then write down your answers on the dotted spaces:**

١- هَلْ تَدْرُسُ الْعَرَبِيَّةَ ؟ ....................................

٢- مَنْ أَنْتَ / أَنْتِ ؟ ....................................

٣- مِنْ أَيْنَ أَنْتَ / أَنْتِ ؟ ....................................

٤- كَيْفَ حَالُكَ / حَالُكِ ؟ ....................................

٥- مَا هَذَا الْكِتَابُ ؟ ....................................

٦- كَيْفَ سَافَرْتَ إِلَى نِيُويُورك ؟ ....................................

٧- هَلْ أَنْتَ طَالِبٌ ؟ ....................................

\* \* \*

**2. Translate the following sentences into Arabic (orally and written):**

1. Where are you studying Arabic? = ؟....................................

2. Are you a new student? = ؟....................................

3. Where are you (female) from? = ؟....................................

4. Who is your (female) father? = ؟....................................

5. How is your (male) health? = ؟....................................

6. Where are you (male) going? = ؟....................................

7. What is this sheet of paper? = ؟....................................

\* \* \*

**3. (Chain Oral Drill)** One student asks the question, the next student answers; then the next student asks the next question and a third one answers, and so on the process continues as a chain oral drill:

(١) مَنْ أَنْتَ ؟ (٢) مَا اسْمُكَ ؟ (٣) مَا مِهْنَتُكَ ؟ (٤) كَيْفَ حَالُكَ ؟ (٥) أَيْنَ كِتَابُكَ ؟ (٦) هَلْ أَنْتَ عَرَبِيٌّ ؟ (٧) مِنْ أَيْنَ أَنْتَ ؟ (٨) مَنْ هَذِهِ الأُسْتَاذَةُ ؟ (٩) مَا هَذَا الْكِتَابُ ؟ (١٠) هَلْ أَنْتِ عَرَبِيَّةٌ ؟

* * *

**4.** Match each question from the sentences in the right-hand with its appropriate answer from the sentences in the left-hand: (*this a general drill using all the interrogative particles learned thus far*):

| | |
|---|---|
| ١- هَلْ أَنْتَ طَالِبٌ ؟ | أَهْلِي بِخَيْرٍ ، اَلْحَمْدُ لِله ! |
| ٢- أَيْنَ تَدْرُسُ الْعَرَبِيَّةَ ؟ | سَافَرْتُ بِالسَّيَّارَةِ . |
| ٣- كَيْفَ أَهْلُكَ ؟ | هَذَا الأُسْتَاذُ الْجَدِيدُ . |
| ٤- مَا اسْمُكَ ؟ | أَنَا ذَاهِبٌ إِلَى الْبَيْتِ . |
| ٥- مِنْ أَيْنَ أَنْتَ ؟ | لاَ ، أَنَا أُخْتُ لَيْلَى . |
| ٦- كَيْفَ سَافَرْتَ إِلَى شِيكَاغُو ؟ | أَنَا مِنْ أَمْرِيكَا . |
| ٧- مَا هَذَا الْكِتَابُ ؟ | إِسْمِي آدَمُ (مَرْيَمُ) . |
| ٨- إِلَى أَيْنَ أَنْتَ ذَاهِبٌ ؟ | أَدْرُسُ الْعَرَبِيَّةَ فِي الْجَامِعَةِ . |
| ٩- مَنْ هَذَا الرَّجُلُ ؟ | نَعَمْ ، أَنَا طَالِبٌ . |
| ١٠- هَلْ أَنْتِ لَيْلَى ؟ | هَذَا كِتَابُ اللُّغَةِ الْعَرَبِيَّةِ . |

**5.** Unscramble the following sets of words to make from each of them a full meaningful sentence, as in the given example, and then translate the resultant sentences into English:

كَيْفَ سَافَرْتَ إِلَى الْقَاهِرَةِ ؟ = الْقَاهِرَةِ / سَافَرْتَ / كَيْفَ / إِلَى
How did you travel to Cairo?

١- أَنْتَ / مِنْ / أَيْنَ / قَادِمٌ ................................ ؟ =

٢- كَيْفَ / سَافَرْتَ / الْقَاهِرَةِ / إِلَى ................................ ؟ =

٣- هَذَا / الْكِتَابُ / مَا / الْجَدِيدُ ................................ ؟ =

٤- هَلْ / طَالِبٌ / جَدِيدٌ / أَنْتَ ................................ ؟ =

٥- اسْمُكِ / مَا / وَمَا / مِهْنَتُكِ ................................ ؟ =

٦- أُسْتَاذُكَ / هُوَ / الْعَرَبِيُّ / مَنْ ................................ ؟ =

٧- إِلَى / أَنْتِ / ذَاهِبَةٌ / أَيْنَ ................................ ؟ =

٨- الرَّجُلُ / مَنْ / هَذَا / الطَّوِيلُ ................................ ؟ =

71

**Lesson 12** ━━━━━━━━━━━━━━━━━━━━━━━━━━━ الدَّرْسُ الثَّانِي عَشَرَ

> تَرَاكِيبُ الإِسْتِفْهَام وَأَدَوَاتُهُ : (٢)
> (مَتَى) و (كَمْ) و (مَاذَا) و (لِمَاذَا) ؟
>
> **The Interrogative (Question) Structures and Its Particles:**
>
> (مَتَى ... ؟) = When? / (كَمْ ... ؟) = How many...?
>
> (لِمَاذَا ... ؟) = Why ...? / (مَاذَا ... ؟) = What ...?

❖ In this lesson, we introduce four more commonly used interrogative particles, and we learn about their characteristics through using them in full meaningful contexts.

❖ Following, you will see examples of the usage of these question particles in full context; then you will see parallel to each question a typical answer:

| An Answer / جَوَابٌ | | A Question / سُؤَالٌ |
|---|---|---|
| فِي السَّاعَةِ الْوَاحِدَةِ . | مَتَى ؟ | مَتَى يَبْدَأُ الدَّرْسُ ؟ |
| At one o'clock. | When? | When does the lesson start? |
| فِي السَّاعَةِ الثَّانِيَةِ وَالرُّبْعِ . | | مَتَى مَوْعِدُ وُصُولِ الطَّائِرَةِ ؟ |
| At quarter past two o'clock. | | When is the arrival time of the plane? |
| بَعْدَ سَاعَةٍ . | | مَتَى تُرِيدُ أَنْ تَأْكُلَ ؟ |
| After an hour. | | When do you want to eat? |

* * *

| | | |
|---|---|---|
| خَمْسُ غُرَفٍ . | كَمْ ؟ | كَمْ غُرْفَةً فِي الْبَيْتِ ؟ |
| Five rooms. | How many? | How many rooms are there in the house |
| عَشَرَةَ كُتُبٍ . | | كَمْ كِتَابًا قَرَأْتَ ؟ |
| Ten books. | | How many books did you read? |

| | | |
|---|---|---|
| أَكْتُبُ رِسَالَةً. | | مَاذَا تَفْعَلُ؟ |
| I am writing a letter. | **مَاذَا؟** What? | What are you doing? |
| أُرِيدُ طَعَامًا وَشَرَابًا. | | مَاذَا تُرِيدِينَ؟ |
| I want food and drink. | | What do you (fem.) want? |
| قَرَأْتُ قِصَّةً. | | مَاذَا قَرَأْتَ؟ |
| I read (past tense) a story | | What did you read? |

\* \* \*

| | | |
|---|---|---|
| لِأَنَّ زَوْجَتِي مَاتَتْ. | | لِمَاذَا أَنْتَ حَزِينٌ؟ |
| Because my wife died. | **لِمَاذَا؟** Why? | Why are you sad? |
| لِأَنَّهُ مَرِيضٌ. | | لِمَاذَا هُوَ غَائِبٌ؟ |
| Because he is sick. | | Why is he absent? |
| أُسَافِرُ إِلَى أَمْرِيكَا لِلدِّرَاسَةِ. | | لِمَاذَا تُسَافِرُ إِلَى أَمْرِيكَا؟ |
| I am traveling to America for studying. | | Why are you traveling to America? |
| لِأَنَّكَ تَأَخَّرْتَ عَنِ الْمَوْعِدِ. | | لِمَاذَا ذَهَبْتَ وَحْدَكَ؟ |
| Because you were late for the appointment. | | Why did you go alone? |

\* \* \*

❖ **Explanatory Notes:** While examining the four sets of examples above, you need to observe the following points:

1. Like the English "When...?", the Arabic (مَتَى ...؟), is used to ask about the time of an event or an action; therefore it could be followed by either a verb or a noun. In the answer to a question starting with (مَتَى ...؟), one is expected to use a preposition or an adverb of time followed by a noun that refers to time; such as hour, day, month, etc.

2. The Arabic (كَمْ ...؟), like the English "How many...?" is used to ask about the number of some thing; therefore it is only followed by a noun, and that noun must always be in its singular, accusative *nunated* form, (i.e. it bears *Tanween* of *Fathah*.) However, the number in response to the question must be in its plural form.

73

3. The Arabic (مَاذَا ...؟), shares with the previously introduced Arabic interrogative particle (مَا ...؟), the English meaning of "<u>What</u>...?." However, whereas (مَا ...؟) is followed by nouns, (مَاذَا ...؟) <u>must always be followed by verbs only.</u>

4. The Arabic (لِمَاذَا ...؟), like the English "<u>Why</u>...?" is used to ask about the <u>reason for someone's specific state or, or why a certain action happened. In this sense it can be equally followed by a noun or a verb.</u> In the answer to a question started with (لِمَاذَا ...؟) one is bound to use a word that has the meaning of "because"; and in Arabic one of the following two devices are used: (لِـ) or (لِأَنَّ) followed by a <u>noun</u> or a <u>suffix pronoun</u>.

\* \* \*

### ❖ New Vocabulary:

( أَسْمَاء / Nouns )

| | |
|---|---|
| ساعَة = hour, watch | السَّاعَة = o'clock, the hour |
| الْوَاحِدَة = (the) first, one | مَوْعِد / الْمَوْعِد = appointed time |
| وُصُول = arrival | الثَّانِيَة = the second, two |
| رُبْع / الرُّبْع = quarter | خَمْس = five |
| غُرَف (غُرْفَة) = rooms (a room) | عَشْرَة = ten |
| كُتُب (كِتَاب) = books (a book) | طَعَامًا = food |
| شَرَابًا = drink | قِصَّة = a story |
| حَزِينٌ = sad | زَوْجَتِي (زَوْجَة+ي) = my wife |

غَائِب = absent        مَرِيض = sick, ill

لِلدِّرَاسَةِ (لِ+ال+دِرَاسَة) = for studying        وَحْدَكَ (وَحْدَ+كَ) = by your self, alone

## أَفْعَال / Verbs

يَبْدَأُ = begins        تُرِيدُ (أَنْ) = want (to) (you, masculine)

تَأْكُلَ = eat (you, masculine)        قَرَأْتَ = read (past tense, you, masculine)

تَفْعَلُ = you do        أَكْتُبُ = I write, I am writing

تُرِيدِينَ (أَنْ) = you want (present tense)        أُرِيدُ = I want

قَرَأْتُ = I read (past tense)        مَاتَتْ = she died

تُسَافِرُ = you are traveling (masculine)        أُسَافِرُ = I am traveling

تَأَخَّرْتَ (عَنْ) = you were late (masculine)        يَفْعَلُ = he does (present tense)

## حُرُوف / Particles

مَتَى ... ؟ = When...?        كَمْ ...؟ = How many...?

مَاذَا ... ؟ = What... do (did)?        لِمَاذَا ...؟ = Why...?

بَعْدَ = after        لِأَنَّ = because

لِأَنَّهُ (لِأَنَّ+هُ) = because he        لِأَنَّكَ (لِأَنَّ+كَ) = because you

\* \* \*

## Remember! / تَذَكَّرْ- تَذَكَّرِي!

1. Arabic, like English, has a set of "Interrogative Particles"; each with its specific meaning which determines its usage.

2. Like English too, the place of the "Interrogative Particle" is at the beginning of the question linguistic structure.

3. "Interrogative Particles" can be followed by a proper name, noun, pronoun or a verb if the question is related to action.

4. (مَتَى ...؟) means "When…?" and it is used to ask about the timing of an event or an action. The response to a question with this particle will require an answer containing certain prepositions or adverbs of time.

5. (كَمْ ...؟) means "How many…?" and it is used to ask about the quantity of a noun. Unlike English, the noun following this interrogative particle must be in its singular, accusative 'nunated' form. In the response, however, we revert to the plural form of the noun in question.

6. (مَاذَا ...؟) has the same identical meaning of the previously studied (مَا ...؟) "What…?" in English. However, (مَاذَا ...؟) can be followed only by a verb; so in the translation it should be rendered as implying, "What…do" or "What… did" depending on the tense of the verb. In response to a question with (مَاذَا ...؟), the answer should always start with a verb indicating the action or activity one is doing or has done.

7. (لِمَاذَا ...؟), like the English "Why…?" is used to ask about the reason for someone's specific state or, or why a certain action happened. In this sense it can be equally followed by a noun or a verb. In the answer to a question started with (لِمَاذَا ...؟) one is bound to use a word that has the meaning of "because"; and in Arabic one of the following two devices are used: (لِـ) or (لِأَنَّ) followed by a noun or a suffix pronoun.

\* \* \*

## تَدْريبَاتٌ / Exercises

**1.** Read the following; answer them verbally first, then write down your answers on the dotted spaces:

١- مَتَى تَذْهَبُ إِلَى الْمَدْرَسَةِ ؟ ..................................

٢- كَمْ طَالِبًا فِي الصَّفِّ ؟ ..................................

٣- مَاذَا تُرِيدِينَ ؟ ..................................

٤- لِمَاذَا سَافَرْتَ إِلَى مِصْرَ ؟ ..................................

٥- كَمْ مُعَلِّمَةً فِي الْمَدْرَسَةِ ؟ ..................................

٦- لِمَاذَا أَنْتَ حَزِينٌ ؟ ..................................

٧- مَتَى مَوْعِدُ وُصُولِ الطَّائِرَةِ ؟ ..................................

* * *

**2.** Translate the following sentences into Arabic (Orally and written):

1. What do you (male) want to eat? = ..................................?

2. How many (female) students are in the class? = ..................................?

3. When do you (male) go to the university? = ..................................?

4. Why is she absent today? = ..................................?

5. What do you (female) want? = ..................................?

6. How many rooms are in your (male) house? = ..................................?

7. What do you (female) want? = ..................................?

* * *

77

**3. (Chain Oral Drill)** One student asks the question, the next student answers; then the next student asks the next question and a third one answers, and so the process continues as a chain oral drill (*this a general drill using all the interrogative particles learned thus far*):

(١) هَلْ بَيْتُكَ كَبِيرٌ ؟ (٢) مَاذَا تُرِيدُ ؟ (٣) كَيْفَ حَالُكَ (حَالُكِ) ؟

(٤) أَيْنَ كِتَابُكَ ؟ (٥) هَلْ أَنْتَ عَرَبِيٌّ ؟ (٦) لِمَاذَا تَأَخَّرْتَ عَنِ الْمَوْعِدِ؟

(٧) مَنْ هَذِهِ الأُسْتَاذَةُ ؟ (٨) مَا هَذَا الْكِتَابُ ؟ (٩) هَلْ أَنْتِ مِنْ فَرَنْسَا ؟

\* \* \*

**4.** Match each question from the sentences on the right-hand with its appropriate answer from the sentences on the left-hand: (*this a general drill using all the interrogative particles learned thus far*):

| | |
|---|---|
| أَهْلِي بِخَيْرٍ ، اَلْحَمْدُ لله ! | ١- هَلْ أَنْتَ طَالِبٌ ؟ |
| أَسْتَعِدُّ لِلإِمْتِحَانِ جَيِّدًا . | ٢- أَيْنَ تَدْرُسُ الْعَرَبِيَّةَ ؟ |
| هَذَا الأُسْتَاذُ الْجَدِيدُ . | ٣- كَيْفَ أَهْلُكَ ؟ |
| نَعَمْ ، أَنَا طَالِبٌ . | ٤- مَا اسْمُكَ ؟ |
| لاَ ، أَنَا أُخْتُ لَيْلَى . | ٥- كَمْ طَالِبًا فِي الصَّفِّ ؟ |
| فِي الصَّفِّ عَشْرُ طُلاَّبٍ . | ٦- كَيْفَ تَنْجَحُ فِي الإِمْتِحَانِ ؟ |
| لأَنِّي فَائِزَةٌ بِالْجَائِزَةِ . | ٧- مَاذَا تَكْتُبُ (تَكْتُبِينَ) ؟ |
| أَدْرُسُ الْعَرَبِيَّةَ فِي الْجَامِعَةِ . | ٨- لِمَاذَا أَنْتَ سَعِيدَةٌ ؟ |
| نَعَمْ ، أَنَا طَالِبٌ . | ٩- مَنْ هَذَا الرَّجُلُ ؟ |
| أَكْتُبُ رِسَالَةً إِلَى أُمِّي . | ١٠- هَلْ أَنْتِ لَيْلَى ؟ |

**5.** Unscramble the following sets of words to make from each of them a full meaningful sentence, as in the given example, and then translate the resultant sentences into English:

> عَنْ / تَأَخَّرْتَ / لِمَاذَا / الْمَوْعِدِ ⟵ لِمَاذَا تَأَخَّرْتَ عَنِ الْمَوْعِدِ ؟ =
> Why were you late for the appointment?

١- الأَحْمَرُ / قَلَمُكَ / أَيْنَ ⟵ ..................... ؟ =

٢- حَالُ / أُسْرَتِكِ / كَيْفَ ⟵ ..................... ؟ =

٣- صَدِيقُكِ / هَلْ / هَذَا / الْمِصْرِيُّ ⟵ ..................... ؟ =

٤- أَنْ / تُرِيدُ / تَأْكُلَ / مَاذَا ⟵ ..................... ؟ =

٥- تُسَافِرُ / فَرَنْسَا / مَتَى / إِلَى ⟵ ..................... ؟ =

٦- حَزِينَةٌ / أَنْتِ / لِمَاذَا ⟵ ..................... ؟ =

٧- الْكَبِيرُ / هَذَا / الْبِنَاءُ / مَا ⟵ ..................... ؟ =

٨- الطَّوِيلُ / هَذَا / مَنْ / الرَّجُلُ ⟵ ..................... ؟ =

# Lesson 13 — الدَّرْسُ الثَّالِثَ عَشَرَ

## الظَّرْفُ (عِنْدَ) وَخُصُوصِيَّاتُهُ
### The Adverb (عِنْدَ) and Its Particulars

❖ Arabic linguists consider the word (عِنْدَ) as an <u>adverb</u>; the closest meaning of which is '**at**', '**with**' or '**by**'.

❖ Depending of what noun follows it, it can be an '**adverb of time**' or an '**adverb of place.**'

❖ Now let's study the following examples:

| As Adverb of Place | As Adverb of Time |
|---|---|
| قَابَلْتُهُ عِنْدَ الْمَكْتَبَةِ. | قَابَلْتُهُ عِنْدَ الظُّهْرِ. |
| I met him at (by) the library. | I met him at noon. |
| رَأَيْتُ مَرْيَمَ عِنْدَ دُكَّانِ الْفَوَاكِهِ. | رَأَيْتُ مَرْيَمَ عِنْدَ غُرُوبِ الشَّمْسِ. |
| I saw Maryam at the fruit shop. | I saw Maryam at sunset time. |

❖ What is further unique about this particle is that it assumes the special meaning of the verb 'have / has' when is is attached to one of the Arabic 'Suffix Pronouns' which we studied earlier. Let's now study the following sentences:

| | |
|---|---|
| He has a new car. | عِنْدَهُ سَيَّارَةٌ جَدِيدَةٌ. |
| She has a beautiful cat. | عِنْدَهَا هِرَّةٌ جَمِيلَةٌ. |
| Do you (male) have an Arabic dictionary? | هَلْ عِنْدَكَ قَامُوسٌ عَرَبِيٌّ؟ |
| Do you (female) have children? | هَلْ عِنْدَكِ أَوْلَادٌ؟ |
| I have a pleasant piece of news. | عِنْدِي خَبَرٌ سَارٌّ. |

\* \* \*

❖ **Explanatory Notes:**

1. The particle(عِنْدَ), is designated by Arab linguists as an '**adverb**.'

2. When used by itself, without an attached pronoun, it can be an '**adverb** of time' or an 'adverb of place', depending on the meaning of the noun that follows it and on the conext in general, as the examples given above illustrate.

3. When this paricle is attached to one of the suffix pronouns, it assumes the possessive meaning of the verb '**has**' or '**have**.' This is, of course, an idiomatic meaning, and the literal meaning would be something like, '*with me there is a new car*' or '*in my possession I have a new car*' for example.

4. Note also that when used with suffix pronouns, the object of possession follows and is always in the indefinite form; such as (سَيَّارَةٌ جَدِيدَةٌ), (هِرَّةٌ جَمِيلَةٌ), (قَامُوسٌ) and (خَبَرٌ سَارٌّ), (عَرَبِيٌّ), (أَوْلَادٌ) in the examples given above.

5. The particle(عِنْدَ) itself is invariable in the since that it does not change the *Fathah* vowel over its finál letter the *Daal*; but when the attached pronoun is the 1st person suffix pronoun (ي) the vowel is changed as a matter of necessity to harmonize with it, thus becoming a *Kasrah* instead of the *Fathah*.

\* \* \*

❖ **New Vocabulary:**

Nouns / أَسْمَاء

the library = الْمَكْتَبة                (the) noon = الظُّهْرِ

shop = دُكَّان                (the) sunset = غُرُوبِ الشَّمْسِ

cat (male/ female) = هِرٌّ / هِرَّةٌ                the fruits = الْفَوَاكِهِ

a piece of news = خَبَرٌ                a dictionary = قَامُوسٌ

pleasant, pleasing = سَارٌّ                children, boys = أَوْلَادٌ

question = سُؤَالٌ                a dog = كَلْبٌ

81

## Verbs / أَفْعَال

I saw = رَأَيْتُ     I met him = قَابَلْتُهُ

\* \* \*

### Remember! / تَذَكَّرْ- تَذَكَّرِي!

1. The particle (عِنْدَ), is designated by Arab linguists as an '**adverb**.'

2. When used by itself, without an attached pronoun, it can be an '**adverb of time**' or an 'adverb of place', depending on the meaning of the noun that follows it and on the conext in general, as the examples given above illustrate.

3. When this paricle is attached to one of the suffix pronouns, it assumes the possessive meaning of the verb '**has**' or '**have**.' This is, of course, an idiomatic meaning, and the literal meaning would be something like, '*with me there is a new car*' or '*in my possession I have a new car*' for example.

4. Note also that when used with suffix pronouns, the object of possession follows and is always in the indefinite.

5. The particle (عِنْدَ) itself is invariable in the since that it does not change the *Fathah* vowel over its finál letter the *Daal*; but when the attached pronoun is the 1st person suffix pronoun (ي) the vowel is changed as a matter of necessity to harmonize with it, thus becoming a *Kasrah* instead of the *Fathah*.

\* \* \*

### Exercises / تَدْرِيبَاتٌ

1. Answer the following questions affirmatively using the suitable form of (عِنْدَ), either by itself or with a suitable attached pronoun:

١- هَلْ عِنْدَكَ سَيَّارَةٌ جَدِيدَةٌ ؟ ...........................................

٢- هَلْ عِنْدَكِ كَلْبٌ ؟ ...........................................

٣– هَلْ عِنْدَهَا أَوْلادٌ ؟ ..................................... .

٤– هَلْ عِنْدَهُ قَامُوسٌ ؟ ..................................... .

٥– هَلْ عِنْدَكَ (عِنْدَكِ) سُؤَالٌ ؟ ..................................... .

٦– أَيْنَ قَابَلْتَهُ ؟ ..................................... .

٧– مَتَى قَابَلْتَهُ ؟ ..................................... .

\* \* \*

## 2. Translate the following sentences into Arabic (Orally and written):

1. I have a new Arabic dictionary. = ……………………………………

2. She has a beautiful house. = ……………………………………

3. He has a pleasant piece of news. = ……………………………………

4. Do you (*mas.*) have a good teacher? = ……………………………………

5. She has a sister and a brother. = ……………………………………

6. I have an old car. = ……………………………………

7. Do you (female) have children? = ……………………………………

\* \* \*

## 3. Translate the following sentences into English (Orally):

١– رَأَيْتُهُ عِنْدَ بَابِ الْمَدْرَسَةِ .    ٢– هَلْ عِنْدَكَ قَلَمٌ وَوَرَقَةٌ ؟

٣– رَأَيْتُهُ عِنْدَ غُرُوبِ الشَّمْسِ .    ٤– هَلْ عِنْدَكَ قَامُوسٌ عَرَبِيٌّ ؟

٥– قَابَلْتُهُ عِنْدَ دُكَّانِ الْفَوَاكِهِ .    ٦– عِنْدِي ثَلاثَةُ أَوْلادٍ .

٧- هَلْ عِنْدَكَ سُؤَالٌ يَا لَيْلَى ؟ ٨- عِنْدَهُ عَائِلَةٌ كَبِيرَةٌ .

٩- عِنْدَهَا كَلْبٌ صَغِيرٌ . ١٠- هَلْ عِنْدَكَ طَعَامٌ وَشَرَابٌ ؟

\* \* \*

**4.** Identify the mistakes in the following sentences, and then correct them:

١- عِنْدَهُ كُرْسِيٌّ كَبِيرَةٌ . ٢- عِنْدَهَا هِرَّةٌ صَغِيرٌ .

٣- هَذِهِ كَلْبٌ كَبِيرٌ . ٤- تِلْكَ صَحْنٌ مَكْسُورٌ .

٥- هُوَ تَاجِرَةٌ غَنِيَّةٌ . ٦- هَلْ أَنْتَ قَامُوسٌ ؟

٧- هَلْ عِنْدَكَ سَيَّارَةٌ جَدِيدٌ ؟ ٨- عِنْدِي أُخْتٌ صَغِيرٌ .

٩- قَابَلْتُ مَرْيَمَ عِنْدَهَا الْبَابِ ؟ ١٠- هَلْ عِنْدَكَ سَيَّارَةٌ يَا لَيْلَى ؟

\* \* \*

**5.** Vocalize the following sentences:

١- عنده ولد وبنت . ٢- تلك سفينة كبيرة .

٣- هذا فنجان نظيف . ٤- عندي سيارة جميلة .

٥- هذه طائرة صغيرة . ٦- هو معلم مخلص .

٧- أنت بنت كريمة . ٨- أنت رجل متواضع .

٩- ذلك تلميذ ذكي . ١٠- عندها أسرة كبيرة .

\* \* \*

**6.** Use each of the following words in a full meningful sentence (verbally):

١- عِنْدَ ٢- عِنْدَهُ ٣- عِنْدِي ٤- عِنْدَكَ ٥- عِنْدَكِ

٦- عِنْدَهَا ٧- أَوْلَادٌ ٨- قَامُوسٌ ٩- سُؤَالٌ ١٠- هِرَّةٌ

\* \* \*

**Lesson 14**

الدَّرْسُ الرَّابِعَ عَشَرَ

حُرُوفُ الْجَرِّ وَعَمَلُهَا:
مِنْ / إِلَى / عَلَى / فِي / عَنْ / بِـ / لِـ
**The Prepositions and Their Grammatical Function**

- Like English, Arabic has a set of particles called (حُرُوفُ الْجَرِّ) "Prepositions" in English.
- Though their total number is more than the seven listed above, these seven are the most commonly used that we will cover in this lesson.
- Now let's use these "Prepositions" in full meaningful sentences to learn their meanings and how they affect the nouns following them.
- Now, let's read and examine the following examples:

| | | |
|---|---|---|
| هَذِهِ رِسَالَةٌ مِنَ الْجَامِعَةِ . | = | This is a letter from the university. |
| هَذِهِ هَدِيَّةٌ مِنْ صَدِيقٍ . | = | This is a gift from a friend. |

\* \* \*

| | | |
|---|---|---|
| ذَهَبَ إِلَى الْمَدْرَسَةِ . | = | He went to the school. |
| ذَهَبَتْ إِلَى حَدِيقَةٍ عَامَّةٍ . | = | She went to a public park. |

\* \* \*

| | | |
|---|---|---|
| اَلْكِتَابُ عَلَى الْمَكْتَبِ . | = | The book is on the desk. |
| اَلْقَلَمُ عَلَى كِتَابٍ . | = | The pen is on a book. |

\* \* \*

| | | |
|---|---|---|
| أُمِّي فِي الْبَيْتِ . | = | My mother is in the house. |
| اَلْبَيْضُ فِي صُنْدُوقٍ . | = | The eggs are in a box. |

\* \* \*

مِنْ = from
إِلَى = to
عَلَى = on
فِي = in, at

85

يَتَحَدَّثُ عَنْ أُسْرَتِهِ . = He is talking about his family.

تَتَحَدَّثُ عَنْ خَبَرٍ هَامٍّ . = She is talking about an important news.

* * *

قَطَعْتُ اللَّحْمَ بِالسِّكِّينِ . = I cut the meat with the knife.

سَافَرْتُ بِسَيَّارَةٍ . = I traveled by car.

* * *

اَلْجَائِزَةُ لِلْفَائِزِ . = The prize is for the winner.

اَلْمَقْعَدُ لِطَالِبٍ جَدِيدٍ . = The seat is for a new student.

* * *

| | |
|---|---|
| عَنْ = | about |
| بِ = | by, with |
| لِ = | for, belongs to |

❖ **Explanatory Notes:**

1. Like English, each Arabic preposition has a specific meaning, which the student should learn for a proper meaningful usage of it.

2. Each Arabic preposition was used in full context twice; in the first context the <u>noun following the preposition</u> is in a <u>definite form,</u> and in the second context the <u>noun following the preposition</u> is in an <u>indefinite form</u>.

3. In all cases, the nouns following the prepositions are said to be the objects of these prepositions, and thus they are in the "**Genitive Mood**"; known in Arabic as (مَجْرُور).

4. The sign of being (مَجْرُور / Genitive) is "*Tanween* of *Kasrah*" if the noun is indefinite, and one "*Kasrah*" if the noun is definite.

5. Note that the two prepositions (بِ / لِ) consist of one letter; therefore they are written connected to the beginning of the following nouns.

* * *

❖ **New Vocabulary:**

## Nouns / أَسْمَاء

| | | | |
|---|---|---|---|
| a gift, a present = هَدِيَّةٌ | | a letter, a message = رِسَالَةٌ | |
| a box = صُنْدُوقٌ | | eggs (an egg) = بَيْضٌ (بَيْضَةٌ) | |
| important = هَامٌّ | | a piece of news = خَبَرٌ | |
| a knife = سِكِينٌ | | meat = لَحْمٌ | |
| winner = فَائِزٌ | | a prize, a reward = جَائِزَةٌ | |
| a refrigerator = ثَلَّاجَةٌ | | a seat = مَقْعَدٌ | |

## Verbs / أَفْعَال

| | | | |
|---|---|---|---|
| she went = ذَهَبَتْ | | he went = ذَهَبَ | |
| she talks, she speaks = تَتَحَدَّثُ | | he talks, he speaks = يَتَحَدَّثُ | |
| I traveled = سَافَرْتُ | | I cut (past tense) = قَطَعْتُ | |

## Particles / حُرُوف

| | | | |
|---|---|---|---|
| to = إِلَى | | from = مِنْ | |
| in, at = فِي | | on = عَلَى | |
| with, by = بِ | | about, of = عَنْ | |
| | | for, belongs to = لِ | |

\* \* \*

## Remember! / تَذَكَّرْ- تَذَكَّرِي!

1. Like English, prepositions in Arabic has specific meanings that need to be learned for proper usage.

2. Like English too, they precede the nouns and form with them special relationship.

3. The nouns after the prepositions are the objects of these prepositions and must be in the genitive case-ending.

4. The two prepositions (ـب / ـل) consist of one letter; therefore they are written connected to the beginning of the following nouns.

5. The preposition and the noun that follows it constitute together what is known as a "prepositional phrase."

* * *

## تَدْرِيبَاتٌ / Exercises

**1. Read the following sentences; underline the "Prepositional Phrase"; then translate them into English; one is done for you as an example:**

١- اَلْبَيْضُ فِي الثَّلاَّجَةِ . ← The eggs are in the refrigerator.

٢- اَلْكِتَابُ عَلَى الطَّاوِلَةِ . ← ...........................................

٣- هُوَ عَرَبِيٌّ مِنَ الْعِرَاقِ . ← ...........................................

٤- ذَهَبَتْ أُخْتِي إِلَى الْجَامِعَةِ . ← ...........................................

٥- تَتَحَدَّثُ عَنْ خَبَرٍ هَامٍّ . ← ...........................................

٦- هَذِهِ السَّيَّارَةُ لِلأُسْتَاذِ . ← ...........................................

٧- سَافَرْتُ بِالطَّائِرَةِ . ← ...........................................

88

**2. Translate the following sentences into Arabic (orally and written):**

1. My book is in my bag. = ..................................................

2. She is an Arab from Egypt. = ..................................................

3. The pen is on the desk. = ..................................................

4. She is talking about her school. = ..................................................

5. He traveled to Iraq. = ..................................................

6. I traveled to the village by car. = ..................................................

7. This house is for the president. = ..................................................

\* \* \*

**3. Translate the following sentences into English (orally):**

(١) قَطَعْتُ الْخُبْزَ بِالسِّكِّينِ . (٢) ذَهَبَ إِلَى مَطْعَمٍ عَرَبِيٍّ . (٣) يَتَحَدَّثُ عَنِ الْمَسْجِدِ الْجَدِيدِ . (٤) السَّيَّارَةُ الْقَدِيمَةُ لِلْأُسْتَاذِ . (٥) بَغْدَادُ مَدِينَةٌ فِي الْعِرَاقِ . (٦) سَافَرْتُ إِلَى السُّودَانِ بِالطَّائِرَةِ . (٧) هُوَ مِنْ أَمْرِيكَا . (٨) اَلطَّائِرُ عَلَى الشَّجَرَةِ . (٩) إِبْنِي فِي غُرْفَتِهِ . (١٠) أَنَا عَرَبِيٌّ مِنَ السُّودَانِ .

\* \* \*

**4.** Give answers to the following questions; first orally and then in writing. Note that the answers to these questions will require the usage of one of the prepositions in the shaded box:

أَيْنَ بَغْدَادُ ؟ ⟵ ..................................

كَيْفَ قَطَعْتَ الْخُبْزَ ؟ ⟵ ..................................

مِنْ أَيْنَ أَنْتَ ؟ ⟵ ..................................

| بِـ |
| لِـ |
| إِلَى |

89

هَلْ كِتابُكَ في الْحَقيبَةِ ؟ ..................................

إلى أَيْنَ سافَرْتَ ؟ ..................................

كَيْفَ سافَرْتَ إلى مِصْرَ ؟ ..................................

هَلْ تَحَدَّثْتَ عَنِ الْخَبَرِ الْهامّ؟ ..................................

| مِنْ |
| عَلَى |
| في |
| عَنْ |

* * *

**5. Fill in the blanks with the appropriate preposition from among those given in brackets:**

١- اَلْبَيْضُ ......... الصُّنْدوقِ . (مِنْ / لِـ)

٢- سافَرْتُ ......... الْعِراقِ ......... الطّائِرَةِ . (في / بِـ / عَلَى / إلى)

٣- هَذِهِ رِسالَةٌ ......... صَديقي الْعَرَبيِّ . (عَنْ / مِنْ)

٤- هَذِهِ جائِزَةٌ ......... الْفائِزِ . (لِـ / إلى)

٥- اَلْهَديَّةُ ......... أَبي ......... أُمّي . (في / مِنْ / عَلَى / لِـ)

٦- ذَهَبَ ......... الْجامِعَةِ ......... السَّيّارَةِ . (لِـ / إلى / بِـ / عَلَى)

٧- اَللَّحْمُ ......... الثَّلاّجَةِ . (بِـ / في)

٨- يَتَحَدَّثُ ......... الْخَبَرِ الْهامّ . (عَلَى / عَنْ)

٩- هَذِهِ السَّيّارَةُ ......... الرَّئيسِ . (لِـ / إلى)

١٠- قَطَعْتُ الْخُبْزَ ......... السِّكّينِ . (في / بِـ)

١١- اَلْمَقْعَدُ الْجَديدُ ......... الطّالِبِ الْجَديدِ . (إلى / لِـ)

١٢- ذَهَبْتُ ......... الْمَدْرَسَةِ ......... الدَّرّاجَةِ . (لِـ / إلى / بِـ / عَلَى)

90

**6.** Unscramble the following sets of words to make from each of them a full meaningful sentence, as in the given example, and then translate the resultant sentences into English:

مِنْ / هَذِهِ / صَدِيقٍ / هَدِيَّةٌ ⟵ هَذِهِ هَدِيَّةٌ مِنْ صَدِيقٍ. =

This is a gift from a friend.

١- فِي / اَلْكِتَابُ / حَقِيبَتِي ⟵ ......................... = .........................

٢- السُّودَانِ / أَبِي / إِلَى / سَافَرَ ⟵ ......................... = .........................

٣- الْجَدِيدُ / الْمُحَاسِبُ / بَغْدَاد / مِنْ ⟵ ......................... = .........................

٤- عَلَى / الصَّغِيرُ / الشَّجَرَةِ / الطَّائِرُ ⟵ ......................... = .........................

٥- بِالطَّائِرَةِ / مِصْرَ / إِلَى / سَافَرْتُ ⟵ ......................... = .........................

٦- الْجَدِيدَةُ / لِلْمُدِيرِ / السَّيَّارَةُ / الْجَدِيد ⟵ ......................... = .........................

٧- خَبَرٍ / يَتَحَدَّثُ / مُهِمّ / عَنْ ⟵ ......................... = .........................

٨- صَدِيقٍ / مِنْ / رِسَالَةٌ / هَذِهِ ⟵ ......................... = .........................

# Lesson 15 — الدَّرْسُ الْخَامِسَ عَشَرَ

## تَقْسِيمُ الأَسْمَاءِ مِنْ حَيْثُ الْعَدَدِ: الْمُفْرَدُ وَالْمُثَنَّى
### The Division of Nouns According to Numbers: Singular & Dual

- English nouns have only two numbers: Singular and Plural. Arabic, on the other hand has three numbers: Singular for one; **Dual** specifically for two; and Plural, for three and up. Thus Arabic has the **Dual** number as an extra, which does not Exist in English

- All the nouns introduced thus far were in the singular forms, and few were used in the plural forms. No dual nouns were introduced.

- So in this lesson we are going to introduce the dual forms of nouns in comparative perspective with their singular counterparts, so that you learn how to make duals from singulars.

- Now, let's read and examine the following parallel examples:

| اَلْمُفْرَدُ / The Singular | اَلْمُثَنَّى / The Dual |
|---|---|
| هَذَا كِتَابٌ جَدِيدٌ. | هَذَانِ كِتَابَانِ جَدِيدَانِ. |
| This is a new book. | These are two new books. |
| هَذِهِ طَالِبَةٌ نَشِيطَةٌ. | هَاتَانِ طَالِبَتَانِ نَشِيطَتَانِ. |
| This is an active (female) student. | These are two active (female) students. |
| هُوَ أُسْتَاذٌ مَشْهُورٌ. | هُمَا أُسْتَاذَانِ مَشْهُورَانِ. |
| He is a famous (male) professor. | They are two famous (male) professors. |
| هِيَ ضَيْفَةٌ أَمْرِيكِيَّةٌ. | هُمَا ضَيْفَتَانِ أَمْرِيكِيَّتَانِ. |
| She is an American guest. | They are two American (female) guests. |
| هَلْ أَنْتَ طَالِبٌ عَرَبِيٌّ؟ | هَلْ أَنْتُمَا طَالِبَانِ عَرَبِيَّانِ؟ |
| Are you a (male) Arab student? | Are you (two male) Arab students? |
| هَلْ أَنْتِ طَبِيبَةٌ عِرَاقِيَّةٌ؟ | هَلْ أَنْتُمَا طَبِيبَتَانِ عِرَاقِيَّتَانِ؟ |

| Are you (two female) Iraqi doctors? | Are you a (female) Iraqi doctor? |
|---|---|
| نَحْنُ مُوَظَّفَانِ جَدِيدَانِ. ⟵ | أَنَا مُوَظَّفٌ جَدِيدٌ |
| We are (two male) new employees. | I am a (male) new employee. |

* * *

| الْمُثَنَّى / The Dual | الْمُفْرَدُ / The Singular |
|---|---|
| قَرَأْتُ كِتَابَيْنِ جَدِيدَيْنِ. ⟵ | قَرَأْتُ كِتَابًا جَدِيدًا. |
| I read two new books. | I read a new book. |
| كَافَأْتُ طَالِبَتَيْنِ نَشِيطَتَيْنِ. ⟵ | كَافَأْتُ طَالِبَةً نَشِيطَةً. |
| I rewarded two active (female) students. | I rewarded an active (female) student. |
| تَعَلَّمْتُ مِنْ أُسْتَاذَيْنِ مَشْهُورَيْنِ. ⟵ | تَعَلَّمْتُ مِنْ أُسْتَاذٍ مَشْهُورٍ. |
| I learned from two famous (male) professors. | I learned from a famous (male) professor. |
| سَلَّمْتُ عَلَى ضَيْفَتَيْنِ أَمْرِيكِيَّتَيْنِ. ⟵ | سَلَّمْتُ عَلَى ضَيْفَةٍ أَمْرِيكِيَّةٍ. |
| I greeted two (female) American guests. | I saluted an American (female) guest. |
| قَابَلْتُ الطَّالِبَيْنِ الْعَرَبِيَّيْنِ. ⟵ | قَابَلْتُ الطَّالِبَ الْعَرَبِيَّ. |
| I met the (two male) Arab students. | I met the (male) Arab student. |
| سَمِعْتُ عَنِ الطَّبِيبَتَيْنِ الْعِرَاقِيَّتَيْنِ. ⟵ | سَمِعْتُ عَنِ الطَّبِيبَةِ الْعِرَاقِيَّةِ. |
| I heard about the (two female) Iraqi doctors. | I heard about the (female) Iraqi doctor. |

❖ **Explanatory Notes:**

1. By examining the first set of the sentences above and focusing on the words or suffixes shown at the end, we will notice that all singular demonstrative as well as personal pronouns have dual forms, which need to be learned if we need to use them in connection to dual nouns and adjectives.

2. If you examine the suffixes at the end of each noun or adjective in the first group, you will notice that all these suffixes are identical; that is the ending

(ان / *āni*), which is the dual sign for nouns and adjectives when they are in a "Nominative Mood" (i.e. functioning as subjects or predicates in nominal sentences.)

3. If you examine these same nouns and adjectives used in the second group, you will notice that they were used in contexts were they <u>were preceded by either a verb or a preposition</u>; therefore they are functioning as the <u>objects of the verbs or the objects of preposition</u>; the first is said to be in an "<u>Accusative Mood</u>" and the second is said to be in "<u>Genitive Mood</u>"; and the suffix in these two cases is (يْنِ / *ayni*).

4. Thus there are two ending signs for recognizing dual nouns or adjectives; (ان / *āni*) if they are in a "<u>Nominative Mood</u>" or (يْنِ / *ayni*) if they are in an "<u>Accusative Mood</u>" or in a "<u>Genitive Mood</u>".

5. Dual nouns and adjectives may appear in their indefinite forms, without the definite article, or they might receive the definite article as in singular nouns.

\* \* \*

❖ **New Vocabulary:**

### أَسْمَاء / Nouns

these two (feminine) = هَاتَانِ     these two (masculine) = هَذَانِ

you two (masculine + feminine) = أَنْتُمَا     they two (masculine + feminine) = هُمَا

employee (m + f) = مُوَظَّفٌ / مُوَظَّفَةٌ     we (for dual & plural) = نَحْنُ

### أَفْعَال / Verbs

I learned = تَعَلَّمْتُ     I rewarded = كَافَأْتُ

I met = قَابَلْتُ     I greeted, I saluted = سَلَّمْتُ (عَلَى)

I heard (about) = سَمِعْتُ (عَنْ)

**Note:** The dual forms of previously studied nouns and adjectives are not going to be listed as new vocabulary, since they are based on the singulars, which you can obtain by stripping them from the dual suffixes.

## Remember! / تَذَكَّرْ- تَذَكَّري!

1. Unlike English, Arabic has extra number, specifically for two, which is called "Dual", Arabic (مُثَنَّى).

2. The demonstrative pronouns and the subject pronouns have their own dual forms related specifically to two in number.

3. The dual nouns and adjectives result by adding one of two suffixes to the end of their singulars; (ان) for the nominative case-ending and (ـَيْن) for the genitive case-ending.

4. If a dual noun is followed by an adjective, the adjective must be also dual and in the same form as the noun it describes.

\* \* \*

## Exercises / تَدْرِيبَاتٌ

**1.** Read the following sentences; underline all the words that appear to be in dual forms; then attempt an English translation; one is done for you as an example:

١- اَلْبَيْضَتَانِ في الثَّلَّاجَةِ .        The two eggs are in the refrigerator.

٢- اَلْكِتَابَانِ الْجَدِيدَانِ عَلَى الطَّاوِلَةِ .      ............................................

٣- هُمَا عَرَبِيَّانِ مِنَ الْعِرَاقِ .        ............................................

٤- هَلْ أَنْتُمَا طَالِبَتَانِ جَدِيدَتَانِ ؟      ............................................

٥- تَتَحَدَّثُ عَنْ خَبَرَيْنِ هَامَّيْنِ .      ............................................

٦- هَاتَانِ السَّيَّارَتَانِ لِلْأُسْتَاذِ .        ............................................

٧- قَرَأْتُ الدَّرْسَيْنِ الْجَدِيدَيْنِ .       ............................................

٨- نَحْنُ طَبِيبَانِ عَرَبِيَّانِ .         ............................................

## 2. Translate the following sentences into Arabic (orally and written):

1. The two new books are on the table. = ..................................................
2. These two houses are old. = ..................................................
3. Are you (two / female) Americans? = ..................................................
4. I read two short stories. = ..................................................
5. I met the two (female) guests. = ..................................................
6. These two lessons are easy. = ..................................................
7. I saluted the two new (male) teachers. = ..................................................

\* \* \*

## 3. Translate the following sentences into English (orally):

(١) الْمُوَظَّفَتَانِ الْجَدِيدَتَانِ أُخْتَانِ .   (٢) ذَهَبَ إِلَى مَطْعَمَيْنِ عَرَبِيَّيْنِ .

(٣) يَتَحَدَّثُ عَنِ الْمَسْجِدَيْنِ الْجَدِيدَيْنِ .   (٤) السَّيَّارَتَانِ الْقَدِيمَتَانِ لِلْأُسْتَاذِ .

(٥) بَغْدَادُ وَالْبَصْرَةُ مَدِينَتَانِ فِي الْعِرَاقِ .   (٦) الطَّبَّاخَانِ الْمَاهِرَانِ مِنْ فَرَنْسَا .

(٧) هُمَا جُنْدِيَّانِ أَمْرِيكِيَّانِ .   (٨) هَلْ أَنْتُمَا طَالِبَانِ عَرَبِيَّانِ ؟

(٩) هُمَا صَدِيقَتَانِ مُخْلِصَتَانِ .   (١٠) تَعَلَّمْتُ فِي مَدْرَسَتَيْنِ صَغِيرَتَيْنِ .

\* \* \*

## 4. Change the singular pronouns, nouns and adjectives of the following sentences into appropriate dual forms; the first is done for you as an example:

أَيْنَ الصُّنْدُوقَانِ الْكَبِيرَانِ ؟   ⟵   أَيْنَ الصُّنْدُوقُ الْكَبِيرُ ؟

.................................................   ⟵   قَرَأْتُ قِصَّةً قَصِيرَةً .

هِيَ صَدِيقَةٌ مُخْلِصَةٌ . ................................
هَلْ أَنْتَ عَرَبِيٌّ ؟ ................................
قَابَلْتُ الْأُسْتَاذَ الْجَدِيدَ . ................................
سَلَّمْتُ عَلَى الْوَلَدِ الصَّغِيرِ . ................................
هَلْ تَحَدَّثْتَ عَنِ الْخَبَرِ الْهَامِّ؟ ................................

\* \* \*

**5. Fill in the blanks with the appropriate form of the <u>dual adjectives</u> from among those given in brackets, to match with the form of the dual nouns:**

١- اَلْقَلَمَانِ ................ عَلَى الْمَكْتَبِ . (الْأَحْمَرَيْنِ / الْأَحْمَرَانِ)

٢- سَمِعْتُ خَبَرَيْنِ ................ . (هَامَّيْنِ / هَامَّانِ)

٣- نَحْنُ مُوَظَّفَانِ ................ . (جَدِيدَانِ / جَدِيدَيْنِ)

٤- سَلَّمْتُ عَلَى الضَّيْفَتَيْنِ ................ . (الْعَرَبِيَّتَانِ / الْعَرَبِيَّتَيْنِ)

٥- هَلْ أَنْتُمَا جُنْدِيَّانِ ................ ؟ (أَمْرِيكِيَّيْنِ / أَمْرِيكِيَّانِ)

٦- كَافَأْتُ التِّلْمِيذَتَيْنِ ................ . (الْمُجْتَهِدَتَيْنِ / الْمُجْتَهِدَتَانِ)

٧- قَرَأْتُ الدَّرْسَيْنِ ................ . (الْقَصِيرَانِ / الْقَصِيرَيْنِ)

٨- هَذَانِ سُؤَالَانِ ................ . (سَهْلَانِ / السَّهْلَيْنِ)

٩- هَاتَانِ السَّيَّارَتَانِ ................ لِلرَّئِيسِ . (الْجَدِيدَتَيْنِ / الْجَدِيدَتَانِ)

١٠- هُمَا لَاعِبَانِ ................ . (مَاهِرَانِ / الْمَاهِرَيْنِ)

١١- اَلْمَقْعَدَانِ ................ لِلطَّالِبَيْنِ . (الْجَدِيدَيْنِ / الْجَدِيدَانِ)

\* \* \*

**6.** Unscramble the following sets of words to make from each of them a full meaningful sentence, as in the given example, and then translate the resultant sentences into English:

عَلَى / الصَّغِيرَانِ / الطَّاوِلَة / الصُّنْدُوقَانِ     الصُّنْدُوقَانِ الصَّغِيرَانِ عَلَى الطَّاوِلَةِ.

The two small boxes are on the table.

١- فِي / اَلْكِتَابُ / حَقِيبَتِي     = ..................................

٢- جَدِيدَتَانِ / هَاتَانِ / طَالِبَتَانِ     = ..................................

٣- هَامَّيْنِ / خَبَرَيْنِ / سَمِعْتُ     = ..................................

٤- عَلَى / الصَّغِيرَانِ / الشَّجَرَةِ / الطَّائِرَانِ     = ..................................

٥- عَنْ / هَذَانِ / سُؤَالَيْنِ / جَوَابَانِ     = ..................................

٦- الْجَدِيدَةُ / لِلْمُدِيرِ / السَّيَّارَةُ / الْجَدِيدِ     = ..................................

٧- عَرَبِيَّانِ / هَلْ / أَنْتُمَا     = ..................................؟

٨- صَدِيقَيْنِ / مِنْ / رِسَالَتَانِ / هَاتَانِ     = ..................................

98

6. Fill in the blank cells either with the dual to a given singular or the singular to a given dual:

| مُثَنَّى / Dual | مُفْرَد / Singular | مُثَنَّى / Dual | مُفْرَد / Singular |
|---|---|---|---|
| شَارِعَانِ |  |  | طَبِيبٌ |
|  | بَيْتٌ | بَابَانِ |  |
| قَلَمَانِ |  |  | رَجُلٌ |
|  | مُعَلِّمٌ | جَمَلَانِ |  |
| عَزِيزَانِ |  |  | جَمِيلٌ |
|  | يَوْمٌ | حِمَارَانِ |  |
| دَجَاجَتَانِ |  |  | مِصْرِيٌّ |
|  | مَدْرَسَةٌ | سَفِينَتَانِ |  |
| مَطْبَخَانِ |  |  | مَسْجِدٌ |
|  | شَرِكَةٌ | مَلْعَبَانِ |  |
| سَاعَتَانِ |  |  | شَجَرَةٌ |
|  | بِنَاءٌ | بُسْتَانَانِ |  |
| بَحْرَانِ |  |  | قَامُوسٌ |
|  | مُزَارِعٌ | غُرْفَتَانِ |  |
| شُرْطِيَّانِ |  |  | أُسْرَةٌ |
|  | مُهَنْدِسٌ | مَرِيضَانِ |  |

99

Lesson 16

## الدَّرْسُ السَّادِسَ عَشَرَ

### اَلْجُمْلَةُ الإِسْمِيَّةُ : الْمُبْتَدَأُ وَالْخَبَرُ مَعَ الْمُثَنَّى

### The Nominal (Equational) Sentences:
### The Subject & the Predicate with Dual Nouns

- Previously, in lesson 10, we mentioned that Arabic has a type of sentences that does not have exact equivalent in English.

- In such sentences, there are no actual physical verbs, though when we translate them into English, we need to use the English verb to be "*are*". We called these "Nominal" or "Equational"; since they only consist of nouns, pronouns or adjectives, and no verbs.

- Each "Nominal" sentence consists of two main parts: The first part is called "Subject" and the second part is called "Predicate."

- Now, let's read and examine the following examples where the "Subjects" and "Predicates" are of the "Dual" number.

١

| | |
|---|---|
| These are (two) books. | هَذَانِ كِتَابَانِ . |
| These are (two) sheets of paper. | هَاتَانِ وَرَقَتَانِ . |
| They are (two) professors (male). | هُمَا أُسْتَاذَانِ . |
| They are (two) beautiful (female). | هُمَا جَمِيلَتَانِ . |
| You are (two) industrious (male). | أَنْتُمَا مُجْتَهِدَانِ . |

٢

| | |
|---|---|
| The (two) carpenters are skilful (male). | اَلنَّجَّارَانِ مَاهِرَانِ . |

| | |
|---|---|
| آدَمُ وَعُمَرُ طَالِبَانِ . | Adam and Omar are students. |
| مَرْيَمُ وَلَيْلَى أُسْتَاذَتَانِ . | Maryam and Layla are professors. |

٣

| | |
|---|---|
| اَلنَّجَّارَانِ الْمَاهِرَانِ عَرَبِيَّانِ . | The (two) skilful carpenters are Arabs (male). |
| الْمُعَلِّمَتَانِ النَّشِيطَتَانِ عَرَبِيَّتَانِ . | The (two) active teachers (female) are Arabs. |
| هُمَا الطَّالِبَانِ الْجَدِيدَانِ . | They are the (two) new (male) students. |
| أَنْتُمَا الطَّالِبَتَانِ الْفَائِزَتَانِ . | You are the (two) winning (female) students. |

### ❖ Explanatory Notes:

1. By examining the two sets of examples above, you will notice that all the examples of group one above and the first two examples of group two are structures consisting of just two words, yet they all constitute full meaningful sentences.

2. The first word in each of these sentences is called the "subject", (مُبْتَدَأٌ) in Arabic, and the second word gives information about the "subject" and is called the "predicate", (خَبَرٌ) in Arabic.

3. In these sentences, the "subject" is either a dual personal subject pronoun, a dual demonstrative pronoun, a dual noun with the definite article or two proper names, and the "predicate" is either a regular noun or an adjectival noun that must agree with the "subject" in gender and in being a dual number, but not in definiteness.

4. In the sentences of group three above, the "subject" is either a noun defined with the definite article followed by an adjective, as in the first two examples of this group. The subject and its adjective must agree in gender, number and definiteness, since they constitute noun-adjective phrases; but the predicate does not have to be definite.

5. In the last two examples of group three above, the "subject" is a pronoun and the predicate is a noun-adjective phrase both in the definite form, which is allowed in such case.

6. In all cases, the "subjects" must be one of the definite nouns categories and the "predicates" are indefinite but they also can be definte.

7. In all cases, the "predicates" must agree with the "subjects" in gender, though not in definiteness.

8. Both the "subjects" and the "predicates" must be in the nominative case-ending, which in this case with duals is an (ـَان) at the end.

9. In all the "Nominal" sentences with duals, the verb to be (*are*) is not actually there; it is only implied in the English translation.

10. "Nominal" sentences can be made longer by adding an adjective to either the "subjects" or the "predicates", as in the examples of group (3) above.

* * *

**New Vocabulary:**

**أَسْمَاء / Nouns**

| | | | |
|---|---|---|---|
| truthful = صَادِقٌ | | liar = كَاذِبٌ | |
| a believer = مُؤْمِنٌ | | non-believer = كَافِرٌ | |
| present, ready = حَاضِرٌ | | absent = غَائِبٌ | |
| open = مَفْتُوحٌ | | closed = مُغْلَقٌ | |
| just = عَادِلٌ | | unjust = ظَالِمٌ | |
| early = مُبَكِّرٌ | | late = مُتَأَخِّرٌ | |

**أَفْعَال / Verbs**

| | | | |
|---|---|---|---|
| he went = ذَهَبَ | | she went = ذَهَبَتْ | |
| he ate = أَكَلَ | | she ate = أَكَلَتْ | |
| he drank = شَرِبَ | | she drank = شَرِبَتْ | |

* * *

❖ **New Vocabulary Used in Full Meaningful Nominal Sentences:**

١- اَلْمُؤْمِنَانِ صَادِقَانِ . = The (two male) believers are truthful.

٢- اَلْكَافِرَتَانِ كَاذِبَتَانِ . = The (two female) non-believers are liars.

٣- اَلطَّالِبَانِ حَاضِرَانِ . = The (two male) students are present.

٤- اَلطَّالِبَتَانِ غَائِبَتَانِ . = The (two female) students are absent.

٥- اَلْبَابَانِ مَفْتُوحَانِ . = The (two) doors are open.

٦- اَلشُّبَّاكَانِ مُغْلَقَانِ . = The (two) windows are closed.

٧- اَلْمَلِكَانِ عَادِلَانِ . = The (two) kings are just.

٨- اَلرَّئِيسَانِ ظَالِمَانِ . = The (two) presidents are unjust.

٩- اَلْمُعَلِّمَتَانِ مُبَكِّرَتَانِ . = The (two female) teachers are early.

١٠- اَلْمُعَلِّمَانِ مُتَأَخِّرَانِ . = The (two male) teachers are late.

١١- ذَهَبَ التِّلْمِيذَانِ إِلَى الْمَدْرَسَةِ . = The (two male) pupils went to the school.

١٢- ذَهَبَتْ التِّلْمِيذَتَانِ إِلَى الْمَلْعَبِ . = The (two female) pupils went to the playground.

١٣- أَكَلَ الْوَلَدَانِ الطَّعَامَ . = The (two) boys ate the food.

١٤- أَكَلَتْ الْبِنْتَانِ الطَّعَامَ . = The (two) girls ate the food.

١٥- شَرِبَ الطَّالِبَانِ الْمَاءَ . = The (two male) students drank the water.

١٦- شَرِبَتْ الطَّالِبَتَانِ الْمَاءَ . = The (two female) students drank the water.

١٧- يُسَافِرُ الطَّبِيبَانِ الْعَرَبِيَّانِ إِلَى أَمْرِيكَا . = The (two male) doctors travel to America.

## تَذَكَّرْ- تَذَكَّرِي! / Remember!

1. If the "subject" in a "Nominal Sentence" is either a dual personal subject pronoun, a dual demonstrative pronoun, a dual noun with the definite article or two proper names, then the "predicate" is either a regular noun or an adjectival noun that must agree with the "subject" in gender and in being a dual number, but not in definiteness.

2. If the sentence has a "subject" which is a noun defined with the definite article followed by an adjective, the subject and its adjective must agree in gender, number and definiteness, since they constitute a noun-adjective phrase; but the predicate does not have to be definite.

3. In the last two examples of group three above, the "subject" is a pronoun and the "predicate" is a noun-adjective phrase both in the definite form and the indefinite form are allowed in the "predicate".

4. In all cases, the "predicates" must agree with the "subjects" in gender, though not in definiteness.

5. Both the "subjects" and the "predicates" must be in the nominative case-ending, which in this case with duals is an (ـَان) at the end.

6. In all the "Nominal" sentences with duals, the verb to be (*are*) is not actually there; it is only implied in the English translation.

7. "Nominal" sentences can be made longer by adding an adjectives to either the "subjects" or the "predicates".

\* \* \*

## تَدْرِيبَاتٌ / Exercises

**1. Read the following "Nominal Sentences"; underline the "Dual Subjects" once and the "Dual Predicates" twice; then translate them into English:**

١- اَلدَّرْسَانِ سَهْلَانِ . ← ....................... .

٢- أَنْتُمَا مُمْتَازَانِ . ← ....................... .

٣- اَلْمُزَارِعَانِ نَشِيطَانِ . ← ..................................

٤- هُمَا أُسْتَاذَتَانِ مَشْهُورَتَانِ . ← ..................................

٥- هُمَا طَالِبَانِ عَرَبِيَّانِ . ← ..................................

٦- هَذَانِ مِفْتَاحَانِ جَدِيدَانِ . ← ..................................

٧- اَلْمَعْهَدَانِ كَبِيرَانِ . ← ..................................

٨- اَلْقَرْيَتَانِ صَغِيرَتَانِ . ← ..................................

٩- أَنْتُمَا بِنْتَانِ جَمِيلَتَانِ . ← ..................................

\* \* \*

2. Translate the following sentences into Arabic (orally and written):

1. The two women are Muslims. = ................................................. •

2. The two men are Arabs. = ................................................. •

3. They are two famous (female) professors. = ................................. •

4. They are two generous men. = ................................................. •

5. Are the two doors open? = ................................................. ?

6. Where are the two new (male) students? = ................................. ?

7. These are two beautiful houses. = ................................................. •

8. The two women are Muslims. = ................................................. •

9. The two presidents are unjust. = ................................................. •

\* \* \*

**3. Translate the following sentences into English (orally):**

(١) اَلنَّهْرَانِ صَغِيرَانِ . (٢) هُمَا حَزِينَانِ . (٣) اَلْقَامُوسَانِ نَافِعَانِ .

(٤) الشَّجَرَتَانِ طَوِيلَتَانِ . (٥) هُمَا عَرَبِيَّتَانِ . (٦) اَلنَّهْرَانِ طَوِيلَانِ .

(٧) اَلْبُحَيْرَةُ جَمِيلَةٌ . (٨) أَنْتُمَا صَدِيقَانِ عَزِيزَانِ . (٩) هَلِ الْمُدَرِّسَانِ غَائِبَانِ؟

(١٠) هَاتَانِ اللُّغَتَانِ سَهْلَتَانِ . (١١) هُمَا طَبِيبَانِ مَاهِرَانِ .

* * *

**4.** Pair each <u>dual subject</u> from group (1) with a suitable <u>dual predicate</u> from group (2) to form full meaningful sentences; then write down the sentence in the dotted space, and then translate it verbally into English:

| (١) | (٢) | |
|---|---|---|
| اَلْمَطْبَخَانِ | بَخِيلَانِ | .................................. |
| اَلطَّائِرَتَانِ | أُسْتَاذَانِ | .................................. |
| اَلرَّجُلَانِ | عَادِلَانِ | .................................. |
| هُمَا | وَسِخَانِ | .................................. |
| هُمَا | بَعِيدَتَانِ | .................................. |
| عُمَرُ وَآدَمُ | كَرِيمَانِ | .................................. |
| اَلْقَرْيَتَانِ | كَبِيرَتَانِ | .................................. |
| اللُّغَتَانِ | صَدِيقَانِ | .................................. |
| الْمَلِكَانِ | سَهْلَتَانِ | .................................. |

106

* * *

**5. Fill in the blanks with the appropriate word from those given in brackets:**

١- اَلصَّديقانِ ............... (مُخْلِصانِ / مُخْلِصَتانِ .)

٢- ............... (هُمَا / هُوَ) أَسْتاذانِ جَديدانِ .

٣- أَنْتُمَا ............... (صَديقانِ / صَديقَتانِ) عَزيزَتانِ .

٤- ............... (اَلْقَامُوسُ / اَلْقَامُوسَانِ) نَافِعَانِ .

٥- اَلْبَحْرانِ ............... (جَميلانِ / جَميلٌ .)

٦- ............... (اَلْجُمْلَتانِ / اَلدَّرْسانِ) سَهْلانِ .

٧- اَلطَّالِبَانِ ............... (غَائِبَانِ / غَائِبَيْنِ) .

\* \* \*

**6. Change the following sentences into "Dual" forms; orally first, and then in writing; the first one is done as an example:**

١- هِيَ أُمٌّ كَريمَةٌ .        هُمَا أُمَّانِ كَريمَتانِ .

٢- هَلِ الْبابُ مَفْتوحٌ ؟        ............... ؟

٣- هَذَا سُؤَالٌ سَهْلٌ .        ............... .

٤- أَيْنَ الْقَلَمُ الأَحْمَرُ ؟        ............... ؟

٥- هَذَا كِتابٌ جَديدٌ .        ............... .

٦- مَنِ الطَّالِبُ الْعَرَبِيُّ ؟        ............... ؟

٧- مَا هَذَا الْبِنَاءُ الْكَبِيرُ ؟        ............... ؟

Lesson 17

## أَنْوَاعُ الْجَمْعِ : جَمْعُ الْمُذَكَّرِ السَّالِمِ
### The Types of Plurals: Masculine Sound Plural

الدَّرْسُ السَّابِعَ عَشَرَ

- ❖ Like English, Arabic has "Plural" nouns and adjectives which refer to three and up in number.

- ❖ However, plural in Arabic has three types or forms: one is called "Masculine Sound Plural"; the other is called "Feminine Sound Plural"; and the third is called "Broken Plural".

- ❖ In this lesson we will deal with the "Masculine Sound Plural"; which is a regular plural for masculine gender only. It is regular, hence "Sound" because it results from suffixing certain suffixes (two) to the end of the singular form. This would be parallel to the English regular, which results from adding an (…*s*) or an (…*es*) at the end of the singular.

- ❖ So in the following examples we introduce the "Masculine Sound Plural" forms of nouns in comparative perspective with their singular counterparts, so that you learn how to make plurals from singulars.

- ❖ Now, let's read and examine the following parallel examples:

| Masculine Sound Plural / جَمْعُ الْمُذَكَّرِ السَّالِمِ | | The Singular / اَلْمُفْرَدُ |
|---|---|---|
| هَؤُلَاءِ مُعَلِّمُونَ مُخْلِصُونَ . <br> These are sincere teachers. | ← | هَذَا مُعَلِّمٌ مُخْلِصٌ . <br> This is a sincere teacher. |
| هُمْ مُسْلِمُونَ . <br> They are Muslims. | ← | هُوَ مُسْلِمٌ . <br> He is a Muslim. |
| هُمْ مُؤْمِنُونَ مُخْلِصُونَ . <br> They are sincere believers. | ← | هُوَ مُؤْمِنٌ مُخْلِصٌ . <br> He is a sincere believer. |
| هَلْ أَنْتُمْ مُهَنْدِسُونَ ؟ <br> Are you engineers? | ← | هَلْ أَنْتَ مُهَنْدِسٌ ؟ <br> Are you an engineer? |

| | | |
|---|---|---|
| نَحْنُ أَمْرِيكِيُّونَ. | ← | أَنَا أَمْرِيكِيٌّ؟ |
| We are Americans. | | I am an American. |
| هُمْ فَلاَّحُونَ نَشِيطُونَ. | ← | هُوَ فَلاَّحٌ نَشِيطٌ. |
| They are active peasants. | | He is an active peasant. |
| هَلْ أَنْتُمْ مُوَظَّفُونَ هُنَا؟ | ← | هَلْ أَنْتَ مُوَظَّفٌ هُنَا؟ |
| Are you employees here? | | Are you an employee here? |

\* \* \*

| Masculine Sound Plural / جَمْعُ الْمُذَكَّرِ السَّالِمِ | | The Singular / اَلْمُفْرَدُ |
|---|---|---|
| قَابَلْتُ مُهَنْدِسِينَ مِصْرِيِّينَ. | ← | قَابَلْتُ مُهَنْدِسًا مِصْرِيًّا. |
| I met Egyptian engineers. | | I met an Egyptian engineer. |
| كَافَأْتُ الْمُعَلِّمِينَ الْمُخْلِصِينَ. | ← | كَافَأْتُ الْمُعَلِّمَ الْمُخْلِصَ. |
| I rewarded the sincere teachers. | | I rewarded the sincere teacher. |
| قَابَلْتُ اللاَّعِبِينَ الْمَشْهُورِينَ. | ← | قَابَلْتُ اللاَّعِبَ الْمَشْهُورَ. |
| I met the famous players. | | I met the famous player. |
| تَعَرَّفْتُ عَلَى الْمُسْلِمِينَ الْمُخْلِصِينَ. | ← | تَعَرَّفْتُ عَلَى الْمُسْلِمِ الْمُخْلِصِ. |
| I got acquainted with the sincere Muslims. | | I got acquainted with the sincere Muslim. |

\* \* \*

### ❖ Explanatory Notes:

1. By examining the first set of the sentences above and focusing on the underlined words, and those with underlined suffixes, we will notice that all singular demonstrative as well as personal pronouns have plural forms, which need to be learned if we need to use them in connection to plural nouns and adjectives. However, these plural pronouns are not representative of "Masculine Sound Plurals."

2. If you examine the words with underlined suffixes at the end of each noun or adjective in the first group, you will notice that all these suffixes are identical; that is the ending (ُونَ / ūna), which is the "Masculine Sound Plurals' " sign for nouns and adjectives when they are in a "Nominative Mood" (i.e. functioning as subjects or predicates in nominal sentences.)

3. If you examine these same nouns and adjectives used in the second group, you will notice that they are used in contexts were they <u>are preceded by either a verb or a preposition</u>; therefore they are functioning as the <u>objects of the verbs or the objects of prepositions</u>; the first is said to be in an "**Accusative Mood**" and the second is said to be in "<u>**Genitive Mood**</u>"; and the suffix in these two cases is (ِينَ / īna).

4. Thus there are two ending signs for recognizing "Masculine Sound Plural" nouns or adjectives; (ُونَ / ūna) if they are in a "<u>Nominative Mood</u>" or (ِينَ / īna) if they are in an "<u>**Accusative Mood**</u>" or in a "<u>**Genitive Mood**</u>".

5. "Masculine Sound Plural" nouns and adjectives may appear in their indefinite forms, without the definite article, or they might receive the definite article as in singular nouns, as you can see in some examples of the second group.

6. Also, "Masculine Sound Plural" nouns can be followed by adjectives that should agree with these nouns in gender, number and definiteness or indefiniteness.

7. <u>Important Note</u>: Not all masculine singular nouns or adjectives may have "Masculine Sound Plural" endings; for the "Broken Plurals" are more dominant with nouns that are made of three letters in the singular.

\* \* \*

❖ **New Vocabulary:**

أَسْمَاء / Nouns

هَؤُلاَءِ = these

أَنْتُمْ = you (plural)

مُعَلِّمُونَ / مُعَلِّمِينَ = teachers

مُسْلِمُونَ / مُسْلِمِينَ = Muslims

مُهَنْدِسُونَ / مُهَنْدِسِينَ = engineers

هُمْ = they

نَحْنُ = we

مُخْلِصُونَ / مُخْلِصِينَ = sincere ones

مُؤْمِنُونَ / مُؤْمِنِينَ = believers

أَمْرِيكِيُّونَ / أَمْرِيكِيِّينَ = Americans

مُوَظَّفُونَ / مُوَظَّفِينَ = employees   مِصْرِيُّونَ / مِصْرِيِّينَ = Egyptians

لاَعِبُونَ / لاَعِبِينَ = players   مَشْهُورُونَ / مَشْهُورِينَ = famous ones

## أَدَوَات / Particles

هُنَا = here

### تَذَكَّرْ - تَذَكَّرِي! / Remember!

1. Arabic has three types of plurals: one is called "Masculine Sound Plural"; the other is called "Feminine Sound Plural"; and the third is called "Broken Plural." The first two are regular, but the third is an irregular plural

2. The demonstrative pronouns and the subject pronouns have their own plural forms related specifically to three and up in number.

3. The "Masculine Sound Plural" nouns and adjectives result by adding one of two suffixes to the end of their singulars; (ـُونَ) for the nominative case-ending and (ـِينَ) for the genitive case-ending.

4. If a plural noun is followed by and adjective, the adjective must be also plural and in the same form as the noun it describes.

5. Not all masculine singular nouns can be made into "Masculine Sound Plurals"; the singulars must refer to human beings, and their singulars must consist of more than three letters; that is why the "Broken Plurals" are more dominant in Arabic.

### تَدْرِيبَاتٌ / Exercises

1. Read the following sentences; underline all the words that appear to be in "Masculine Sound Plural" forms; then attempt an English translation; one is done for you as an example:

١- هُمْ مُهَنْدِسُونَ نَاجِحُونَ .   ⟵   They are successful engineers .

111

٢- كَافَأْتُ الْعَامِلِينَ الْمُخْلِصِينَ . ← ..................................... .

٣- هَؤُلَاء طَبَّاخُونَ مَاهِرُونَ . ← ..................................... .

٤- مَنِ الْمُسَافِرُونَ عَلَى هَذِهِ الطَّائِرَةِ؟ ← ..................................... .

٥- قَابَلْتُ الْمُتَرْجِمِينَ الْأَمْرِيكِيِّينَ . ← ..................................... .

٦- أَيْنَ الصَّحَافِيُّونَ الزَّائِرُونَ ؟ ← ..................................... .

٧- قَابَلْتُ الْمُزَارِعِينَ النَّشِيطِينَ . ← ..................................... .

٨- اَلْمُجْتَهِدُونَ فَائِزُونَ بِالْجَائِزَةِ . ← ..................................... .

\* \* \*

**2. Translate the following sentences into Arabic (orally and written):**

1. They are American engineers. = ................................................. .

2. Are you travelers on this plane? = ................................................. .

3. Are you Egyptian teachers? = ................................................. .

4. They are sincere workers. = ................................................. .

5. These are famous writers. = ................................................. .

6. We are sincere believers. = ................................................. .

7. I saluted the visiting Muslims. = ................................................. .

\* \* \*

**3. Translate the following sentences into English (orally):**

١- اَلْمُوَظَّفُونَ مُخْلِصُونَ .

٢- قَابَلْتُ اللَّاعِبِينَ فِي الْمَلْعَبِ .

٣- تَحَدَّثْتُ عَنِ الْمُؤْمِنِينَ الْفَائِزِينَ .

٤- هُمْ صِحَافِيُّونَ فَرَنْسِيُّونَ .

٥- هٰؤُلَاءِ نَجَّارُونَ مَاهِرُونَ .

٦- أَيْنَ السَّائِقُونَ الْمِصْرِيُّونَ ؟

٧- هُمْ مُعَلِّمُونَ لُبْنَانِيُّونَ .

٨- هَلْ أَنْتُمْ مُسَافِرُونَ ؟

٩- نَحْنُ مُمَرِّضُونَ هُنَا .

١٠- كَافَأْتُ اللَّاعِبِينَ الْفَائِزِينَ .

\* \* \*

**4. Change the sentences with singular pronouns, nouns and adjectives to "Dual" first; then to "Masculine Sound Plural", as in the given examples:**

| | | |
|---|---|---|
| هُمْ لَاعِبُونَ مَشْهُورُونَ . | هُمَا لَاعِبَانِ مَشْهُورَانِ . | هُوَ لَاعِبٌ مَشْهُورٌ . |
| قَابَلْتُ مُهَنْدِسِينَ أَمْرِيكِيِّينَ . | قَابَلْتُ مُهَنْدِسَيْنِ أَمْرِيكِيَّيْنِ . | قَابَلْتُ مُهَنْدِسًا أَمْرِيكِيًّا . |
| | | هٰذَا النَّجَّارُ الْمَاهِرُ . |
| | | هَلْ أَنْتَ الْمُعَلِّمُ ؟ |
| | | هُوَ فَلَّاحٌ نَشِيطٌ . |
| | | كَافَأْتُ اللَّاعِبَ الْفَائِزَ . |
| | | هُوَ مُؤْمِنٌ صَادِقٌ . |
| | | سَلَّمْتُ عَلَى الطَّبَّاخِ الْمَاهِرِ . |
| | | أَنَا مُوَظَّفٌ مُخْلِصٌ . |

\* \* \*

**5.** Unscramble the following sets of words to make from each of them a full meaningful sentence, as in the given example, and then translate the resultant sentences into English:

مُخْلِصُونَ / مُعَلِّمُونَ / هُمْ ⟵ هُمْ مُعَلِّمُونَ مُخْلِصُونَ.

They are sincere teachers.

١- في / الْمُسْلِمُونَ / هَلْ / الْمَسْجِدِ ⟵ .................... ؟ =

٢- الْبُسْتَانِ / في / هَلْ / الْمُزَارِعُونَ ⟵ .................... ؟ =

٣- عَلَى / الصَّادِقِينَ / الْمُؤْمِنِينَ / سَلَّمْتُ ⟵ .................... . =

٤- مَاهِرُونَ / طَبَّاخُونَ / هَؤُلَاءِ ⟵ .................... . =

٥- النَّشِيطُونَ / الْفَلَّاحُونَ / أَيْنَ ⟵ .................... ؟ =

\* \* \*

**6. Fill in the blank cells either with the singular, dual, or masculine sound plural:**

| جَمْعُ مُذَكَّرٍ سَالِمٍ / M.S.P. | مُثَنَّى / Dual | مُفْرَد / Singular |
|---|---|---|
|  |  | مِصْرِيٌّ |
|  | الْمُسْلِمَانِ |  |
| مُهَنْدِسِينَ |  |  |
|  | مُسَافِرَانِ |  |
|  |  | مُزَارِعٌ |
|  | مُجْتَهِدَيْنِ |  |
| الصَّادِقُونَ |  |  |
|  | مُهَنْدِسَانِ |  |

115

**Lesson 18** ﺍَﻟﺪَّﺭْﺱُ ﺍﻟﺜَّﺎﻣِﻦَ ﻋَﺸَﺮَ

اَلْجُمْلَةُ الإِسْمِيَّةُ : الْمُبْتَدَأُ وَالْخَبَرُ مَعَ جَمْعِ الْمُذَكَّرِ السَّالِمِ

**The Nominal (Equational) Sentences:**

**The Subject & the Predicate with Masculine Sound Plurals**

❖ Previously, in lesson 10, we mentioned that Arabic has a type of sentences that does not have exact equivalent in English.

❖ In such sentences, there are no actual physical verbs, though when we translate them into English, we need to use the English verb to be "*are*". We called these "Nominal" or "Equational"; since they only consist of nouns, pronouns or adjectives, and no verbs.

❖ Each "Nominal" sentence consists of two main parts: The first part is called "Subject" and the second part is called "Predicate."

❖ Now, let's read and examine the following examples where the "Subjects" and "Predicates" are of the "Masculine Sound Plural" type.

١

| | |
|---|---|
| These are engineers. | هَؤُلاءِ مُهَنْدِسُونَ . |
| They are teachers. | هُمْ مُعَلِّمُونَ . |
| You are sincere (ones). | أَنْتُمْ مُخْلِصُونَ . |
| We are Muslims. | نَحْنُ مُسْلِمُونَ . |
| They are pilots. | هُمْ طَيَّارُونَ . |

## ٢

| | |
|---|---|
| The engineers are famous. | اَلْمُهَنْدِسُونَ مَشْهُورُونَ . |
| The teachers are active. | اَلْمُعَلِّمُونَ نَشِيطُونَ . |
| Adam, Omar and Khalid are Muslims. | آدَمُ وَعُمَرُ وَخَالِدٌ مُسْلِمُونَ . |

## ٣

| | |
|---|---|
| The skilful carpenters are Egyptians. | اَلنَّجَّارُونَ الْمَاهِرُونَ مِصْرِيُّونَ . |
| The pious believers are beloved. | اَلْمُؤْمِنُونَ الصَّالِحُونَ مَحْبُوبُونَ . |
| They are hypocrite employees. | هُمْ مُوَظَّفُونَ مُنَافِقُونَ . |
| You are sincere workers. | أَنْتُمْ عَامِلُونَ مُخْلِصُونَ . |

❖ **Explanatory Notes:**

1. By examining the first two sets of examples above, you will notice that all the examples of group one above and the first two examples of group two are structures consisting of just two words, yet they all constitute full meaningful sentences.

2. The first word in each of these sentences is called the "subject", (مُبْتَدَأٌ) in Arabic, and the second word gives information about the "subject" and is called the "predicate", (خَبَرٌ) in Arabic.

3. In these sentences, the "subject" is either a plural personal subject pronoun, a plural demonstrative pronoun, a plural noun with the definite article or proper names, and the "predicate" is either a regular noun or an adjectival noun that must agree with the "subject" in gender and in being plural in number, but not in definiteness.

4. In the sentences of group three above, the "subject" is either a noun defined with the definite article followed by an adjective, as in the first two examples of this group. The subject and its adjective must agree in gender, number and definiteness, since they constitute noun-adjective phrases; but the predicate does not have to be definite.

5. In the last two examples of group three above, the "subject" is a pronoun and the "predicate" is a noun-adjective phrase both in the indefinite form.

6. In all cases, the "subjects" must be one of the definite nouns categories and the "predicate" is indefinite and it can be definite also.

6. In all cases, the "predicates" must agree with the "subjects" in gender, though not in definiteness.

7. Both the "subjects" and the "predicates" must be in the nominative case-ending, which in this case with "Masculine Sound Plurals" is an (ـُونَ) at the end.

8. In all the "Nominal" sentences with "Masculine Sound Plurals" the verb to be (*are*) is not actually there; it is only implied in the English translation.

9. "Nominal" sentences can be made longer by adding an adjective to either the "subjects" or the "predicates", as in the examples of group (3) above.

\* \* \*

❖ **New Vocabulary:**

أَسْمَاء / Nouns

a pilot = طَيَّارٌ        pilots = طَيَّارُونَ / طَيَّارِينَ

a hypocrite = مُنَافِقٌ        hypocrites = مُنَافِقُونَ / مُنَافِقِينَ

pure = طَاهِرٌ        pure ones = طَاهِرُونَ / طَاهِرِينَ

happy = مَسْرُورٌ        happy ones = مَسْرُورُونَ / مَسْرُورِينَ

just = عَادِلٌ        just ones = عَادِلُونَ / عَادِلِينَ

disbeliever = كَافِرٌ        disbelievers = كَافِرُونَ / كَافِرِينَ

ignorant = جَاهِلٌ        ignorant ones = جَاهِلُونَ / جَاهِلِينَ

emigrant = مُهَاجِرٌ        emigrants = مُهَاجِرُونَ / مُهَاجِرِينَ

مَحْبُوبٌ = beloved, liked     مَحْبُوبُونَ / مَحْبُوبِينَ = beloved ones

صَالِحٌ = righteous     صَالِحُونَ / صَالِحِينَ = righteous ones

**أَفْعَال / Verbs**

أُحِبُّ = I like, I love

**حُرُوف / Particles**

لاَ = do not (when followed by a verb)

\* \* \*

❖ <u>**New Vocabulary Used in Full Meaningful Sentences:**</u>

١- اَلْمُؤْمِنُونَ طَاهِرُونَ . = The (male) believers are pure.

٢- اَلْكَافِرُونَ مُنَافِقُونَ . = The (male) non-believers are hypocrites.

٣- هُمْ طَيَّارُونَ أَمْرِيكِيُّونَ . = They (male) are American pilots.

٤- هَلْ أَنْتُمْ مَسْرُورُونَ ؟ = Are you (male) happy?

٥- اَلْمُوَظَّفُونَ مُبَكِّرُونَ . = The (male) employees are early.

٦- اَلْعَامِلُونَ مُتَأَخِّرُونَ . = The (male) workers are late.

٧- اَلْجَاهِلُونَ كَثِيرُونَ . = The (male) ignorant ones are many.

٨- هَلْ أَنْتُمْ مُهَاجِرُونَ لُبْنَانِيُّونَ ؟ = Are you (male) Lebanese emigrants?

٩- أُحِبُّ الْمُؤْمِنِينَ الصَّالِحِينَ . = I like the righteous believers.

١٠- لاَ أُحِبُّ الْمُنَافِقِينَ . = I do not like the hypocrites.

١١- هُمْ مُعَلِّمُونَ مَحْبُوبُونَ . = They (male) are beloved teachers.

١٢- أُحِبُّ الْحَاكِمِينَ الْعَادِلِينَ . = I like the just rulers.

119

### Remember! / تَذَكَّرْ – تَذَكَّرِي!

1. If the "subject" in a "Nominal Sentence" is either a plural personal subject pronoun, a plural demonstrative pronoun, a plural noun with the definite article or three proper names, then the "predicate" is either a regular noun or an adjectival noun that must agree with the "subject" in gender and in being plural in number, but not in definiteness.

2. If the sentence has a "subject" which is a noun defined with the definite article followed by an adjective, the subject and its adjective must agree in gender, number and definiteness, since they constitute a noun-adjective phrase; but the predicate does not have to be definite.

3. In the last two examples of group three above, the "subject" is a pronoun and the "predicate" is a noun-adjective phrase both in the indefinite form.

4. In all cases, the "predicates" must agree with the "subjects" in gender and number, though not in definiteness.

4. Both the "subjects" and the "predicates" must be in the nominative case-ending, which in this case with "Masculine Sound Plurals" is an (ونَ) at the end.

5. In all the "Nominal" sentences with "Masculine Sound Plurals", the verb to be (*are*) is not actually there; it is only implied in the English translation.

6. "Nominal" sentences can be made longer by adding an adjective to either the "subjects" or the "predicates".

### Exercises / تَدْرِيبَاتٌ

**1. Read the following "Nominal Sentences"; underline the "Masculine Sound Plural Subjects" once and the "Masculine Sound Plural Predicates" twice; then translate them into English:**

١- اَلصَّالِحُونَ مَحْبُوبُونَ . ← ...................................

٢- هَلْ أَنْتُمْ طَيَّارُونَ ؟ ← ...................................

٣- اَلْمُزَارِعُونَ نَشِيطُونَ . ⟵ ..................

٤- هُمْ كَافِرُونَ جَاهِلُونَ . ⟵ ..................

٥- هَلْ أَنْتُمْ مَسْرُورُونَ ؟ ⟵ ..................

٦- اَلْمُهَاجِرُونَ مُسْلِمُونَ . ⟵ ..................

٧- اَلْمُؤْمِنُونَ طَاهِرُونَ . ⟵ ..................

٨- اَلْكَافِرُونَ مُنَافِقُونَ . ⟵ ..................

\* \* \*

**2. Translate the following sentences into Arabic (orally and written):**

1. The Muslims are sincere. = ..................

2. The engineers are Americans. = ..................

3. They are Sudanese emigrants. = ..................

4. Are you (plural) happy? = ..................

5. Are the pure (ones) beloved (ones)? = ..................

6. I do not like the hypocrites = ..................

7. I like the virtuous Muslims. = ..................

8. We are Egyptian visitors. = ..................

9. They are famous engineers. = ..................

\* \* \*

**3. Translate the following sentences into English (orally):**

(١) لاَ أُحِبُّ الْمُنَافِقِينَ . (٢) الزَّائِرُونَ حَاضِرُونَ . (٣) اللَّاعِبُونَ مَاهِرُونَ .

(٤) الْمُزَارِعُونَ نَشِيطُونَ . (٥) أُحِبُّ الْعَامِلِينَ الْمُخْلِصِينَ . (٦) هَؤُلاَءِ مُسْلِمُونَ أَمْرِيكِيُّونَ . (٧) هُمْ لاَعِبُونَ مِصْرِيُّونَ . (٨) هَلْ أَنْتُمْ مُهَنْدِسُونَ ؟

(٩) هُمْ طَيَّارُونَ سُورِيُّونَ . (١٠) الصَّالِحُونَ مَحْبُوبُونَ . (١١) لاَ أُحِبُّ الْمُنَافِقِينَ وَلاَ الْجَاهِلِينَ . (١٢) هَلْ أَنْتُمْ مَسْرُورُونَ أَمْ حَزِينُونَ ؟

\* \* \*

**4. Pair each <u>Masculine Sound Plural Subject</u> from group (1) with a suitable <u>Masculine Sound Plural Predicate</u> from group (2) to form full meaningful sentences; then write down the sentence in the dotted space, and then translate it verbally into English:**

| (٢) | (١) |
|---|---|
| عِرَاقِيُّونَ | الطَّبَّاخُونَ |
| مَحْبُوبُونَ | اللَّاعِبُونَ |
| مَشْهُورُونَ | الْمُهَاجِرُونَ |
| صَالِحُونَ | الصَّالِحُونَ |
| مَاهِرُونَ | الْمُجْتَهِدُونَ |
| مُنَافِقُونَ | الْمُؤْمِنُونَ |
| نَاجِحُونَ | الْكَافِرُونَ |

**5. Fill in the blanks with the appropriate word from those given in brackets:**

١- الصَّدِيقانِ ............... (مُخْلِصَانِ / مُخْلِصُونَ) .

٢- ............... (هُمْ / هُمَا) مُمْتَازُونَ .

٣- هَلْ أَنْتُمْ ............... (مُسْلِمَانِ / مُسْلِمُونَ) ؟

٤- أُحِبُّ العَامِلِينَ ............... (النَّشِيطُونَ / النَّشِيطِينَ) .

٥- هُمْ ............... (مَسْرُورُونَ / مَسْرُورَانِ) .

٦- لاَ أُحِبُّ ............... (الْمُنَافِقِينَ / الْمُنَافِقُونَ) .

\* \* \*

**6. Change the following sentences into "Plural" forms; orally first, and then in writing; the first one is done as an example:**

١- هُوَ طَيَّارٌ مَاهِرٌ .  ⟵  هُمْ طَيَّارُونَ مَاهِرُونَ .

٢- هَلْ أَنْتَ مَسْرُورٌ ؟  ⟵  ............... ؟

٣- هَذَا مُهَاجِرٌ عِرَاقِيٌّ .  ⟵  ............... .

٤- الْمُؤْمِنُ صَادِقٌ .  ⟵  ............... .

٥- لاَ أُحِبُّ الْمُنَافِقَ .  ⟵  ............... .

٦- مَنِ الْمُهَنْدِسُ الأَمْرِيكِيُّ ؟  ⟵  ............... ؟

٧- أَيْنَ الْفَلَّاحُ النَّشِيطُ ؟  ⟵  ............... ؟

\* \* \*

**6. Fill in the blank cells either with the singular, dual, or masculine sound plural:**

| جَمْعُ مُذَكَّرٍ سَالِمٍ / M.S.P. | مُثَنَّى / Dual | مُفْرَد / Singular |
|---|---|---|
| | | عَادِلٌ |
| | طَاهِرَانِ | |
| كَافِرِينَ | | |
| | مَحْبُوبَانِ | |
| | | جَاهِلٌ |
| | مُهَاجِرَيْنِ | |
| صَالِحُونَ | | |

# Lesson 19 — الدَّرْسُ التَّاسِعَ عَشَرَ

## أَنْوَاعُ الْجَمْعِ : جَمْعُ الْمُؤَنَّثِ السَّالِمِ
### The Types of Plurals: Feminine Sound Plural

- Unlike English, Arabic has special plural nouns and adjectives which refer exclusively to three and up of feminine gender.

- In this lesson we will deal with the "Feminine Sound Plural"; which is a regular plural for feminine gender only. It is regular, hence "Sound" because it results from suffixing a certain suffix to the end of the singular form. This would be parallel to the English regular, which results from adding an (…*s*) or an (…*es*) at the end of the singular.

- So in the following examples we introduce the "Feminine Sound Plural" forms of nouns in comparative perspective with their singular counterparts, so that you learn how to make plurals from singulars.

- Now, let's read and examine the following parallel examples:

| اَلْمُفْرَدُ / The Singular | جَمْعُ الْمُؤَنَّثِ السَّالِمِ / Feminine Sound Plural |
|---|---|
| هَذِهِ مُعَلِّمَةٌ مُخْلِصَةٌ . <br> This is a sincere (female) teacher. | هَؤُلاَءِ مُعَلِّمَاتٌ مُخْلِصَاتٌ . <br> These are sincere (female) teachers. |
| هِيَ مُسْلِمَةٌ . <br> She is a Muslim. | هُنَّ مُسْلِمَاتٌ . <br> They are (female) Muslims. |
| هِيَ مُؤْمِنَةٌ مُخْلِصَةٌ . <br> She is a sincere believer. | هُنَّ مُؤْمِنَاتٌ مُخْلِصَاتٌ . <br> They are sincere (female) believers. |
| هَلْ أَنْتِ مُهَنْدِسَةٌ ؟ <br> Are you (female) an engineer? | هَلْ أَنْتُنَّ مُهَنْدِسَاتٌ ؟ <br> Are you (female) engineers? |

| | | |
|---|---|---|
| نَحْنُ عَرَبِيَّاتٌ . | ← | أَنَا عَرَبِيَّةٌ . |
| We are Arabs (female). | | I am an Arab (female). |
| هُنَّ فَلَّاحَاتٌ نَشِيطَاتٌ . | ← | هِيَ فَلَّاحَةٌ نَشِيطَةٌ . |
| They are active (female) peasants. | | She is an active peasant. |
| هَلْ أَنْتُنَّ مُوَظَّفَاتٌ هُنَا ؟ | ← | هَلْ أَنْتِ مُوَظَّفَةٌ هُنَا ؟ |
| Are you (female) employees here? | | Are you (female) an employee here? |

* * *

| جَمْعُ الْمُؤَنَّثِ السَّالِمِ / Feminine Sound Plural | | اَلْمُفْرَدُ / The Singular |
|---|---|---|
| قَابَلْتُ سَيِّدَاتٍ مِصْرِيَّاتٍ . | ← | قَابَلْتُ سَيِّدَةً مِصْرِيَّةً . |
| I met Egyptian ladies. | | I met an Egyptian lady. |
| كَافَأْتُ الْمُعَلِّمَاتِ الْمُخْلِصَاتِ . | ← | كَافَأْتُ الْمُعَلِّمَةَ الْمُخْلِصَةَ . |
| I rewarded the sincere (female) teachers. | | I rewarded the sincere (female) teacher. |
| قَابَلْتُ اللَّاعِبَاتِ الْمَشْهُورَاتِ . | ← | قَابَلْتُ اللَّاعِبَةَ الْمَشْهُورَةَ . |
| I met the famous (female) players. | | I met the famous (female) player. |
| تَعَرَّفْتُ عَلَى الزَّائِرَاتِ الأَمْرِيكِيَّاتِ . | ← | تَعَرَّفْتُ عَلَى الزَّائِرَةِ الأَمْرِيكِيَّةِ . |
| I got acquainted with the (female) American visitors. | | I got acquainted with the (female) American visitor. |

* * *

❖ **Explanatory Notes:**

1. By examining the first set of the sentences above and focusing on the words with suffixes underlined, we will notice that all feminine singular demonstrative as well as personal pronouns have plural forms, which need to be learned if we need to use them in connection to plural nouns and adjectives. However, these plural pronouns are not representative of "Feminine Sound Plurals."

2. If you examine the words with suffixes at the end of each noun or adjective in the first group, you will notice that all these suffixes are identical; that is the ending (ـَاتٌ / *ātun*), which is the "Feminine Sound Plural'" sign for nouns and adjectives when they are in a "Nominative Mood" (i.e. functioning as subjects or predicates in nominal sentences) and without the definite article.

3. If you examine the nouns and adjectives used in the second group, you will notice that they were used in contexts were they were preceded by either a verb or a preposition; therefore they are functioning as the objects of the verbs or the objects of prepositions; the first is said to be in an **Accusative Mood** and the second is said to be in "**Genitive Mood**"; and the suffix in these two cases is (ـَاتٍ / *ātin*) if they are without the definite article, or (ـَاتِ / *āti*) if they are with the definite article.

4. Thus there is basically one ending sign for recognizing "Feminine Sound Plural" nouns or adjectives; (ـَات / *āt*).

5. "Feminine Sound Plural" nouns and adjectives, like other nouns, may appear in their indefinite forms, without the definite article, and in this case the "*Tanween of Dammah*" or the "*Tanween of Kasrah*" will appear on top of the last "*Taa*". If they receive the definite article, then only one "*Dammah*" or one "*Kasrah*" will appear over the last "*Taa*"; as you can see in some examples of the second group.

6. Also, "Feminine Sound Plural" nouns can be followed by adjectives that should agree with these nouns in gender, number and definiteness or indefiniteness if the noun is referring to humans.

7. Important Note: Not all feminine singular nouns or adjectives may have "Feminine Sound Plural" endings; for they might have "Broken Plurals" forms.

\* \* \*

❖ **New Vocabulary:**

| | | | |
|---|---|---|---|
| you (feminine plural) = أَنْتُنَّ | | they (feminine) = هُنَّ | |
| sincere ones (female) = مُخْلِصَات | | teachers (female) = مُعَلِّمَات | |
| believers (female) = مُؤْمِنَات | | Muslims (female) = مُسْلِمَات | |
| Arabs (female) = عَرَبِيَّات | | engineers (female) = مُهَنْدِسَات | |
| active ones (female) = نَشيطَات | | peasants (female) = فَلاَّحَات | |
| lady / ladies = سَيِّدَة / سَيِّدَات | | employees (female) = مُوَظَّفَات | |
| the players (female) = اللاَّعِبَات | | Egyptians (female) = مِصْرِيَّات | |
| the visiting ones (females) = الزَّائِرَات | | the famous ones (females) = الْمَشْهُورَات | |
| | | the Americans (females) = الأَمْرِيكِيَّات | |

## Remember! / تَذَكَّرْ – تَذَكَّرِي!

1. Arabic has a special plural for an exclusively female group, called "Feminine Sound Plural"; and it is a regular plural resulting from adding a certain suffix to the end of the singular.

2. The "Feminine Sound Plural" nouns and adjectives result by adding the suffix (ـَات) after dropping the *"Taa' Marbut*ah" of the singular.

3. The demonstrative pronouns and the subject pronouns have their own feminine plural forms related specifically to three and up in number.

4. <u>Feminine Sound Plurals have only two case-endings</u>, instead of three in regular nouns; the *"Tanween Damm*ah" or "on*e Damm*ah" for the <u>nominative</u>, and *"Tanween Kasr*ah" or "on*e Kasr*ah" for both <u>accusative</u> and <u>genitive</u>.

5. If a feminine plural noun referring to human beings is followed by an adjective, the adjective must be also feminine sound plural and in the same form as the noun it describes.

6. Not all feminine singular nouns can be made into "Feminine Sound Plurals" if they happened to have an established "Broken Plural" form for non-human nouns.

## تَدْرِيبَاتٌ / Exercises

**1.** Read the following sentences; underline all the words that appear to be in "Feminine Sound Plural" forms; then attempt an English translation; one is done for you as an example:

١- هُنَّ مُهَنْدِسَاتٌ نَاجِحَاتٌ .   They are successful (female) engineers.

٢- كَافَأْتُ الْعَامِلَاتِ الْمُخْلِصَاتِ .   ..................................

٣- هَؤُلَاءِ طَبَّاخَاتٌ مَاهِرَاتٌ .   ..................................

٤- مَنِ الْمُسَافِرَاتُ عَلَى هَذِهِ الطَّائِرَاتِ ؟   .................................. ؟

٥- قَابَلْتُ الْمُتَرْجِمَاتِ الْأَمْرِيكِيَّاتِ .   ..................................

٦- أَيْنَ الصَّحَافِيَّاتُ الزَّائِرَاتُ ؟   .................................. ؟

٧- قَابَلْتُ الْمُزَارِعَاتِ النَّشِيطَاتِ .   ..................................

٨- اَلْمُجْتَهِدَاتُ فَائِزَاتٌ بِالْجَائِزَةِ .   ..................................

129

## 2. Translate the following sentences into Arabic (orally and written):

1. They are (female) American engineers. = ..........................................

2. Are you (female) travelers on this plane? = ؟..........................................

3. Are you Egyptian (female) players? = ؟..........................................

4. They are sincere (female) teachers. = ..........................................

5. These are famous (female) writers. = ..........................................

6. We are sincere (female) workers. = ..........................................

7. I saluted the visiting (female) Muslims. = ..........................................

\* \* \*

## 3. Translate the following sentences into English (orally):

١- الْمُوَظَّفَاتُ مُخْلِصَاتٌ .

٢- قَابَلْتُ اللاَّعِبَاتِ فِي الْمَلْعَبِ .

٣- تَحَدَّثْتُ عَنِ الْمُؤْمِنَاتِ الْفَائِزَاتِ .

٤- هُنَّ صَحَافِيَّاتٌ فَرَنْسِيَّاتٌ .

٥- هَؤُلَاءِ طَبَّاخَاتٌ مَاهِرَاتٌ .

٦- أَيْنَ الطَّبِيبَاتُ الْمِصْرِيَّاتُ ؟

٧- هُنَّ مُعَلِّمَاتٌ لُبْنَانِيَّاتٌ .

٨- هَلْ أَنْتُنَّ مُسَافِرَاتٌ ؟

٩- نَحْنُ مُمَرِّضَاتٌ هُنَا .

١٠- كَافَأْتُ اللاَّعِبَاتِ الْفَائِزَاتِ .

\* \* \*

**4. Change the sentences with singular pronouns, nouns and adjectives to "Dual" first; then to "Feminine Sound Plural", as in the given examples:**

| | | |
|---|---|---|
| هُنَّ لاعِبَاتٌ مَشْهُورَاتٌ . | هُمَا لاعِبَتَانِ مَشْهُورَتَانِ . | هِيَ لاعِبَةٌ مَشْهُورَةٌ . |
| قَابَلْتُ مُهَنْدِسَاتٍ أَمْرِيكِيَّاتٍ . | قَابَلْتُ مُهَنْدِسَتَيْنِ أَمْرِيكِيَّتَيْنِ . | قَابَلْتُ مُهَنْدِسَةً أَمْرِيكِيَّةً . |
| | | هَذِهِ طَبَّاخَةٌ مَاهِرَةٌ . |
| | | هَلْ أَنْتِ الْمُعَلِّمَةُ ؟ |
| | | هِيَ سَيِّدَةٌ نَشِيطَةٌ . |
| | | كَافَأْتُ اللاَّعِبَةَ الْفَائِزَةَ . |
| | | هِيَ مُؤْمِنَةٌ صَادِقَةٌ . |
| | | سَلَّمْتُ عَلَى الأُسْتَاذَةِ . |
| | | أَنَا مُوَظَّفَةٌ مُخْلِصَةٌ . |

\* \* \*

131

**5.** Unscramble the following sets of words to make from each of them a full meaningful sentence, as in the given example, and then translate the resultant sentences into English:

> مُخْلِصَاتٌ / مُعَلِّمَاتٌ / هُنَّ     هُنَّ مُعَلِّمَاتٌ مُخْلِصَاتٌ .
> They are sincere (female) teachers.

١- فِي / الْمُسْلِمَاتُ / هَلْ / الْمَسْجِدِ    = ؟ ..................................................

..................................................

٢- الْبُسْتَانِ / فِي / هَلْ / الْمُزَارِعَاتُ    = ؟ ..................................................

..................................................

٣- عَلَى / الصَّادِقَاتِ / الْمُؤْمِنَاتِ / سَلَّمْتُ    = . ..................................................

..................................................

٤- مَاهِرَاتٌ / طَبَّاخَاتٌ / هَؤُلَاءِ    = . ..................................................

..................................................

٥- النَّشِيطَاتُ / الْفَلَّاحَاتُ / أَيْنَ    = ؟ ..................................................

..................................................

\* \* \*

**6. Fill in the blank cells either with the singular, dual, or feminine sound plural:**

| جَمْعُ مُؤَنَّثٍ سَالِمٍ / F.S.P. | مُثَنَّى / Dual | مُفْرَد / Singular |
|---|---|---|
| عِرَاقِيَّاتٌ | عِرَاقِيَّتَانِ | عِرَاقِيَّةٌ |
| الْمُسْلِمَاتُ | الْمُسْلِمَتَانِ | الْمُسْلِمَةُ |
| مُهَنْدِسَاتٌ | مُهَنْدِسَتَانِ | مُهَنْدِسَةٌ |
| مُسَافِرَاتٌ | مُسَافِرَتَانِ | مُسَافِرَةٌ |
| مُزَارِعَاتٌ | مُزَارِعَتَانِ | مُزَارِعَةٌ |
| مُجْتَهِدَاتٌ | مُجْتَهِدَتَيْنِ | مُجْتَهِدَةٌ |
| الصَّادِقَاتُ | الصَّادِقَتَانِ | الصَّادِقَةُ |
| سَيِّدَاتٌ | سَيِّدَتَانِ | سَيِّدَةٌ |

**Lesson 20**

الدَّرْسُ الْعِشْرُونَ

> التَّعْبِيرُ النَّعْتِيُّ مَعَ جَمْعِ الْمُؤَنَّثِ السَّالِمِ لِلْعَاقِلِ وَغَيْرِ الْعَاقِلِ
>
> The Adjectival Phrase with Feminine Sound Plurals for Humans and Non-Humans

❖ Previously, in lesson 18, we have seen examples of adjectival phrases where the nouns are "Feminine Sound Plurals" referring to human beings and the adjectives modifying them were also in the "Feminine Sound Plural" forms.

❖ However, there are many nouns that take the "Feminine Sound Plural" forms, but they refer to non-human entities. With these nouns the adjectives modifying them remain in the "Feminine Singular" form, with the "*Taa' Marbutah*" of the singular.

❖ Now, let's read and examine the following sets of parallel sentences to observe this rule in context:

| Adjectival Phrases with Feminine Sound Plurals for Non-Humans | Adjectival Phrases with Feminine Sound Plurals for Humans |
|---|---|
| هَذِهِ جَامِعَاتٌ عَرَبِيَّةٌ . | هَؤُلَاءِ مُهَنْدِسَاتٌ عَرَبِيَّاتٌ . |
| These are Arabic universities. | These are (female) Arabic engineers. |
| هَذِهِ سَيَّارَاتٌ جَدِيدَةٌ . | هَؤُلَاءِ مُعَلِّمَاتٌ جَدِيدَاتٌ . |
| These are new cars. | These are (female) new teachers. |
| هِيَ مَكْتَبَاتٌ مَشْهُورَةٌ . | هُنَّ طَبِيبَاتٌ مَشْهُورَاتٌ . |
| They are famous libraries. | They are (female) famous doctors. |
| رَأَيْتُ طَائِرَاتٍ صَغِيرَةً . | رَأَيْتُ تِلْمِيذَاتٍ صَغِيرَاتٍ . |
| I saw small airplanes. | I saw (female) small pupils. |
| الْوَرَدَاتُ الْجَمِيلَةُ فِي الْحَدِيقَةِ . | السَّيِّدَاتُ الْجَمِيلَاتُ فِي الْحَدِيقَةِ . |
| The beautiful roses are in the garden. | The beautiful ladies are in the garden. |
| أَيْنَ الْبَقَرَاتُ الْكَبِيرَةُ ؟ | أَيْنَ الطَّالِبَاتُ الْكَبِيرَاتُ ؟ |
| Where are the older cows? | Where are the (female) older students? |

## ❖ Explanatory Notes:

1. By examining the sentences on the right above, you will notice that all these contain noun-adjective phrases (underlined). All the nouns of this group appear in the "Feminine Sound Plural" forms and all of them refer to human beings. Therefore, the adjectives modifying them must also be in the "Feminine Sound Plural" forms.

2. However, by examining the parallel sentences on the left, you will notice that all these also contain noun-adjective phrases (underlined). All the nouns of this group appear in the "Feminine Sound Plural" forms, but <u>all of them refer to non-human beings</u>. Therefore, the adjectives modifying them <u>must be used in their</u> <u>"Feminine Singular"</u> forms.

\* \* \*

### ❖ New Vocabulary:

**أَسْمَاء / Nouns**

| | |
|---|---|
| جَامِعَات = universities | جَدِيدَات = new ones |
| سَيَّارَات = cars | طَبِيبَات = (female) doctors |
| مَكْتَبَات = libraries, bookstores | تِلْمِيذَات = (female) pupils |
| صَغِيرَات = small ones, little ones | طَائِرَات = airplanes |
| الْجَمِيلَاتُ = the beautiful ones | الْوَرْدَات = the roses |
| الطَّالِبَات = the female students | الْكَبِيرَات = the older ones, the bigger ones |
| الْبَقَرَات = the cows | |

**أَفْعَال / Verbs**

رَأَيْتُ = I saw

\* \* \*

135

# تَذَكَّرْ – تَذَكَّرِي! / Remember!

1. In noun-adjective phrases involving "Feminine Sound Plural Nouns", we need to consider whether these nouns refer to human beings or to non-human beings.

2. If they refer to human beings, then the adjectives modifying them must also be in the "Feminine Sound Plural" forms.

3. However, if the nouns refer to non-human beings, then the adjectives modifying them must be in their "Feminine Singular" forms.

## تَدْرِيبَاتٌ / Exercises

**1. Read the following "Nominal Sentences"; underline the noun-adjective phrases then explain the relationship of the noun to its adjective:**

١- الطَّالِبَاتُ الْعَرَبِيَّاتُ فِي الصَّفِّ .

٢- هَلْ أَنْتُنَّ مُمَرِّضَاتٌ جَدِيدَاتٌ؟

٣- أَيْنَ الْمَكْتَبَاتُ الْجَدِيدَةُ ؟

٤- سَلَّمْتُ عَلَى الصَّحَافِيَّاتِ الزَّائِرَاتِ .

٥- هَذِهِ بُحَيْرَاتٌ كَبِيرَةٌ .

٦- التِّلْمِيذَاتُ الصَّغِيرَاتُ فِي الصَّفِّ .

٧- أَيْنَ الطَّبِيبَاتُ الْأَمْرِيكِيَّاتُ ؟

٨- هَذِهِ جَامِعَاتٌ مَشْهُورَةٌ .

٩- لَا أُحِبُّ الْمُحَاضَرَاتِ الطَّوِيلَةَ .

١٠- كَافَأْتُ الْمُوَظَّفَاتِ الْمُخْلِصَاتِ .

* * *

**2. Translate the following sentences into Arabic (orally and written):**

1. Where are the beautiful roses? = ................................................ ؟

2. The older (female) students are in the class. = ................................................ .

3. They are famous (female) doctors. = ................................. .

4. Are these new libraries? = ................................. ؟

5. I saw the famous (female) players. = ................................. .

\* \* \*

**3. Translate the following sentences into English (orally):**

(١) لاَ أُحِبُّ الْمُنَافِقَاتِ .   (٢) الْمُوَظَّفَاتُ الْجَدِيدَاتُ نَشِيطَاتٌ .

(٣) اللَّاعِبَاتُ الْمَاهِرَاتُ فِي الْمَلْعَبِ .   (٤) الْمَكْتَبَاتُ الْجَدِيدَةُ كَبِيرَةٌ .

(٥) أُحِبُّ الْعَامِلَاتِ الْمُخْلِصَاتِ .   (٦) هَؤُلَاءِ مُسْلِمَاتٌ أَمْرِيكِيَّاتٌ .

(٧) هُنَّ سَيِّدَاتٌ مِصْرِيَّاتٌ .   (٨) هَلْ أَنْتُنَّ طَالِبَاتٌ جَدِيدَاتٌ ؟

(٩) هَذِهِ سَيَّارَاتٌ قَدِيمَةٌ .   (١٠) رَأَيْتُ الطَّائِرَاتِ الْكَبِيرَةَ .

\* \* \*

**4. Fill in the blanks with the appropriate adjective from those given in brackets:**

١- اَلصَّدِيقَاتُ ................ مَحْبُوبَاتٌ .   (الْمُخْلِصَةُ / الْمُخْلِصَاتُ)

٢- هَذِهِ جَامِعَاتٌ ................ .   (مَشْهُورَاتٌ / مَشْهُورَةٌ)

٣- هَلْ أَنْتُنَّ سَيِّدَاتٌ ................ ؟   (عِرَاقِيَّاتٌ / عِرَاقِيَّةٌ)

٤- رَأَيْتُ الْمَكْتَبَاتِ ................ .   (الْكَبِيرَاتِ / الْكَبِيرَةَ)

٥- هُنَّ تِلْمِيذَاتٌ ................ .   (مَسْرُورَةٌ / مَسْرُورَتٌ)

٦- لاَ أُحِبُّ الْمُحَاضَرَاتِ ................ .   (الطَّوِيلَةَ / الطَّوِيلَاتِ)

٧- أُحِبُّ الطَّالِبَاتِ ................ .   (الْمُجْتَهِدَةَ / الْمُجْتَهِدَاتِ)

**5.** Change the following sentences into "Feminine Sound Plural" forms; orally first, and then in writing; the first one is done as an example. *Note also that personal pronouns and demonstrative pronouns need to be made plural too*:

١- هِيَ طَبَّاخَةٌ مَاهِرَةٌ .    هُنَّ طَبَّاخَاتٌ مَاهِرَاتٌ .

٢- هَلْ أَنْتِ مَسْرُورَةٌ ؟    ................................ ؟

٣- هَذِهِ مُهَاجِرَةٌ عِرَاقِيَّةٌ .    ................................ .

٤- الْمُؤْمِنَةُ صَادِقَةٌ .    ................................ .

٥- هِيَ طَالِبَةٌ مُجْتَهِدَةٌ .    ................................ .

٦- مَنِ السَّيِّدَةُ الْعَرَبِيَّةُ ؟    ................................ ؟

٧- أَيْنَ الْفَلَّاحَةُ النَّشِيطَةُ ؟    ................................ ؟

* * *

**6.** Fill in the blank cells either with the singular, dual, or feminine sound plural:

| جَمْعُ مُؤَنَّثٍ سَالِمٍ / F.S.P. | مُثَنَّى / Dual | مُفْرَد / Singular |
|---|---|---|
|  |  | نَظِيفَةٌ |
|  | طَاهِرَتَانِ |  |
| كَافِرَاتٌ |  |  |
|  | مَحْبُوبَتَانِ |  |
|  |  | جَاهِلَتَانِ |
|  | مُهَاجِرَتَانِ |  |
| صَالِحَاتٌ |  |  |

138

**Lesson 21** ──────────────── الدَّرْسُ الْحَادِيَ وَالْعِشْرُونَ

> ## أَنْوَاعُ الْجَمْعِ : جَمْعُ التَّكْسِيرِ
> ### The Types of Plurals: Broken Plural

- Arabic has a third type of plural, called "Broken Plural."

- "Broken Plurals" result by internal vowel changes as well as by eliminating or adding letters to the singulars. In this sense they are irregular plurals such as the English, "oxen" from the singular "ox" or "children" from the singular "child" or "geese" from the singular "goose"

- However, Arabic has so many plural of this type to the point that the best way to learn "Broken Plurals" is to learn them in conjunction with their singulars. Thus dictionaries and language educational books make the point of listing them after their singulars.

- Though theoretically, "Broken Plurals" are labeled as irregular, they, in fact, fall neatly under certain patterns, which make it easy to categorize and predict them when the student reaches a certain level of familiarity with the language and its pattern system.

- Following, you will find a number of tables representing samples of some of the most common patterns:

| جَمْعُ التَّكْسِيرِ / Broken Plural | الْمُفْرَدُ / The Singular | جَمْعُ التَّكْسِيرِ / Broken Plural | الْمُفْرَدُ / The Singular |
|---|---|---|---|
| جُيُوشٌ | جَيْشٌ = an army | أَقْلَامٌ | قَلَمٌ = pen |
| وُعُودٌ | وَعْدٌ = a promise | أَعْلَامٌ | عَلَمٌ = flag |
| قُلُوبٌ | قَلْبٌ = a heart | أَخْبَارٌ | خَبَرٌ = a piece of news |
| طُبُولٌ | طَبْلٌ = a drum | أَبْطَالٌ | بَطَلٌ = a hero |
| سُهُولٌ | سَهْلٌ = plain | أَوْلَادٌ | وَلَدٌ = a boy |
| فُعُولٌ | فَعْلٌ | أَفْعَالٌ | فَعَلٌ |

139

| جَمْعُ التَّكْسِيرِ<br>Broken Plural | اَلْمُفْرَدُ / The Singular | جَمْعُ التَّكْسِيرِ<br>Broken Plural | اَلْمُفْرَدُ / The Singular |
|---|---|---|---|
| كُتَّابٌ | كَاتِبٌ = a writer | حُمْرٌ | أَحْمَرُ = red |
| حُرَّاسٌ | حَارِسٌ = a guard | خُضْرٌ | أَخْضَرُ = green |
| عُمَّالٌ | عَامِلٌ = a worker | صُفْرٌ | أَصْفَرُ = yellow |
| زُرَّاعٌ | زَارِعٌ = a planter | زُرْقٌ | أَزْرَقُ = blue |
| جُهَّالٌ | جَاهِلٌ = an ignorant | سُمْرٌ | أَسْمَرُ = tawny |
| فُعَّالٌ | فَاعِلٌ | فُعْلٌ | أَفْعَلُ |

❖ **Explanatory Notes:**

1. By examining the four sets of the singular nouns or adjectives above in comparative perspective with their "Broken Plurals" counterparts, you will notice that a group of singulars that have the same "pattern" might have one certain pattern in the plurals. For example, group one has the pattern of (أَفْعَلُ) with the singulars, has the pattern of (فُعْلٌ) with the plurals. Likewise, group two has the pattern of (فَعْلٌ) with the singulars, has the pattern of (فُعُولٌ) with the plurals, and so on with the other two groups.

2. However, it is important to caution that this patterning paradigm does not work always in absolute terms. Therefore, in the initial stages of learning Arabic a student is advised to learn "Broken Plurals" as vocabulary in conjunction with their singulars.

3. Also, it is possible for certain singulars to have more than one broken plural; such as (أُسُودٌ) and (أُسْدٌ) for the singular (أَسَدٌ), which means "lion".

4. Like "Feminine Sound Plurals", if "Broken Plurals" refer to non-humans, then the pronouns and adjectives related to them must be in the "Feminine Singular" forms.

5. In terms of "Case-Ending" signs, "Broken Plurals" are like regular nouns; they show the "*Dammah*" or "*Tanween Dammah*" in the nominative; the "*Fathah*" or "*Tanween Fathah*" in the accusative; and the "*Kasrah*" or "*Tanween Kasrah*" in the genitive.

❖ **Examples of Broken Plurals Used in Full Sentences:**

| Used with Humans | Used with Non-Humans |
|---|---|

**Used with Humans**

١- الأَوْلَادُ سُمْرٌ .

The boys are tawny.

٢- الأَبْطَالُ مُخْلِصُونَ .

The heroes are sincere.

٣- الْعُمَّالُ نَشِيطُونَ .

The workers are active.

٤- الْحُرَّاسُ مُمْتَازُونَ .

The guards are excellent.

٥- قَابَلْتُ الْكُتَّابَ الْمَشْهُورِينَ .

I met the famous writers.

٦- لَا أُحِبُّ الطُّلَّابَ الْجُهَّالَ .

I do not like the ignorant students.

**Used with Non-Humans**

١- الأُسُودُ قَوِيَّةٌ .

The lions are strong.

٢- هَذِهِ وُعُودٌ صَادِقَةٌ .

These are true promises.

٣- السُّهُولُ الْخَضْرَاءُ جَمِيلَةٌ .

The green plains are beautiful.

٤- هَذِهِ أَخْبَارٌ طَيِّبَةٌ .

These are good news.

٥- هَذِهِ الأَعْلَامُ عَرَبِيَّةٌ .

These flags are Arabic.

٦- الأَقْلَامُ الْجَدِيدَةُ فِي الْحَقِيبَةِ .

The new pens are in the bag.

\* \* \*

**New Vocabulary:**

pen / pens = قَلَمٌ / أَقْلَامٌ     army / armies = جَيْشٌ / جُيُوشٌ

flag / flags = عَلَمٌ / أَعْلَامٌ     promise / promises = وَعْدٌ / وُعُودٌ

item of news / news = خَبَرٌ / أَخْبَارٌ     heart / hearts = قَلْبٌ / قُلُوبٌ

hero / heroes = بَطَلٌ / أَبْطَالٌ     boy / boys = وَلَدٌ / أَوْلَادٌ

| | |
|---|---|
| plain / plains = سَهْلٌ / سُهُولٌ | red / red ones = أَحْمَرُ / حُمْرٌ |
| green / green ones = أَخْضَرُ / خُضْرٌ | yellow / yellow ones = أَصْفَرُ / صُفْرٌ |
| blue / blue ones = أَزْرَقُ / زُرْقٌ | tawny / tawny ones = أَسْمَرُ / سُمْرٌ |
| writer / writers = كَاتِبٌ / كُتَّابٌ | guard / guards = حَارِسٌ / حُرَّاسٌ |
| worker / workers = عَامِلٌ / عُمَّالٌ | planter / planters = زَارِعٌ / زُرَّاعٌ |
| ignorant / ignorant ones = جَاهِلٌ / جُهَّالٌ | lion / lions = أَسَدٌ / أُسْدٌ ، أُسُودٌ |
| student / students = طَالِبٌ / طُلَّابٌ | good = طَيِّبَةٌ |
| blond, blonds = أَشْقَرُ / شُقْرٌ | |

## Remember! / تَذَكَّرْ - تَذَكَّرِي!

1. Arabic has a third type of plural called "Broken Plural"; and it is an irregular plural resulting from internal changes of vowels and consonants.

2. "Broken Plurals", however, fall under a large number of patterns that become easier to predict as the student of Arabic advances in his / her studies.

3. Students in the initial stages should learn "Broken Plurals" as vocabulary in conjunction with their singulars.

4. "Broken Plurals", whether nouns or adjectives may refer to humans or non-human things and entities. If they are referring to non-humans, then demonstrative pronouns and adjectives used in conjunction with them must be used in their feminine singular forms.

5. "Broken Plurals" show their case-ending like regular nouns; i.e. by a *"Dammah"* or *"Tanween Dammah"*, a *"Fathah"* or *"Tanween Fathah"*, or a *"Kasrah"* or *"Tanween Kasrah"*

6. Some nouns might take more than one "Broken Plural" pattern.

7. Your dictionary should be used frequently to look up the "Broken Plurals" of singulars that do not take either "Masculine Sound Plurals" or "Feminine Sound Plurals"

# Exercises / تَدْرِيبَاتٌ

**1.** Read the following sentences; underline all the words that appear to be in the "Broken Plural" forms; then attempt English translations; one is done for you as an example:

١- هُمْ عُمَّالٌ نَشِيطُونَ .  They are industrious workers.

٢- كَافَأْتُ الْكُتَّابَ الْمُمْتَازِينَ .

٣- هَؤُلَاءِ طُلَّابٌ مُجْتَهِدُونَ .

٤- هَذِهِ وُعُودٌ صَادِقَةٌ .

٥- قُلُوبُ الْمُؤْمِنِينَ طَاهِرَةٌ .

٦- هَذِهِ طُبُولٌ جَمِيلَةٌ .

٧- هَؤُلَاءِ حُرَّاسٌ مُخْلِصُونَ .

٨- هَذِهِ أَخْبَارٌ طَيِّبَةٌ .

**2. Translate the following sentences into Arabic (orally and written):**

1. These flags are beautiful. = ..................................................

2. Are you American boys? = ؟ ..................................................

3. Are you Egyptian workers? = ؟ ..................................................

4. These are new pens. = ..................................................

5. They are Muslim heroes. = ..................................................

6. We are sincere workers. = ..................................................

7. These are big lions. = ..................................................

**3. Translate the following sentences into English (orally):**

١- هَذِهِ أَعْلامٌ عَرَبِيَّةٌ .   ٢- هَذِهِ جُيُوشٌ عَرَبِيَّةٌ .

٣- هَؤُلاءِ طُلّابٌ مُجْتَهِدُونَ .   ٤- هُمْ أَبْطَالٌ مَشْهُورُونَ .

٥- هَؤُلاءِ أَوْلادٌ شُقْرٌ .   ٦- الأَوْلادُ السُّمْرُ مِصْرِيُّونَ .

٧- هَؤُلاءِ عُمَّالٌ أَمْرِيكِيُّونَ .   ٨- لا أُحِبُّ الْجُهَّالَ .

٩- نَحْنُ حُرَّاسٌ مُخْلِصُونَ .   ١٠- كَافَأْتُ الزُّرَّاعَ النَّشِيطِينَ .

**4. Change the underlined parts of the following sentences to correspond to their "Plural" forms; these plurals might be "Broken Plurals" or "Masculine Sound Plurals"; the first one is done as an example:**

١- هُوَ عَامِلٌ نَشِيطٌ .  ←  هُمْ عُمَّالٌ نَشِيطُونَ .

٢- هَذَا خَبَرٌ طَيِّبٌ .  ←  ..................................

٣- هُوَ كَاتِبٌ مَشْهُورٌ .  ←  ..................................

٤- هُوَ طَالِبٌ مُجْتَهِدٌ .  ←  ..................................

٥- هَذَا وَلَدٌ أَسْمَرُ .  ←  ..................................

٦- هُوَ بَطَلٌ مَعْرُوفٌ .  ←  ..................................

٧- هَذَا حَارِسٌ مُخْلِصٌ .  ←  ..................................

٨- أَيْنَ الْقَلَمُ الْجَدِيدُ ؟  ←  .................................. ؟

٩- الْوَلَدُ جَاهِلٌ .  ←  ..................................

١٠- هَلْ أَنْتَ زَارِعٌ ؟  ←  .................................. ؟

١١- هَذَا أَسَدٌ كَبِيرٌ .  ←  ..................................

145

5. Fill in the blank cells either with the singular, dual, or broken plural:

| Broken Plural / جَمْعُ تَكْسِيرٍ | Dual / مُثَنَّى | Singular / مُفْرَد |
|---|---|---|
| | | جَيْشٌ |
| | طِبْلانِ | |
| قُلُوبٌ | | |
| | | سَهْلٌ |
| | بَطَلانِ | |
| وُعُودٌ | | |
| | | أَشْقَرُ |
| | خَبَرانِ | |
| سُمْرٌ | | |
| | | عَلَمٌ |
| | هُمَا | |
| أَنْتُمْ | | |
| | | أَنَا |
| | هَذانِ | |
| زُرْقٌ | | |
| | | حَارِسٌ |

146

**Lesson 22** ━━━━━━━━━━━━━━━━━━━━━━━━━ الدَّرْسُ الثَّانِي وَالعِشْرُونَ

> تَرَاكِيبُ الْعَطْفِ وَحُرُوفُهُ:
> (وَ) ، (أَوْ) ، (أَمْ) ، (ثُمَّ) ، (فَـ) ، (بَلْ) ، (لَكِنْ) ، (حَتَّى)
> **The Conjunction Structures and Its Particles:**
> (وَ) = and / (أَوْ) = or / (أَمْ) = or / (ثُمَّ) = then / (فَـ) = then / (بَلْ) = rather / (لَكِنْ) = but rather / (حَتَّى) = even

❖ The conjunction structures are two words, two phrases or two sentences joined together to form more complex structures. The particles that join these parts together are called "Conjunction Particles," Arabic (حُرُوفُ الْعَطْفِ).

❖ The word, phrase, or sentence that follows the "Conjunction Particle" is called (مَعْطُوفٌ) in Arabic, which roughly means "*Conjunctioned*".

❖ The word, phrase, or sentence that precedes the "Conjunction Particle" is called (مَعْطُوفٌ عَلَيْهِ) in Arabic, which roughly means "*Conjunctioned to*".

❖ The following section contains four sentences with each of the eight conjunction particles to show the process in context:

> وَ
> **and**

|  |  |
|---|---|
| I ate an apple and I drank juice. | أَكَلْتُ تُفَّاحَةً وَشَرِبْتُ عَصِيرًا . |
| The figs and the grapes are from among the summer fruits. | التِّينُ وَالْعِنَبُ مِنْ فَاكِهَةِ الصَّيْفِ . |
| The red pen and the blue pen are in the bag. | الْقَلَمُ الْأَحْمَرُ وَالْقَلَمُ الْأَزْرَقُ فِي الْحَقِيبَةِ . |
| This is a light box and that is a heavy box. | هَذَا صُنْدُوقٌ خَفِيفٌ وَذَلِكَ صُنْدُوقٌ ثَقِيلٌ . |

147

\* \* \*

| | |
|---|---|
| Read or write your lesson! | اِقْرَأْ أَوْ اُكْتُبْ دَرْسَكَ ! |

**أَوْ**
or

| | |
|---|---|
| I want a sheet of paper or a writing pad. | أُرِيدُ وَرَقَةً أَوْ دَفْتَرًا . |
| Where is the principal or his assistance? | أَيْنَ الْمُدِيرُ أَوْ مُساعدُهُ ؟ |
| I will travel today or tomorrow. | سَأُسَافِرُ الْيَوْمَ أَوْ غَدًا . |

**أَمْ**
(either) or

| | |
|---|---|
| Do you want tea or coffee? | هَلْ تُرِيدُ شَايًا أَمْ قَهْوَةً ؟ |
| Is your father at home or in the shop? | هَلْ أَبُوكَ فِي الْبَيْتِ أَمْ الدُّكَانِ ؟ |
| Are you a student or a professor? | هَلْ أَنْتَ طَالِبٌ أَمْ أُسْتَاذٌ؟ |
| Is this your sister or your mother? | هَلْ هَذِهِ أُخْتُكَ أَمْ أُمُّكَ؟ |

**ثُمَّ**
then

| | |
|---|---|
| I ate my food then reviewed my lessons. | أَكَلْتُ طَعَامِي ثُمَّ رَاجَعْتُ دُرُوسِي . |
| I went to the mosque then to the market. | ذَهَبْتُ إِلَى الْمَسْجِدِ ثُمَّ السُّوقِ . |
| My mother traveled then my father traveled after her. | سَافَرَتْ أُمِّي ثُمَّ سَافَرَ أَبِي بَعْدَهَا . |

جَاءَ آدَمُ أَوَّلاً ثُمَّ مَرْيَمُ .

Adam came first, then Maryam (came).

> **فَـ**
> then

جَاءَ نَبِيلٌ فَسَعِيدٌ .

Nabeel came then Sa'id (came).

دَخَلَ الْمُدِيرُ فَسَلَّمَ عَلَيْنَا .

The director entered then he greeted us.

قَرَأْتُ الدَّرْسَ الأَوَّلَ فَالثَّانِيَ .

I read the first lesson then the second.

سَمِعْتُ الأَذَانَ فَقُمْتُ إِلَى الصَّلاةِ .

I heard the prayer's call, so I stood up for praying.

> **بَلْ**
> rather

اشْتَرَيْتُ كِتَابًا بَلْ دَفْتَرًا .

I bought a book, rather a notebook.

أَذْهَبُ إِلَى الْبَيْتِ بَلِ الْمَدْرَسَةِ .

I am going to the house, rather the school.

قَرَأْتُ الدَّرْسَ الأَوَّلَ بَلِ الثَّالِثَ .

I read the first lesson, rather the third.

جَاءَ الأُسْتَاذُ بَلِ الْمُدِيرُ .

The teacher came, rather the principal.

> **لَكِنْ**
> but rather

مَا جَاءَ الرَّئِيسُ لَكِنْ نَائِبُهُ .

The president did not come, but rather his deputy.

مَا ضَحِكَ الأَوْلادُ لَكِنْ عُمَرُ .

The boys did not laugh, but rather 'Umar.

مَا قَرَأْتُ الدَّرْسَ لَكِنْ بَعْضَهُ .

I did not read the lesson, but rather some of it.

مَا سَمِعْتُ الْجَوَابَ لَكِنِ السُّؤَالَ .

I did not hear the answer, but rather the question.

## حَتَّى
**even**

| | |
|---|---|
| The soldiers fled even the commander. | هَرَبَ الجُنُودُ حَتَّى القَائِدُ . |
| I ate the fish, even its head. | أَكَلْتُ السَّمَكَةَ حَتَّى رَأْسَهَا . |
| All are in the class even the principal. | الْجَمِيعُ فِي الصَّفِّ حَتَّى الْمُدِيرُ . |
| I heard the talk even the last word. | سَمِعْتُ الْحَدِيثَ حَتَّى آخِرَ كَلِمَةٍ . |

\* \* \*

❖ <u>**Explanatory Notes:**</u> While examining the sentences above, you need to observe the following points:

1. The nouns following the "Conjunction Particle" must agree with the noun preceding it in its grammatical function (i.e. being nominative, accusative or genitive.)

2. If the "Conjunction Particle" is connecting two verbs or verbal sentences, then both verbs must be of the same tense (i.e. past, present, or imperative.)

3. The conjunction (وَ) is, like the English (and), a simple connector of two parts, without any implication of priority or time sequence.

4. The conjunction (أَوْ), like the English (or), implies the meaning of choice between two choices.

5. The conjunction (أَمْ), which also means (or), shares the same basic meaning of (أَوْ), but with the extra <u>specification to choose between two choices given in a question format</u>.

6. The conjunction (ثُمَّ) is equivalent to the English "then" and it is used to specify that two events took place in a specific sequence order but with some lapse of time between them.

7. The conjunction (فَ) is equivalent to the English "then" and it shares with (ثُمَّ) the concept that two events took place in a specific sequence order, but with the (فَ) there is no lapse of time between them.

150

8. The conjunction (بَلْ) is equivalent to the English "rather" and it used to rectify an error or a slip of tongue whereby the information given is cancelled in regard to the subject before (بَلْ), and it is affirmed in regard to the subject which follows it.

9. The conjunction (لَكِنْ) is equivalent to the English "but rather" and it is also close in meaning to the conjunction (بَلْ). However, in the case of (لَكِنْ), we specifically use a negating particle (مَا) to negate the application of an action to the subject before it, and then affirming it to the subject after it.

10. The conjunction (حَتَّى) is equivalent to the English "even" which is used to specify the application of the action to some particular subject after a generalization involving a more general subject.

❖ <u>New Vocabulary:</u>

### Nouns / أَسْمَاء

| | |
|---|---|
| juice = عَصِيرًا | an apple = تُفَّاحَةً |
| the grapes (coll.n) = الْعِنَبُ | the figs (coll.n) = التِّينُ |
| the summer = الصَّيْف | fruit = فَاكِهَة |
| your lesson = دَرْسَكَ (دَرْس+كَ) | the bag = الْحَقِيبَة |
| his assistance = مُسَاعِدُهُ (مُسَاعِدُ+هُ) | a sheet of paper = وَرَقَةً |
| day / today = يَوْمٌ / الْيَوْمَ | tomorrow = غَدًا |
| coffee = قَهْوَةً | tea = شَايًا |
| the shop, the store = الدُّكَّان | your father = أَبُوكَ (أَبُو+كَ) |
| your sister = أُخْتُكَ (أُخْتُ+كَ) | professor = أُسْتَاذ |
| my food = طَعَامِي (طَعَام+ي) | your mother = أُمُّكَ (أُمُّ+كَ) |
| the market = السُّوق | my lessons = دُرُوسِي (دُرُوس+ي) |

| | | | |
|---|---|---|---|
| أُمِّي (أُمّ+ي) = my mother | آدَمُ = Adam |
| أَوَّلاً = first, firstly | الأَذَانُ = the call to prayer |
| الصَّلاَةُ = the prayer | نَائِبُهُ (نَائِبُ+هُ) = his deputy |
| عُمَرُ = Omar | بَعْضُهُ (بَعْضُ+هُ) = some of it |
| الْجُنُودُ = the soldiers | الْقَائِدُ = the commander, leader |
| الْجَمِيعُ = all, everyone | الْحَدِيثُ = the talk, the speech |
| آخِرُ = last | كَلِمَة = word |

### أَفْعَال / Verbs

| | | | |
|---|---|---|---|
| اقْرَأْ = read (*command verb*) | اُكْتُبْ = write (*command verb*) |
| أُرِيدُ (أَنْ) = I want (to) | سَأُسَافِرُ (سَـ+أُسَافِرُ) = I will travel |
| تُرِيدُ (أَنْ) = you want (to) | قَرَأْتُ = I read |
| رَاجَعْتُ = I reviewed | ذَهَبْتُ = I went |
| سَافَرْتُ = I read (*past tense*) | جَاءَ = he came |
| دَخَلَ = he entered | سَلَّمَ = he greeeted |
| سَمِعْتُ = I heard | قُمْتُ (إِلَى) = I stood up (for) |
| اشْتَرَيْتُ = I bought | أَذْهَبُ = I go |
| ضَحِكَ = he laughed | هَرَبَ = he fled |

152

## حُرُوف / Particles

| | | | |
|---|---|---|---|
| وَ =and | | أَوْ= or | |
| أَمْ = or (either) | | فَـ = then | |
| ثُمَّ = then | | بَلْ = rather | |
| لَكِنْ = but rather | | حَتَّى = even | |
| مِنْ = from among | | بَعْدَهَا (بَعْدَ+هَا) = after her | |
| عَلَيْنَا (عَلَى+نَا) = on us, upon us | | مَا = did not | |

\* \* \*

## تَذَكَّرْ- تَذَكَّرِي! / Remember!

1. Arabic, like English, has a group of words called "Conjunctions"; each has a specific meaning, but they all serve the purpose of connecting words, phrases or sentences together to form larger linguistic units.

2. The nouns following the "Conjunction Particle" must agree with the noun preceding it in its grammatical function (i.e. being nominative, accusative or genitive.)

3. If the "Conjunction Particle" is connecting two verbs or verbal sentences, then both verbs must be of the same tense (i.e. past, present, or imperative.)

4. The "Conjunction Particles" that consist of one letter, such as (وَ) and (فَـ) are written as part of the following words.

5. Each "Conjunction Particle" has a specific meaning that a student needs to know for a proper use; review the examples and explanatory notes above to learn them and gain insight on each particle usage.

\* \* \*

# تَدْرِيبَاتٌ / Exercises

**1. Read the following sentences; identify the conjunction particles by underlining them, and then give their English meanings**

١- أَكَلْتُ تُفَّاحَةً وَمَوْزَةً . .................................................

٢- جَاءَ يُوسُفُ فَآدَمُ . .................................................

٣- هَلْ تَشْرَبُ شَايًا أَمْ قَهْوَةً ؟ .................................................

٤- سَأُسَافِرُ الْيَوْمَ أَوْ غَدًا . .................................................

٥- أَكَلْتُ طَعَامِي ثُمَّ شَرِبْتُ الْعَصِيرَ. .................................................

٦- دَخَلَ الْأُسْتَاذُ بَلِ الْمُدِيرُ . .................................................

٧- أَكَلَ السَّمَكَةَ حَتَّى رَأْسَهَا . .................................................

\* \* \*

**2. Translate the following sentences into Arabic (Orally and written):**

1. I like figs and grapes. = .................................................

2. Are you a professor or a student? = ?.................................................

3. I will travel today or tomorrow. = .................................................

4. The soldiers did not flee, rather the leader. = .................................................

5. I went to the school then to the market. = .................................................

6. I ate the chicken, even its head? = .................................................

7. I like tea, rather coffee. = .................................................

**3. Translate the following Arabic sentences into English**

(١) التِّينُ والعِنَبُ مِن فاكِهَةِ الصَّيْفِ .  ......................................

(٢) جاءَ الرَّئيسُ ، بَلْ نائِبُهُ .  ......................................

(٣) سَمِعْتُ الْحَديثَ حَتَّى آخِرَ كَلِمَةٍ .  ......................................

(٤) ذَهَبْتُ إِلَى الدُّكَّانِ ثُمَّ الْمَدْرَسَةِ .  ......................................

(٥) دَخَلَ الْمُعَلِّمُ الصَّفَ فَسَلَّمَ عَلَيْنا .  ......................................

(٦) ما اشْتَرَيْتُ كِتابًا بَلْ دَفْتَرًا .  ......................................

\* \* \*

**4. Unscramble the following sets of words to make from each of them a full meaningful sentence, as in the given example, and then translate the resultant sentences into English:**

طالِبٌ / أَنْتَ / أَمْ / هَلْ / أُسْتاذٌ ⟵ هَلْ أَنْتَ أُسْتاذٌ أَمْ طالِبٌ ؟ =
Are you a student or a professor?

١- فَقُمْتُ / الأَذانَ / إِلَى / سَمِعْتُ / الصَّلاةِ         = ......................................

٢- لَكِنْ / اشْتَرَيْتُ / ما / عِنَبًا / تينًا         = ......................................

٣- الْكِتابَ / حَتَّى / وَرَقَةٍ / قَرَأْتُ / آخِرَ         = ......................................

155

٤- شَايًا / أُرِيدُ / قَهْوَةً / بَلْ . ................................................ =

٥- الأَحَدِ / يَوْمَ / سَأُسَافِرُ / أَوْ / السَّبْتِ . ................................................ =

* * *

**5.** Join the following pairs of phrases or sentences, using an appropriate "Conjunction Particle" from among those in the shaded column; you might need to modify the combined sentences by eliminating certain words:

أَكَلْتُ طَعَامِي . / شَرِبْتُ شَايًا . ← ................................

سَمِعْتُ الأَذَانَ . / قُمْتُ إِلَى الصَّلَاةِ . ← ................................

مَا شَرِبْتُ قَهْوَةً . / أَكَلْتُ . ← ................................

سَأُسَافِرُ الْيَوْمَ . / سَأُسَافِرُ غَدًا . ← ................................

مَا حَضَرَ الرَّئِيسُ . / نَائِبُهُ . ← ................................

قَرَأْتُ الْكِتَابَ . / آخِرَ صَفْحَةٍ . ← ................................

هَلْ أَنْتَ عَرَبِيٌّ ؟ / هَلْ أَنْتَ أَمْرِيكِيٌّ ؟ ← ................................

سَأَدْرُسُ دُرُوسِي أَوَّلاً . / سَأَلْعَبُ . ← ................................

وَ / أَوْ / ثُمَّ / بَلْ / فَـ / حَتَّى / لكِنْ / أَمْ

* * *

156

**Lesson 23**  الدَّرْسُ الثَّالِثُ والعِشْرُونَ

## تَرَاكِيبُ الإِضَافَة
### The *Idafah* Linguistic Structures

- There is very common Arabic linguistic structure called "*Idafah*", Arabic (الإِضَافة); a word which means '**addition**' or '**annexion**.'

- In its simplist form, the "*Idafah*" is a structure where two nouns are juxtaposed next to each others without anything separating them.

- The "*Idafah*" is the Arabic way to express a **possessive** relationship between two nouns; the **first term** being the **possessed** and the **second term** being the **possessor**.

- The "*Idafah*" usually corresponds to an English linguistic structure with an "*of-relationship*" or to a structure involving the possessive ('s) or (s').

- The **first term** of the "*Idafah*" is called (مُضَافٌ إِلَيْهِ) in Arabic, which roughly means "*added to*", and the **second term** of the "*Idafah*" is called (مُضَافٌ) in Arabic, which roughly means "*added*".

- Let's now examine the following sentences:

| | |
|---|---|
| I am the professor of Arabic. | ١- أَنَا أُسْتَاذُ الْعَرَبِيَّةِ . |
| Muhammad is the Messsenger of God. | ٢- مُحَمَّدٌ رَسُولُ اللهِ . |
| The school's principal is in his office. | ٣- مُدِيرُ الْمَدْرَسَةِ في مَكْتَبِه . |
| I am a seeker of knowledge; not a seeker of wealth. | ٤- أَنَا طَالِبُ عِلْمٍ وَلَسْتُ طَالِبَ مَالٍ . |
| I am a language professor; not a philosophy professor. | ٥- أَنَا أُسْتَاذُ لُغَةٍ وَلَسْتُ أُسْتَاذَ فَلْسَفَةٍ . |
| The director's car is new. | ٦- سَيَّارَةُ الْمُدِيرِ جَدِيدَةٌ . |
| This is the daughter of Salih. | ٧- هَذِهِ ابْنَةُ صَالِحٍ . |

٨- مَكْتَبَةُ الْمَعْهَدِ كَبيرَةٌ.  The library of the institute is big.

٩- سَمِعْتُ صَوْتَ الْبِنْتِ الْجَميلَ.  I heard the beautiful voice of the girl.

١٠- هَذِهِ مَكْتَبَةُ الْجَامِعَةِ الْجَديدَةُ.  This is the new university library.

❖ **Explanatory Notes:** While examining the sentences above, you need to observe the following two essential points:

A. The first term of an "*Idafah*" never receives the definite article (ال) or the "*Tanween*". However, the second term may have either.

B. The second term must always be genitive. However, the first term may be in any of the three cases, depending on its grammatical function within a sentence.

1. Now, if we examine the first three sentences, we notice that the first terms of the "*Idafah*"; namely (مُديرُ), (رَسُولُ) and (أُسْتَاذُ) do not have the definite article (ال), yet they are nevertheless made definite by way of being attached to the second terms which are definite; namely (الْمَدْرَسَةِ), (الْعَرَبيَّةِ) and (اللهِ).

2. If, on the other hand, we examine the four "*Idafah*s" in sentences 3 and 5 above, we will notice that the whole "*Idafah*s" are indefinite by virtue of the second terms being indefinite; namely (فَلْسَفَةٍ), (عِلْمٍ), (مَالٍ), (لُغَةٍ).

3. If the whole "*Idafah*" is functioning as the subject of a nominal sentence, then the predicate adjective must agree with the gender of the first term, as in example 6 above. However, there is no rule that the two terms of the "*Idafah*" need to be of the same gender.

4. If a sentence starts with a pronoun as its subject and followed by an "*Idafah*" as its predicate, the pronoun has to agree with gender of the first term of the "*Idafah*", as in example 7 above.

5. If we need to use an adjective to describe the first term of an "*Idafah*", that adjective must come after the second term, but must agree in gender, number and case-ending with the first term, as in examples 9 and 10 above.

❖ **New Vocabulary:**

### أَسْمَاء / Nouns

his office = مَكْتَبِهِ (مَكْتَبُ + ـهِ)

knowledge = عِلْمٌ

language = لُغَةٌ

library = مَكْتَبَةٌ

voice, sound = صَوْتَ

messenger = رَسُولٌ

seeker, student = طَالِبٌ

wealth, money = مَالٌ

philosophy = فَلْسَفَةٌ

the institute = الْمَعْهَد

the girl = الْبِنْتِ

### أَفْعَال / Verbs

I heard = سَمِعْتُ

I am not = لَسْتُ

\* \* \*

## تَذَكَّرْ - تَذَكَّرِي! / Remember!

1. The <u>first term</u> of an "*Idafah*" never receives the definite article (ال) or the "*Tanween*." However, the <u>second term</u> may have either.

2. The <u>second term</u> must always be <u>genitive</u>. However, the first term may be in any of the three cases, depending on its grammatical function within a sentence.

3. If the whole "*Idafah*" is functioning as the subject of a <u>nominal sentence</u>, then the <u>predicate adjective must agree with the gender of the first term</u>, as in example 6 above. However, <u>there is no rule that the two terms of the "*Idafah*" need to be of the same gender</u>.

4. If a sentence starts with a pronoun as its <u>subject</u> and followed by an "*Idafah*" as its predicate, the pronoun has to agree with gender of the first term of the "*Idafah*.

5. If we need to use an adjective to describe the first term of an "*Idafah*", that <u>adjective must come after the second term</u>, but <u>must agree in gender, number and case-ending with the first term.</u>

\* \* \*

## تَدْرِيبَاتٌ / Exercises

**1.** Read the following sentences; identify the "*Idafah*" by underlining each, and then give their English meanings: (the first is done for you as an example to follow:

١- أَكَلْتُ فِي مَطْعَمِ الْجَامِعَةِ .  ← the university restaurant

٢- جَاءَ مُدِيرُ الْمَدْرَسَةِ .  ← ....................................

٣- هَلْ تَشْرَبُ عَصِيرَ تُفَّاحٍ ؟  ← ....................................

٤- أَيْنَ مَكْتَبَةُ الْجَامِعَةِ ؟  ← ....................................

٥- هَذِهِ أَقْلَامُ الطُّلَّابِ الْجَدِيدَةُ .  ← ....................................

٦- بَابُ الْبَيْتِ مَفْتُوحٌ .  ← ....................................

٧- مَتَى يَوْمُ الْعِيدِ ؟  ← ....................................

**2.** Translate the following sentences into Arabic (Orally and written):

1. I like the fruits of the summer. = • ..............................................

2. I am not a seeker of wealth. = • ..............................................

3. The university library is far away. = • ..............................................

4. She is the daughter of the president. = •..................................................

5. He is a professor of philosophy. = •..................................................

6. The student's book is on the teacher's desk. = •..................................................

7. The school's playground is large. = •..................................................

\* \* \*

**3. Translate the following Arabic sentences into English:**

(١) التِّينُ وَالعِنَبُ مِن فَاكِهَةِ الصَّيْفِ . ← ..................................................

(٢) جَاءَ رَئِيسُ الْجَامِعَةِ . ← ..................................................

(٣) سَمِعْتُ حَدِيثَ الأُسْتَاذِ . ← ..................................................

(٤) سَيَّارَةُ الْمُدِيرِ أَمَامَ الْمَتْحَفِ . ← ..................................................

(٥) مُعَلِّمُ الْعَرَبِيَّةِ في مَكْتَبِ الْمُدِيرَةِ . ← ..................................................

(٦) لَسْتُ طَالِبَ مَالٍ ، بَلْ طَالِبُ عِلْمٍ . ← ..................................................

\* \* \*

**4.** Join the pair of nouns in parenthesis to form actual "*Idafah*" structures **within the rest of the sentences.** You might need to modify one of the two nouns to correspond to the rules of the "*Idafah*"; also vowel the end of both terms of the "*Idafah*" and write the final structure on the dotted space! One is done for you as a model to follow:

١- (كِتَابٌ – طَالِبٌ) عَلَى الْمَكْتَبِ . ← كِتَابُ الطَّالِبِ عَلَى الْمَكْتَبِ .

٢- هَذَا (بَيْتٌ – اللهُ) . ← ..................................................

٣- هَلْ (صَوْتٌ – وَلَدٌ) جَمِيلٌ ؟ ← ..................................................?

٤- هُوَ (أُسْتَاذٌ – لُغَةٌ) . ← ..................................................

161

٥- لَسْتُ (طَالِبَةٌ – مَالٌ) . ................................. .

٦- هَلْ (سُوقُ – الْمَدِينَةِ) قَرِيبٌ . ................................. ؟

٧- هَلْ (صَوْتُ – وَلَدٍ) جَمِيلٌ ؟ ................................. ؟

٨- هُوَ (أُسْتَاذُ – لُغَةٍ) . ................................. .

**5.** Unscramble the following sets of words to make from each of them a full meaningful sentence, as in the given example, and then translate the resultant sentences into English:

١- الْمَدِينَةِ / هَذَا / الْجَدِيدُ / سُوقُ ................................. =

٢- الْبَيْتِ / صَغِيرٌ / مَطْبَخُ ................................. =

٣- فِي / مُدِيرَةُ / مَكْتَبِهَا / الْمَدْرَسَةِ ................................. =

٤- الْعَرَبِيَّة / هُوَ / اللُّغَةِ / أُسْتَاذُ ................................. =

٥- مُجْتَهِدَاتٌ / الْجَامِعَةِ / طَالِبَاتُ / ................................. =

٦- جَدِيدَةٌ / الْوَلَدِ / دَرَّاجَةُ ................................. =

٧- الْجَدِيدُ / أُسْتَاذُ / هُوَ / الْفَلْسَفَةِ ................................. =

٨- سَوْدَاءُ / الْأُسْتَاذِ / سَيَّارَةُ ................................. =

162

**Lesson 24** ━━━━━━━━━━━━━━━ الدَّرْسُ الرَّابِعُ والعِشْرُونَ

> ### الفِعْلُ وأَقْسَامُهُ : الفِعْلُ الْمَاضِي
> ### The Verb and Its Division: The Past (Perfect) Tense

- ❖ The <u>verb</u> is a part of speech that denotes an action. Therfore, it must indicate whether the action was completed some time in the past, whether the action is taking place at the time of speaking, whether the action takes place as a matter of habitual action, or whether the action is expected to take place some time in the future.

- ❖ Based on this criterion, Arabic has three major tenses as follows:

  1. Past (Perfect) Tense (الْمَاضِي): Used to indicate actions that have been completed sometime in the past.

  2. Present (Imperfect) Tense (الْمُضَارِع): Used to indicate actions that are either taking place at the time of speaking or actions that take place as a matter of habitual actions.

  3. Imperative (Command) Tense (الأَمْرُ): This type of tense is derived in a certain formula from the Present (Imperfect) tense to issue a request or command to undertake a certain action sometime in the future following the given command.

- ❖ Besides relating verbs to the time aspect, they also need to be related to the aspects of <u>persons</u> (i.e. 1st person, 2nd person or 3rd person), numbers (i.e. singular, dual or plural) and <u>gender</u> (i.e. masculine or feminine).

- ❖ The process of relating the stem of a verb to all the above mentioned aspects is called in English "Verb Conjugation"; Arabic (تَصْرِيفُ الفِعْلِ).

- ❖ The Arabic verb conjugation is rather very elaborate and complex; certainly more complex than English at least; there are 13 total conjugations for the Arabic verb; however, the formula is very standard that will render the process easy once understood by learners and given enough practice.

- ❖ In this lesson, we will focus on learning the <u>five singular conjugations</u> of the <u>past (perfect) tense</u> verbs:

163

| | |
|---|---|
| ١- (هُوَ) كَتَبَ . | He wrote. |
| كَتَبَ رِسَالةً . | He wrote a letter. |
| ٢- (هِيَ) كَتَبَتْ . | She wrote. |
| كَتَبَتْ مَقَالةً . | She wrote an article. |
| ٣- (أَنْتَ) كَتَبْتَ . | You (masculine) wrote. |
| كَتَبْتَ الدَّرْسَ . | You (male) wrote the lesson. |
| ٤- (أَنْتِ) كَتَبْتِ . | You (feminine) wrote. |
| كَتَبْتِ الكَلِمَةَ . | You (female) wrote the word. |
| ٥- (أَنَا) كَتَبْتُ . | I (male / female) wrote. |
| كَتَبْتُ الْجُمْلَةَ . | I wrote the sentence. |

\* \* \*

❖ **Explanatory Notes:** While examining the sentences above, you need to observe the following two essential points:

1. All the five conjugations of this one verb share a basic three-letter root called the "stem" of the verb; these three consonants are also called the "radicals". The stem or root of all these five conjugations is (ذَهَبْ), and it has the basic underlying meaning of "went", but it does not tell us the number, person or gender of the one undertaking the action.

2. Adding the "*Fathah*" over the last consonant of the stem to replace the "*Sukoon*", will relate the conjugation to the 3rd person masculine singular; thus (ذَهَبَ) means "he went", as in the examples of number one above.

3. The past tense verb conjugated with the 3rd person masculine singular is considered the shortest form of the verb, and it is used as the basis for listing verbs in an Arabic dictionary.

4. If we add an (*at* / ـَتْ) to the stem, then the result is (ذَهَبَتْ), which relates the conjugation to (she) or a 3rd person feminine singular, as in the examples of two above.

5. If If we add an (*ta* / تَ) to the stem, then the result is (ذَهَبْتَ), which relates the conjugation to (you / masculine) or a 2nd person masculine singular, as in the examples of three above.

6. If If we add an (*ti* / ت) to the stem, then the result is (ذَهَبْتِ), which relates the conjugation to (you / féminine) or a 2nd person feminine singular, as in the examples of four above.

7. If If we add an (*tu* / تُ) to the stem, then the result is (ذَهَبْتُ), which relates the conjugation to (I / -masculine & feminine) or a 1st person singular, both masculine or feminine, as in the examples of five above.

8. Every verb will require a subject, which could be an implied pronoun to be understood from the conjugation form, or it could be an expressed subject. If the verb is transitive, then it will also take a direct object, which will be in the accusative mood or case-ending. In the examples above, the nouns, (رِسَالَةً), (مَقَالَةً), (الدَّرْسَ), (الْجُمْلَةَ) and (الْكَلِمَةَ) are the direct objects of the verbs.

9. The subject pronouns appearing in parentheis in the above sentences are used to further assist the learner in identifying the person, but it is not necessary to always use them, because the particular conjugation has built in it the implied subject pronoun.

10. It is important to note that the <u>middle letter of the verb stem does not always bear a "*Fathah*"</u>; there is smaller number of verbs that bear a "*Kasrah*", and yet another smaller number that bear a "*Dammah*". Examples: (فَهِمَ) for "understood", (سَمِعَ) for "heard", (كَرُمَ) for "became generous" and (كَبُرَ) for "grew up"

❖ The table below shows the process explained above with all the verbs introduced above, to help you further in understanding the conceptualization of the verb conjugations in Arabic:

| 1st Person Masculine + Feminine Singular (أَنَا) | 2nd Person Feminine singular (أَنْتِ) | 2nd Person Masculine Singular (أَنْتَ) | 3rd Person Feminine Singular (هِيَ) | 3rd Person Masculine Singular (هُوَ) | Stem (Root) and Basic Meaning |
|---|---|---|---|---|---|
| دَرَسْتُ | دَرَسْتِ | دَرَسْتَ | دَرَسَتْ | دَرَسَ | دَرَسْ (studied) |
| قَرَأْتُ | قَرَأْتِ | قَرَأْتَ | قَرَأَتْ | قَرَأَ | قَرَأْ (read) |
| أَكَلْتُ | أَكَلْتِ | أَكَلْتَ | أَكَلَتْ | أَكَلَ | أَكَلْ (ate) |
| شَرِبْتُ | شَرِبْتِ | شَرِبْتَ | شَرِبَتْ | شَرِبَ | شَرِبْ (drank) |
| عَمِلْتُ | عَمِلْتِ | عَمِلْتَ | عَمِلَتْ | عَمِلَ | عَمِلْ (worked) |
| فَهِمْتُ | فَهِمْتِ | فَهِمْتَ | فَهِمَتْ | فَهِمَ | فَهِمْ (understood) |
| سَمِعْتُ | سَمِعْتِ | سَمِعْتَ | سَمِعَتْ | سَمِعَ | سَمِعْ (heard) |
| كَرُمْتُ | كَرُمْتِ | كَرُمْتَ | كَرُمَتْ | كَرُمَ | كَرُمْ (became generous) |
| كَبُرْتُ | كَبُرْتِ | كَبُرْتَ | كَبُرَتْ | كَبُرَ | كَبُرْ (grew up) |

\* \* \*

❖ **Using One Conjugation of Each of the Verbs Above in a Full Sentence:**

| | |
|---|---|
| He studied the first lesson. | ١- <u>دَرَسَ</u> الدَّرْسَ الأَوَّلَ . |
| She read a short story. | ٢- <u>قَرَأَتْ</u> قِصَّةً قَصِيرَةً . |
| Did you (male) eat the fish? | ٣- هَلْ <u>أَكَلْتَ</u> السَّمَكَةَ ؟ |
| Did you (female) drink the milk? | ٤- هَلْ <u>شَرِبْتِ</u> الْحَلِيبَ ؟ |
| Yes, I did the homework. | ٥- نَعَمْ ، <u>عَمِلْتُ</u> الْوَاجِبَ . |
| I understood the lesson well. | ٦- <u>فَهِمْتُ</u> الدَّرْسَ جَيِّدًا . |
| Did you hear the important piece of news? | ٧- هَلْ <u>سَمِعْتَ</u> الْخَبَرَ الْهَامَّ ؟ |
| The man became <u>generous</u> after being miser. | ٨- <u>كَرُمَ</u> الرَّجُلُ بَعْدَ كَوْنِهِ بَخِيلاً . |
| The boy <u>grew up</u> and became a man. | ٩- <u>كَبُرَ</u> الْوَلَدُ وَأَصْبَحَ رَجُلاً . |

\* \* \*

( أَسْمَاء / Nouns )

❖ <u>New Vocabulary:</u>

| | | | |
|---|---|---|---|
| an article = | مَقَالَةً | a letter = | رِسَالَةً |
| the sentence = | الْجُمْلَةَ | the word = | الْكَلِمَةَ |
| the fish = | السَّمَكَةَ | the first = | الأَوَّلَ |
| the homework = | الوَاجِبَ | the milk = | الْحَلِيبَ |
| the piece of news = | الْخَبَرَ | well, good = | جَيِّدًا |

| | | | |
|---|---|---|---|
| the important = الْهَامّ | | the man / a man = الرَّجُلُ / رَجُلاً | |
| his being = كَوْنِهِ (كَوْنِ + ـهِ) | | miser, stingy = بَخِيلاً | |

## أَفْعَال / Verbs

| | | | |
|---|---|---|---|
| he read = قَرَأَ | | he studied = دَرَسَ | |
| he drank = شَرِبَ | | he ate = أَكَلَ | |
| he understood = فَهِمَ | | he worked = عَمِلَ | |
| he became generous = كَرُمَ | | he heard = سَمِعَ | |
| he became = أَصْبَحَ * | | he grew up = كَبُرَ | |

## أَدَوَاتٌ / Particles

| | | | |
|---|---|---|---|
| did not = مَا | | after = بَعْدَ | |

*__Note:__ The dictionary will not list all the conjugations of a verb; it only lists the verb conjugated in the 3rd person masculine singular.

\* \* \*

❖ <u>Negating the Past Tense Verbs with (مَا):</u>

Past tense verbs can be negated by simply placing the negative particle (مَا) before them; examples:

١- مَا دَرَسَ الدَّرْسَ . He did not study the lesson.

٢- مَا قَرَأَتْ كِتَابَهَا . She did not read her book.

٣- مَا أَكَلْتَ الطَّعَامَ . You (masculine) did not eat the food.

٤ - مَا شَرِبْتِ الْقَهْوَةَ .   You (feminine) did not drink the coffee.

٥ - مَا عَمِلْتُ الْوَاجِبَ .   I did not study the lesson.

٦ - مَا فَهِمَ الدَّرْسَ .   He did not understand the lesson.

٧ - مَا سَمِعَتْ سُؤَالَكَ .   She did not hear your question.

٨ - مَا كَرُمَ الْبَخِيلُ .   The miser did not become generous.

٩ - مَا كَبُرَتْ هَذِهِ الْبِنْتُ .   This girl did not grow up.

*  *  *

## تَذَكَّرْ - تَذَكَّرِي! / Remember!

1. Past (Perfect) Tense (الْمَاضِي) is used to indicate actions that have been completed sometime in the past.

2. Besides relating the verb to the time aspect, it also needs to be related to the aspects of <u>persons</u> (i.e. 1st person, 2nd person or 3rd person), numbers (i.e. singular, dual or plural) and <u>gender</u> (i.e. masculine or feminine).

3. The process of relating the stem of a verb to all the above mentioned aspects is called in English "Verb Conjugation"; Arabic (تَصْرِيفُ الْفِعْلِ).

4. All conjugations of a given verb share a basic three-letter root called the "stem" of the verb; these three consonants are also called the "radicals". The stem or root of a verb has a basic underlying meaning, but it does not tell us the number, person or gender of the one undertaking the action.

5. Adding the "*Fathah*" (*a* / ◌َ ) over the last consonant of the stem will relate the conjugation to the 3rd <u>person masculine singular</u>.

6. The past tense verb conjugated with the 3rd person masculine singular is considered the shortest form of the verb, and it is used as the basis for listing verbs in an Arabic dictionary.

7. If we add an (*at* / ـَتْ) to the stem, then it relates the conjugation to (she) or a 3rd person feminine singular.

8. If If we add an (*ta* / تَ) to the stem, then it relates the conjugation to (you / masculine) or a 2nd person masculine singular.

9. If If we add an (*ti* / تِ) to the stem, then it relates the conjugation to (you / feminine) or a 2nd person feminine singular.

10. If If we add an (*tu* / تُ) to the stem, then it relates the conjugation to (I / -masculine & feminine) or a 1st person singular, both masculine or feminine.

11. Every verb will require a subject, which could be an implied pronoun to be understood from the conjugation form, or it could be an expressed subject. If the verb is transitive, then it will also take a direct object, which will be in the accusative mood or case-ending.

* * *

## تَدْريبَاتٌ / Exercises

**1.** Read the following sentences; identify the "*Verb*" by underlining it, and then give its English meanings: (the first is done for you as an example to follow:

١- <u>أَكَلْتُ</u> فِي مَطْعَمِ الْجَامِعَةِ .  I ate

٢- جَاءَ مُدِيرُ الْمَدْرَسَةِ .

٣- هَلْ شَرِبْتَ عَصِيرَ تُفَّاحٍ ؟

٤- هَلْ دَرَسْتِ الدَّرْسَ ؟

٥- أَكَلَتْ تُفَّاحَةً وَشَرِبَتْ حَلِيبًا .

٦- مَا عَمِلَ التِّلْمِيذُ الْوَاجِبَ .

٧- قَرَأَتْ مَرْيَمُ قِصَّةً قَصِيرَةً .

**2. Translate the following sentences into Arabic (Orally and written):**

1. I wrote a letter to my father. = .................................................

2. The girl did not drink juice. = .................................................

3. Did you (masculine) do the homework? = ؟ .................................

4. She ate bread and drank milk. = .................................................

5. He read the article. = .................................................

\* \* \*

**3. Translate the following Arabic sentences into English:**

(١) أَكَلْتُ تِينًا وَعِنَبًا .   .................................

(٢) جَاءَ رَئِيسُ الْجَامِعَةِ .   .................................

(٣) هَلْ سَمِعْتَ حَدِيثَ الأُسْتَاذِ ؟   .................................

(٤) هَلْ عَمِلْتِ الْوَاجِبَ ؟   .................................

(٥) مَا كَتَبَتْ لَيْلَى مَقَالَةً طَوِيلَةً .   .................................

(٦) أَكَلَ طَعَامَهُ ثُمَّ شَرِبَ قَهْوَةً .   .................................

(٧) قَطَعْتُ اللَّحْمَ بِالسِّكِينِ .   .................................

**4.** Fill in the blank cells of the following table with the appropriate conjugations of the past tense verbs which you were given one of their conjugations; you need to match the conjugation to the subject pronoun provided in the shaded cells at the top of each column:

| (أَنَا) | (أَنْتِ) | (أَنْتَ) | (هِيَ) | (هُوَ) |
|---|---|---|---|---|
|  |  |  |  | أَكَلَ |
|  |  |  | دَرَسَتْ |  |
|  |  | أَكَلْتَ |  |  |
|  | شَرِبْتِ |  |  |  |
| عَمِلْتُ |  |  |  |  |
|  | سَمِعْتِ |  |  |  |
|  |  | فَهِمْتَ |  |  |
|  |  |  | كَرُمَتْ |  |

\* \* \*

**Lesson 25**                                            الدَّرْسُ الْخَامِسَ والعِشْرُونَ

## الْفِعْلُ الْمُضَارِعُ
### The Imperfect (Present) Tense Verb

❖ Imperfect (Present) Tense Verbs (الْمُضَارِع) are used to indicate actions that are either taking place at the time of speaking or actions that take place as a matter of habitual actions.

❖ Thus, they correspond to two types of verbs in English; one is **simple present**, such as: (**he writes, she writes, you write, I write**), and the other is **present continuous** or **progressive**, such as: (**he is writing, she is writing, you are writing, I am writing.**)

❖ In matters of translations, it is the context or certain contextual clues that will determine whether to use the simple present or the progressive.

❖ In this lesson, we will focus on learning the <u>five singular conjugations paradigm</u> of the <u>present (imperfect) tense verbs</u>:

| | |
|---|---|
| He writes. / He is writing. | ١- (هُوَ) يَكْتُبُ . |
| He writes a letter. / He is writing a letter. | يَكْتُبُ رِسَالَةً . |
| She writes. / She is writing. | ٢- (هِيَ) تَكْتُبُ . |
| She writes an article. / She is writing an article. | تَكْتُبُ مَقَالَةً . |
| You (male) write. / You are writing. | ٣- (أَنْتَ) تَكْتُبُ . |
| You (male) write the lesson. / You are writing the lesson. | تَكْتُبُ الدَّرْسَ . |
| You (female) write. / You are writing. | ٤- (أَنْتِ) تَكْتُبِينَ . |

173

| | |
|---|---|
| You (female) write the word. / You are writing the word. | تَكْتُبِينَ الكَلِمَةَ . |
| I (male / female) write. / I am writing. | ٥- (أَنَا) أَكْتُبُ . |
| I write the sentence. / I am writing the sentence. | أَكْتُبُ الْجُمْلَةَ . |

❖ **Explanatory Notes:** While examining the sentences above, you need to observe the following two essential points:

1. Arabic verbs in the present tense, like their past tense counterparts, consist of three-letter root called the "stem" of the verb and a "subject marker". The stem or root indicates the verb's basic meaning and its tense, and the "subject marker" indicates the person, gender and number of the subject.

2. All the five conjugations above have the stem (كْتُبْ), which has the basic underlying meaning of "to write", but it does not tell us the number, person or gender of the one undertaking the action.

3. Adding the prefix "يَـ" before the first radical of the stem, will relate the conjugation to the 3rd person masculine singular; thus (يَكْتُبُ) means "he writes / he is writing", as in the examples of number one above.

4. If we prefix a (تَـ) to the stem, then the result is (تَكْتُبُ), which relates the conjugation to (she) or a 3rd person feminine singular, as in the examples of two above.

5. If If we prefix a (تَـ) to the stem, then the result is (تَكْتُبُ), which relates the conjugation to (you / masculine) or a 2nd person masculine singular, as in the examples of three above.

6. Now note that the conjugations of the 3rd person feminine singular and the 2nd person masculine singular are identical; only the context will determine which we are dealing with.

7. If we prefix an (تَـ) to the stem and suffix (ـِينَ) to it, then the result is (تَكْتُبِينَ), which relates the conjugation to (you / feminine) or a 2nd person feminine singular, as in the examples of four above.

8. Now note that the conjugation of the 2nd person feminine singular is a combination of the prefix (تَـ) and the suffix (ـِينَ) added to the stem of the verb.

9. If we prefix (أَ) to the stem, then the result is (أَكْتُبُ), which relates the conjugation to (I / -masculine & feminine) or a 1st person singular, both masculine or feminine, as in the examples of five above.

10. As was the case with the past tense conjugations, every present tense verb will require a subject, which could be an implied pronoun to be understood from the conjugation form itself, or it could be an expressed subject. If the verb is transitive, then it will also take a direct object, which will be in the accusative mood or case-ending. In the examples above, the nouns (الْكَلِمَةَ), (الدَّرْسَ), (مَقَالَةً), (رِسَالَةً) and (الْجُمْلَةَ) are the direct objects of the verb's conjugations.

11. The subject pronouns appearing in parentheis in the above sentences are used to further assist the learner in identifying the person, but it is not necessary to always use them, because the particular conjugation has built in it the implied subject pronoun.

10. It is important to note that the <u>middle letter of the verb stem does not always bear a "*Dammah*"</u>; there are other verbs that bear a "*Kasrah*", and yet others that bear a "*Fathah*". Examples: (يَعْمَلُ) for "to work", (يَجْلِسُ) for "to sit.

12. The "*Dammah*" over the last letter of four of these conjugations and the "*Noon*" at the end of the fifth indicate the "**mood**" of these verbs; in this case this is called "**Indicative Moo**d"; in Arabic called (*Marfu'* / مَرْفُوع).

175

❖ The table below shows the process explained above with ten other verbs, to help you further in understanding the conceptualization of the verb conjugations paradigm in Arabic:

| 1st Person Masculine + Feminine Singular (أَنَا) | 2nd Person Feminine singular (أَنْتِ) | 2nd Person Masculine Singular (أَنْتَ) | 3rd Person Feminine Singular (هِيَ) | 3rd Person Masculine Singular (هُوَ) | Stem (Root) and Basic Meaning |
|---|---|---|---|---|---|
| أَدْرُسُ | تَدْرُسِينَ | تَدْرُسُ | تَدْرُسُ | يَدْرُسُ | دْرُسْ (to study) |
| أَقْرَأُ | تَقْرَئِينَ | تَقْرَأُ | تَقْرَأُ | يَقْرَأُ | قْرَأْ (to read) |
| أَشْرَبُ | تَشْرَبِينَ | تَشْرَبُ | تَشْرَبُ | يَشْرَبُ | شْرَبْ (to drink) |
| أَجْلِسُ | تَجْلِسِينَ | تَجْلِسُ | تَجْلِسُ | يَجْلِسُ | جْلِسْ (ti sit) |
| أَعْمَلُ | تَعْمَلِينَ | تَعْمَلُ | تَعْمَلُ | يَعْمَلُ | عْمَلْ (to work) |
| أَفْهَمُ | تَفْهَمِينَ | تَفْهَمُ | تَفْهَمُ | يَفْهَمُ | فْهَمْ (to understod) |
| أَسْمَعُ | تَسْمَعِينَ | تَسْمَعُ | تَسْمَعُ | يَسْمَعُ | سْمَعْ (to hear) |
| أَكْرُمُ | تَكْرُمِينَ | تَكْرُمُ | تَكْرُمُ | يَكْرُمُ | كْرُمْ (to become) (generous) |
| أَكْبُرُ | تَكْبُرِينَ | تَكْبُرُ | تَكْبُرُ | يَكْبُرُ | كَبْرْ (to grow up) |
| آكُلُ * (أَأْكُلُ) | تَأْكُلِينَ | تَأْكُلُ | تَأْكُلُ | يَأْكُلُ | أْكُلْ (to eat) |

* Notice that the conjugation of the 1st person singular (آكُلُ) was slightly modified; since its 1st radical is an (أْ) and the added subject marker is an (أُ), the two "Hamzated Alif" are combined together and written as (آ); called in Arabic as "Hamzat-ul Madd".

\* \* \*

❖ <u>Using One Conjugation of Each of</u> the Verbs Above in a Full Sentence:

| | |
|---|---|
| He studies his lessons before sleeping. | ١- يَدْرُسُ دُرُوسَهُ قَبْلَ النَّوْمِ . |
| She is reading her lessons now. | ٢- تَقْرَأُ دُرُوسَهَا الآنَ . |
| Are you (masculine) eating your breakfast now? | ٣- هَلْ تَأْكُلُ فُطُورَكَ الآنَ ؟ |
| I am sitting now in the kitchen. | ٤- أَجْلِسُ الآنَ فِي الْمَطْبَخِ . |
| Sameer does his homework every day. | ٥- يَعْمَلُ سَمِيرٌ وَاجِبَهُ كُلَّ يَوْمٍ . |
| Maryam understands her lessons well. | ٦- تَفْهَمُ مَرْيَمُ دُرُوسَهَا جَيِّدًا . |
| Do you (masculine) hear what I am telling you? | ٧- هَلْ تَسْمَعُ مَا أَقُولُ لَكَ ؟ |
| Do you (female) become generous in the month of Ramadan? | ٨- هَلْ تَكْرُمِينَ فِي شَهْرِ رَمَضَانَ ؟ |
| The boy grows up and becames a man. | ٩- يَكْبُرُ الْوَلَدُ وَيُصْبِحُ رَجُلاً . |
| I eat my lunch at school. | ١٠- آكُلُ غَدَائِي فِي الْمَدْرَسَةِ . |

\* \* \*

❖ **New Vocabulary:**

## أَسْمَاء / Nouns

دُرُوسُهُ (دُرُوسَ+ـهُ) = his lessons    دُرُوسَهَا (دُرُوسَ+ـهَا) = her lessons

فُطُورَكَ (فُطُورَ+ـكَ) = your breakfast    الْمَطْبَخِ = the kitchen

وَاجِبَهُ (وَاجِبَ+ـهُ) = his homework    كُلَّ يَوْمٍ = every day

الَّذِي = مَا = that which (relative pronoun)    شَهْرِ = month (of)

رَمَضَانَ = Ramadan (9th month of Islamic calendar)

غَدَائِي (غَدَاءِ+ي) = my lunch    غَدًا = tomorrow

السَّنَةَ = the year    الْقَادِمَةَ = the coming

## أَفْعَال / Verbs

Note: Verbs' listing will be based on the 3rd person masculine singular conjugation, as in the case of the past tense, to match the way dictionaries list verbs in their entries:

يَدْرُسُ = he studies / he is studying    يَقْرَأُ = he reads / he is reading

يَأْكُلُ = he eats / he is eating    يَجْلِسُ = he sits / he is sitting

يَعْمَلُ = he works / he is working    يَفْهَمُ = he understands / he is understanding

يَسْمَعُ = he hears / he is hearing    يَكْرُمُ = he becomes generous / he is becoming genero

يَكْبُرُ = he grows up / he is growing up    يُصْبِحُ = he becomes / he is becoming

يَتَخَرَّجُ = he graduates / he is graduating

## أَدَوَاتٌ / Particles

الآنَ = now    لَكَ (لَ+كَ) = to you (masculine)

178

❖ **Negating the Present Tense Verbs with (لاَ):**

Imperfect (present) tense verbs can be simply negated by placing the negative particle (لاَ) before them; examples:

١- لاَ يَدْرُسُ دَرْسَهُ الآنَ .   He is not studying his lesson now.

٢- لاَ تَقْرَأُ دُرُوسَهَا كُلَّ يَوْمٍ .   She does not read her lessons every day.

٣- لاَ تَأْكُلُ كُلَّ طَعَامِكَ .   You (masculine) do not eat all your food.

٤- لاَ تَشْرَبِينَ الْقَهْوَةَ .   You (feminine) do not drink the coffee.

٥- لاَ أَعْمَلُ الْوَاجِبَ الآنَ .   I am not doing my homework now.

٦- لاَ يَفْهَمُ الدَّرْسَ جَيِّدًا .   He does not understand the lesson well.

٧- لاَ أَسْمَعُ سُؤَالَكَ .   I do not hear your question.

٨- لاَ يَكْرُمُ في رَمَضَانَ .   He does not become generous in Ramadan.

٩- لاَ آكُلُ الْفُطُورَ كُلَّ يَوْمٍ .   I do not eat breakfast every day.

\* \* \*

❖ **Forming Direct Future Meaning With the Present Tense Verbs Using (سَـــ) or (سَوْفَ):**

Generally speaking, the imperfect (present) tense verbs can indicate future meaning when used in certain contexts in conjunction with certain adverbs which indicate future meaning; such as:

١- يَذْهَبُ إلى الْجَامِعَةِ غَدًا .   He will go to the university tomorrow.

٢- أَتَخَرَّجُ السَّنَةَ الْقَادِمَةَ .   I will graduate next year.

٣- أَرْجِعُ إلى بَيْتِي بَعْدَ قَلِيلٍ .   I will return to my home after a short time.

However, we can make a present tense directly future if we place one of the two future particles (ﺳَـ) or (ﺳَوْفَ) directly before the verb, as in the following sentences:

١- سَيَذْهَبُ إِلَى السُّوقِ .       سَوْفَ يَذْهُبُ إِلَى السُّوقِ .

He will go to the market.      He will go to the market.

٢- سَأَتَخَرَّجُ السَّنَةَ الْقَادِمَةَ .       سَوْفَ أَتَخَرَّجُ السَّنَةَ الْقَادِمَةَ .

I will graduate next year.      I will graduate next year.

٣- سَآكُلُ بَعْدَ قَلِيلٍ .       سَوْفَ آكُلُ بَعْدَ قَلِيلٍ .

I will eat after a while.      I will eat after a while.

٤- سَتَسْمَعُ الأَخْبَارَ .       سَوْفَ تَسْمَعُ الأَخْبَارَ .

She will hear the news.      She will hear the news.

\* \* \*

## Remember! / تَذَكَّرْ - تَذَكَّرِي!

1. Imperfect (Present) Tense verbs, (الْمُضَارِعُ), are used to indicate actions that are in progress at the time of speaking, or actions that happen as a matter of habitual actions.

2. All conjugations of a given imperfect verb share a basic three-letter root called the "stem" of the verb; these three consonants are also called the "radicals". The stem or root of a verb has a basic underlying meaning, but it does not tell us the number, person or gender of the one undertaking the action.

3. Unlike the past tense where the conjugation results by adding certain suffixes at the end of the verb stem, the imperfect (present) tense results by adding certain prefixes to the beginning of the stem, and in one case (i.e. 2nd person feminine singular) a suffix as well.

4. The three standard prefixes of the singular imperfect conjugations are (يـ), (تـ), and (أ) and the same prefixes will appear with the dual and plural conjugations with an addition of the prefix (نـ) for the 1st person plural. These four prefixes are called collectively (أَحْرُفُ الْمُضَارِعِ), (i.e. the letters of the imperfect conjugations.)

5. The vowels of the middle radical stems of the imperfect verbs might be a "*Dammah*", a "*Fathah*" or a "*Kasrah*" and these vowels might correspond or might not correspond to the same in the perfect stem of the verbs. The dictionaries usually list such vowels for each individual verb for both the perfect and imperfect.

6. The present tense verbs can simply be negated by placing the negating particle (لَا) before the verbs.

7. The imperfect conjugations can be rendered directly into future time by inserting one of the two future particles (سَـ) or (سَوْفَ) before the verb.

8. The final vowel sign "*Dammah*" and the (نْ), in the case of the 2nd person feminine, are considered "**Mood Markers**" for the "**Indicative Mood**" and will be altered when the verb is preceded by a "Jussive" or "Subjunctive" particle; a topic that will be treated in "**Secnd Steps in Arabic Grammer.**"

\* \* \*

## تَدْرِيبَاتٌ / Exercises

**1.** Read the following sentences; identify the "Imperfect Verb" by underlining it, and then give its English meanings: (the first is done for you as an example to follow:

١- <u>آكُلُ</u> فِي مَطْعَمِ الْجَامِعَةِ .  ←  I eat

٢- تَشْرَبُ الْحَلِيبَ كُلَّ يَوْمٍ .  ←  ...............

٣- هَلْ تَشْرَبِينَ عَصِيرَ تُفَّاحٍ ؟  ←  ...............

٤- هَلْ تَدْرُسُ الدَّرْسَ الآنَ ؟  ←  ...............

٥- يَأْكُلُ تُفَّاحَةً وَيَشْرَبُ حَلِيبًا . ← ..............................

٦- لَا يَعْمَلُ التِّلْمِيذُ الْوَاجِبَ . ← ..............................

٧- تَقْرَأُ مَرْيَمُ قِصَّةً قَصِيرَةً . ← ..............................

٨- سَأَذْهَبُ إِلَى السُّوقِ بَعْدَ قَلِيلٍ . ← ..............................

**2. Translate the following sentences into Arabic (Orally and written):**

1. I am writing a letter to my father. = ..............................

2. The girl does not drink juice. = ..............................

3. Are you (masculine) doing the homework? = ..............................?

4. She eats bread and drinks milk. = ..............................

5. He is reading the article now. = ..............................

6. I do not go to the school every day. = ..............................

* * *

**3. Translate the following Arabic sentences into English:**

(١) مَاذَا تَأْكُلُ يَا صَلَاحُ ؟ ← ..............................?

(٢) آكُلُ تِينًا وَعِنَبًا وَخُبْزًا . ← ..............................

(٣) هَلْ تَسْمَعِينَ حَدِيثَ الْأُسْتَاذِ ؟ ← ..............................?

(٤) هَلْ تَعْمَلُ الْوَاجِبَ يَا سَمِيرُ ؟ ← ..............................?

(٥) سَتَكْتُبُ لَيْلَى مَقَالَةً طَوِيلَةً . ← ..............................

(٦) يَأْكُلُ أَبِي طَعَامَهُ ثُمَّ يَشْرَبُ قَهْوَةً . ← ..............................

(٧) لَا أَفْهَمُ الدَّرْسَ جَيِّدًا . ← ..............................

**4.** Fill in the blank cells of the following table with the appropriate conjugations of the imperfect verbs which you were given one of their conjugations; you need to match the conjugation to the subject pronoun provided in the shaded cells at the top of each column:

| (أَنَا) | (أَنْتِ) | (أَنْتَ) | (هِيَ) | (هُوَ) |
|---|---|---|---|---|
|  |  |  |  | يَأْكُلُ |
|  |  |  | تَدْرُسُ |  |
|  |  | تَفْهَمُ |  |  |
|  | تَشْرَبِينَ |  |  |  |
| أَعْمَلُ |  |  |  |  |
|  | تَسْمَعِينَ |  |  |  |
|  |  | تَجْلِسُ |  |  |
|  |  |  | تَكْرُمُ |  |

\* \* \*

183

**5.** Unscramble the following sets of words to make from each of them a full meaningful sentence, as in the given example, and then translate the resultant sentences into English:

رِسَالَةً / إلَى / أَكْتُبُ / صَدِيقِي ⟵ أَكْتُبُ رِسَالَةً إلَى صَدِيقِي =
I a writing a letter to my friend.

١- الآنَ / تَعْمَلِينَ / هَلْ / الْوَاجِبَ ................................ ؟ =

................................................................

٢- الْقَادِمَةَ / سَأَتَخَرَّجُ / السَّنَةَ ................................ . =

................................................................

٣- فِي / أُمِّي / تَعْمَلُ / الْمَطْبَخِ ................................ . =

................................................................

٤- السُّوقِ / إلَى / يَذْهَبُ / كُلَّ / أَبِي / يَوْمٍ ................................ . =

................................................................

٥- غَدًا / أُخْتِي / سَتُسَافِرُ ................................ . =

................................................................

٦- جَيِّدًا / لَا / الدَّرْسَ / أَفْهَمُ ................................ . =

................................................................

٧- الْعَرَبِيَّةَ / تَدْرُسِينَ / أَيْنَ / اللُّغَةَ ................................ ؟ =

................................................................

\* \* \*

**Lesson 26**

الدَّرْسُ السَّادِسُ وَالعِشْرُونَ

## فِعْلُ الأَمْرِ
### The Imperative Tense Verb

- Imperative (Command) Tense Verbs (الأَمْرُ) are used to command a second person to undertake a given action sometime in the future time, after the command is given.

- Theoretically, one can only <u>command directly a second person</u>, both mascululine and feminine, thus the conjugations of the imperative verbs total only five: two for singular, both for masculine and feminine; two for plural masculine and feminine; one for dual, identical for both masculine and feminine.

- There is an indirect way of commanding a third person using a special particle called the (لَامُ الأَمْرِ) (i.e the *Laam* of Command) as we will see later.

- The good news is that the imperative tense verbs are based on and directly related to the present tense conjugations through a specific process which will be explained below.

- In this lesson we will confine ourselves to explaining the imperative paradigm of the singular conjugations <u>directly with two 2ⁿᵈ persons</u> and <u>indirectly with two 3ʳᵈ persons</u>. One does not command him or herself, therefore there is no 1ˢᵗ person conjugation with the imperative tense.

- Let's now study the parallel pairs of sentences in comparative perspective:

| The Imperative Tense / الأَمْرُ | The Imperfect Tense / المُضَارِعُ |
|---|---|
| ١- (أَنْتَ) اُكْتُبْ دَرْسَكَ ! | ١- (أَنْتَ) تَكْتُبُ دَرْسَكَ . |
| You (masculine) write your lesson! | You (masculine) are writing your lesson. |
| ٢- (أَنْتِ) اُكْتُبِي دَرْسَكِ ! | ٢- (أَنْتِ) تَكْتُبِينَ دَرْسَكِ . |
| You (feminine) write your lesson! | You (feminine) are writing your lesson. |

✽ ✽ ✽

185

٣- (أَنْتَ) تَجْلِسُ عَلَى الْكُرْسِيِّ .

You (masculine) are sitting on the chair.

٣- (أَنْتَ) اِجْلِسْ عَلَى الْكُرْسِيِّ !

You (masculine) sit down on the chair!

٤- (أَنْتِ) تَجْلِسِينَ عَلَى الْكُرْسِيِّ .

You (feminine) are sitting down on the chair.

٤- (أَنْتِ) اِجْلِسِي عَلَى الْكُرْسِيِّ !

You (feminine) sit down on the chair!

* * *

٥- (أَنْتَ) تَعْمَلُ وَاجِبَكَ .

You (masculine) are doing your homework.

٥- (أَنْتَ) اِعْمَلْ وَاجِبَكَ !

You (masculine) do your homework!

٦- (أَنْتِ) تَعْمَلِينَ وَاجِبَكِ .

You (feminine) are doing your homework.

٦- (أَنْتِ) اِعْمَلِي وَاجِبَكِ !

You (feminine) do your homework!

* * *

٧- (هُوَ) يَقْرَأُ دَرْسَهُ .

He is reading his lesson.

٧- (هُوَ) لِيَقْرَأْ دَرْسَهُ !

Let him read his lesson!

٨- (هِيَ) تَقْرَأُ دَرْسَهَا .

She is reading his lesson.

٨- (هِيَ) لِتَقْرَأْ دَرْسَهَا !

Let her read her lesson!

❖ **Explanatory Notes:**

1. If we examine the pair of parallel sentences from 1-6, we will notice that in all the imperatives, we dropped the (تَ) of the imperfect and replaced it with (اُ) (*Alif*).

2. We also notice that the vowel of the *Alif* appears with a (*Dammah* اُ), in the first two examples. That is because the middle radical of the root verb (i.e. the (تُ) which is between the *Kaaf* and the *Baa*) bears the *Dammah* vowel.

3. We also notice that in examples 3 and 4, the *Alif* appears with a (*Kasrah* اِ). That is because the middle radical of the root verb (i.e. the (لِ) which is between the *Jeem* and the *Seen*) bears the *Kasrah* vowel.

4. We also notice that in examples 5 and 6, the *Alif* appears also with a (*Kasrah* اِ) when the middle radical of the root verb (i.e. the (مَ) which is between the *'Ayn* and the *Laam*) bears the *Fathah* vowel.

5. If we further examine the ending of the imperative conjugations, as opposed to the imperfect conjugations in examples one through six, we find out that, in the case of the 2nd person masculine conjugations, we dropped the *Dammah* vowel and replaced it with a *Sukoon* to look as (اِجْلِسْ), (اُكْتُبْ) and (اِعْمَلْ) respectively.

6. If we further examine the ending of the imperative conjugations, as opposed to the imperfect conjugation in examples one through six, we find out that, in the case of the 2nd person feminine conjugations, we dropped the (نَ) ending and ended with the long vowel (ـِي) marking all verbs of 2nd person feminine, thus we have: (اُكْتُبِي) (اِجْلِسِي), and (اِعْمَلِي) respectively.

7. The examples 7 and 8 above illustrate how we <u>make imperatives indirectly</u> to relate to <u>3rd persons</u>, both masculine and feminine. The process runs this way: We prefix the <u>Lamm of Command</u> (لِ) to the imperfect stem, but without dropping the subject markers (يَـ) or (تَـ). And then we drop the *Dammah* vowels of the last letters, and replaced it with a *Sukoon* instead; thus the final forms will appear as: (لِيَقْرَأْ), for the masculine (he) and (لِتَقْرَأْ), for the feminine (she).

187

8. <u>Important note</u>: The process explained above <u>applies to trilateral sound verbs</u>; weak verbs and derived forms of verbs have a slightly modified process, which will be treated in <u>Second Steps in Arabic Grammer</u>.

❖ The table below shows the process explained above with ten other verbs, to help you further in understanding the conceptualization of the imperative verb conjugations paradigm in Arabic:

| Indirect Command for 3rd Person Feminine singular (هِيَ) | Indirect Command for 3rd Person Masculine Singular (هُوَ) | Direct Command for 2nd Person Feminine singular (أَنْتِ) | Direct Command for 2nd Person Masculine Singular (أَنْتَ) | Imerfect (Present) Tense Conjugations |
|---|---|---|---|---|
| لِتَضْحَكْ | لِيَضْحَكْ | اِضْحَكِي | اِضْحَكْ | تَضْحَكُ / تَضْحَكِينَ (you laugh, you are laughing) |
| لِتَلْعَبْ | لِيَلْعَبْ | اِلْعَبِي | اِلْعَبْ | تَلْعَبُ / تَلْعَبِينَ (you play, you are playing) |
| لِتَشْرَبْ | لِيَشْرَبْ | اِشْرَبِي | اِشْرَبْ | تَشْرَبُ / تَشْرَبِينَ (you drink, you are drinking) |
| لِتَحْمِلْ | لِيَحْمِلْ | اِحْمِلِي | اِحْمِلْ | تَحْمِلُ / تَحْمِلِينَ (you carry, you are carrying) |
| لِتَدْخُلْ | لِيَدْخُلْ | اُدْخُلِي | اُدْخُلْ | تَدْخُلُ / تَدْخُلِينَ (you enter, you are entering) |
| لِتَفْهَمْ | لِيَفْهَمْ | اِفْهَمِي | اِفْهَمْ | تَفْهَمُ / تَفْهَمِينَ (you understand, you are undrstanding) |
| لِتَسْمَعْ | لِيَسْمَعْ | اِسْمَعِي | اِسْمَعْ | تَسْمَعُ / تَسْمَعِينَ (you hear, you are hearing) |
| لِتَكْرُمْ | لِيَكْرُمْ | اُكْرُمِي | اُكْرُمْ | تَكْرُمُ / تَكْرُمِينَ (you become generous, you are becoming generous) |

| لِتَخْرُجْ | لِيَخْرُجْ | اُخْرُجِي | اُخْرُجْ | تَخْرُجُ / تَخْرُجِينَ (you get out, you are getting out) |
|---|---|---|---|---|
| لِتَشْكُرْ | لِيَشْكُرْ | اُشْكُرِي | اُشْكُرْ | تَشْكُرُ / تَشْكُرِينَ (to eat) |

\* \* \*

❖ **Using One Imperative Verb Conjugation of Each of the Verbs Above in a Full Sentence:**

١- اِضْحَكْ وَقْتَ الضَّحِك فَقَطُ !  Laugh at the time of laughing only!

٢- اِلْعَبِي وَقْتَ اللَّعِب فَقَطُ !  Play at the time of playing only!

٣- اِشْرَبْ حَلِيبًا كُلَّ يَوْمٍ !  Drink milk every day!

٤- اِحْمِلِي حَقِيبَتَك عَلَى ظَهْرِك !  Carry your bag on your back!

٥- اِعْمَلْ وَاجِبَك كُلَّ يَوْمٍ !  Do your homework every day!

٦- اُدْخُلِي مِنَ البَابِ الْخَلْفِي !  Enter from the back door!

٧- اِفْهَمْ سُؤَالِي قَبْلَ الإِجَابَة !  Understand my question before answering!

٨- اِسْمَعِي نَصِيحَتِي جَيِّدًا !  Listen to my advice well!

٩- اُخْرُجِي مِنَ البَابِ الأَمَامِيِّ !  Exit from the front door!

١٠- اُشْكُرْ رَبَّكَ عَلَى نِعَمِه !  Thank your Lord for His blessings!

\* \* \*

❖ <u>New Vocabulary:</u>

## أَسْمَاء / Nouns

| | |
|---|---|
| laughing (v.n). = الضَّحِكِ | time (of) = وَقْتَ |
| your bag = حَقِيبَتَك (حَقِيبَةٌ + كِ) | (the) playing = اللَّعِبِ |
| the back, the rear = الْخَلْفِيِّ | your back = ظَهْرِكِ (ظَهْرِ + كِ) |
| answering (v.n). = الْإِجَابَة | my question = سُؤَالِي (سُؤَالٌ + ي) |
| your Lord = رَبَّكَ (رَبَّ + كَ) | my advice = نَصِيحَتِي (نَصِيحَةٌ + ي) |
| | his blessings = نِعَمِهِ (نِعَم + ــهِ) |

## أَفْعَال / Verbs

**Note:** The following verbs' listing will give you the past tense and present tense conjugation of the 3<sup>rd</sup> person masculine singular and the imperative conjugations of the 2<sup>nd</sup> person masculine!

he laughed / he is laughing / laugh! = ضَحِكَ / يَضْحَكُ / اِضْحَكْ

he carried / he is carrying / carry! = حَمَلَ / يَحْمِلُ / اِحْمِلْ

he entered / he is entering / enter! = دَخَلَ / يَدْخُلُ / أُدْخُلْ

he exited / he is exiting / exit! go out! = خَرَجَ / يَخْرُجُ / أُخْرُجْ

## أَدَوَاتٌ / Particles

| | |
|---|---|
| before = قَبْلَ | only = فَقَطُ |
| | for = عَلَى |

\* \* \*

# Remember! / تَذَكَّرْ – تَذَكَّرِي!

1. Imperative (Command) Tense Verbs, (الأَمْرُ), are used to command a second person to undertake given actions in a future time in relation to the time of speaking.

2. A command <u>can be given directly to second persons only</u>; though by using the *Laam of Command* (لَامُ الأَمْرِ) we can <u>command 3<sup>rd</sup> persons in an indirect way</u>.

2. The imperative tense conjugations are based on the imperfect tense conjugations with some specific alterations as follows:

    (a) The imperfect tense subject marker prefix (تـ) is removed and in its place we add an (*Alif* / ا), which would bear either a (*Dammah* / اُ), if the vowel of the 2<sup>nd</sup> radical is a *Dammah*, or it would bear a (*Kasrah* / اِ), if the vowel of the 2<sup>nd</sup> radical is a *Fathah* or a *Kasrah*.

    (b) The ending *Dammah* of the imperfect conjugation is dropped, becoming a *Sukoon* (sign of a voweless consonant) in the 2<sup>nd</sup> person masculine.

    (c) The ending (نَ) of the 2<sup>nd</sup> person feminine is also dropped, leaving the imperative ending with a long (ـِي).

3. The above mentioned process applies to all sound trilateral verbs; weak verbs and other derived forms of verbs have their own sub-rules which are slightly different and will be covered in "**Second Steps in Arabic Grammar.**"

\* \* \*

## Exercises / تَدْريبَاتٌ

**1.** Read the following sentences; identify the "Imperative Verb" by underlining it, and then give its English meanings with the gender of the person: (the first is done for you as an example to follow:

Drink! (you-feminine)            ١- اِشْرَبِي الْحَلِيبَ كُلَّ يَوْمٍ !

                                            ٢- اُدْرُسْ دَرْسَكَ الآنَ !

٣- اعْمَلي وَاجبَكَ بَعْدَ قَليلٍ ! ..................................

٤- اُدْخُلْ مِنْ هَذَا الْبَابِ ! ..................................

٥- اُشْكُري اللهَ كَثيراً ! ..................................

٦- اُخْرُجْ مِنَ الصَّفِّ ! ..................................

٨- لِيَذْهَبْ إِلَى بَيْتِه ! ..................................

٩- لِتَسْمَعْ نَصيحَةَ الْمُعَلِّمَةِ ! ..................................

١٠- اُكْتُبي رِسَالَةً إِلَى صَديقَتِكِ ! ..................................

١١- اِذْهَبْ وَالْعَبْ فِي الْحَديقَةِ ! ..................................

\* \* \*

**2. Translate the following sentences into Arabic (Orally and written):**

1. Write (masculine) a letter to my father! = ! ..................................

2. Drink (feminine) juice and milk! = ! ..................................

3. Do (masculine) your homework now! = ! ..................................

4. Read (feminine) this article! = ! ..................................

5. Sit down (masculine) in your chair! = ! ..................................

6. Open (feminine) the door now! = ! ..................................

7. Thank (feminine) God every day! = ! ..................................

\* \* \*

**3. Translate the following Arabic sentences into English:**

(١) اِسْمَعْ نَصِيحَتِي يَا صَلَاحُ ! ...................................

(٢) اعْمَلِي وَاجِبَكِ الآنَ ! ...................................

(٣) اقْرَأْ دَرْسَكَ قَبْلَ اللَّعِبِ ! ...................................

(٤) اُكْتُبِي رِسَالَةً إِلَى أُمِّكِ ! ...................................

(٥) اُشْكُرْ صَدِيقَكَ عَلَى الْهَدِيَّةِ ! ...................................

(٦) اِشْرَبْ قَهْوَتَكَ بَعْدَ الْأَكْلِ ! ...................................

(٧) افْهَمِي سُؤَالِي قَبْلَ الْإِجَابَةِ ! ...................................

(٨) اجْلِسْ عَلَى هَذَا الْكُرْسِيِّ ! ...................................

(٩) اُخْرُجِي مِنَ الْبَابِ الْخَلْفِيِّ ! ...................................

(١٠) اِلْعَبْ وَقْتَ اللَّعِبِ فَقَطْ ! ...................................

\* \* \*

**4.** Fill in the blank cells of the following table with the appropriate conjugations of the <u>perfect (past) tense verbs</u>, <u>imperfect (present) tense verbs</u>, or <u>imperative (command) tense verbs</u>; note that all the conjugations you will provide are confined to 2<sup>nd</sup> person singular, either masculine or feminine:

| فِعْلُ الْأَمْرِ<br>Imperative Tense | الْفِعْلُ الْمُضَارِعُ<br>Present Tense | الْفِعْلُ الْمَاضِي<br>Past Tense |
|---|---|---|
|  |  | ذَهَبْتَ |
|  | تَكْتُبِينَ |  |
| اِسْمَعْ |  |  |
|  | تَشْكُرُ |  |

193

|  |  | حَمَلْتِ |
|---|---|---|
|  | تَشْرَبُ |  |
| اُخْرُجِي |  |  |
|  | تَدْخُلِينَ |  |
|  |  | قَرَأْتَ |
|  | تَجْلِسِينَ |  |
| اِضْحَك |  |  |
|  | تَعْمَلُ |  |
|  |  | دَرَسْتِ |
|  | تَفْعَلِينَ |  |

* * *

**5. Unscramble the following sets of words to make from each of them a full meaningful sentence, as in the given example, and then translate the resultant sentences into English:**

دَرْسَكَ / اُكْتُبْ / الآنَ  ⟵  اُكْتُبْ دَرْسَكَ الآنَ ! =
Write your lesson now!

١- فِي / اِعْمَلِي / الْبَيْتِ / الْوَاجِب ............................... ! =

................................................

194

٢- الْإِجَابَةِ / قَبْلَ / افْهَمْ / سُؤَالِي ................... = !

٣- عَلَى / حَقِيبَتِكِ / ظَهْرِكِ / احْمِلِي ................... = !

٤- اسْمَكَ / اللَّوْحِ / اُكْتُبْ / عَلَى ................... = !

٥- هُنَاكَ / إِلَى / اِذْهَبِي / وَالْعَبِي / الْمَلْعَبِ ................... = !

٦- جَيِّدًا / الدَّرْسَ / افْهَمْ ................... = !

٧- عَلَى / الْكُرْسِيِّ / هَذَا / اِجْلِسْ ................... = !

٨- الْخَلْفِيِّ / مِنَ / اُخْرُجْ / الْبَابِ ................... = !

195

**Lesson 27**

الدَّرْسُ السَّابِعُ وَالْعِشْرُونَ

## الْفِعْلُ مَعَ الضَّمَائِرِ الْمُتَّصِلَةُ
### The Verb with Suffix (Attached) Pronouns

❖ In an ealier lesson we have learned that <u>suffix</u> or <u>attached pronouns</u> can be attached to the end of nouns to express possessive relationship; in this sense they would be equivalent to the English <u>possessive pronouns</u>: (**his**, **her**, **your**, **my**).

❖ To refresh our memories about the usage of these pronouns with nouns in Arabic, let's consider the following examples:

| | | |
|---|---|---|
| His book is new. | ـهُ | ١- كِتَابُهُ جَدِيدٌ . = |
| Her pen is red. | ـهَا | ٢- قَلَمُهَا أَحْمَرُ . = |
| Is this your (masculine) car? | ـكَ | ٣- هَلْ هَذِهِ سَيَّارَتُكَ ؟ = |
| Is this your (feminine) house? | ـكِ | ٤- هَلْ هَذَا بَيْتُكِ ؟ = |
| This is my school. | ـِي | ٥- هَذِهِ مَدْرَسَتِي . = |

❖ In this lesson, we will learn that these same suffix pronouns can be attached to the end of a special group of verbs called "Transitive Verbs" (i.e verbs that take direct object).

❖ In this case they are not used any more to express possessive meaning, but to <u>function as direct objects of transitive verbs</u>, as replacement for an object noun. Therefore, they are called, when attached to verbs, as "<u>Object Pronouns</u>"; Arabic (ضَمَائِرُ الْمَفْعُولِيَّة).

❖ Now, let's examine the following parallel sentences to see how this process works:

| | |
|---|---|
| ١- قَرَأَ الْكِتَابَ . | قَرَأَهُ . |
| He read the book. | He read it. |
| ٢- كَتَبَ الرِّسَالَةَ . | كَتَبَهَا . |
| He wrote the letter. | He wrote it. |
| ٣- أَعْرِفُ مَنْ أَنْتَ . | أَعْرِفُكَ . |
| I know who you are. | I know you. (*Masculine*) |
| ٤- أَعْرِفُ مَنْ أَنْتِ . | أَعْرِفُكِ . |
| I know who you are. | I know you. (*Feminine*) |
| ٥- هَلْ تَعْرِفُ مَنْ أَنَا ؟ | هَلْ تَعْرِفُنِي ؟ |
| Do you know who I am? | Do you know me? |

\* \* \*

### ❖ Explanatory Notes:

1. If we examine the numbered sentences on the right, we will notice that each has a transitive verb that takes a direct object. The underlined parts of these sentences, whether they consist of one word or a phrase, are functioning as the direct objects of these verbs.

2. In the parallel linguistic structures on the left, we used the corresponding attached pronouns to replace the nouns or phrases in the first group. These pronouns have the same fuction of the nouns or phrases they replaced, therefore they are now the <u>objects of the verbs they were attached to</u>.

3. If you take a closer look, you will find that these are exactly the same attached pronouns used with nouns, <u>with the exception of the 1st person pronoun for (me)</u> where there is an extra (نِ) inserted between the end of the verb and the (ي) of the pronoun. This inserted (نِ) is needed to bear the *Kasrah* which must precede the *Yaa*; because the last letter of a verb will never bear a *Kasrah*.

197

4. The two 3rd person suffix pronouns (ﻪ / ـﻪ), for masculine, and (ـﻬَﺎ), for feminine, may refer either to humans or to non-humans. If they refer to humans, then they are rendered in English as (**him**) and (**her**); if they refer to non-humans, however, they are rendered into English as the neuter (**it**).

5. The suffix pronouns for 2nd persons, both masculine and feminine, (ﻚَ) and (ﻚِ), as well as the 1st person pronoun (ﻧﻲ) refer only to human beings, and they are rendered into English as (**you**) for the 2nd persons, and as (**me**) for the 1st person.

6. It is important to note that, in real language, not all these pronouns can be attached to specific verbs; for example, we may say, (ﻛَﺘَﺒَﻪ) or (ﻛَﺘَﺒَﻬَﺎ) "he wrote **it**" if referring to a book or a letter, for example, but you cannot say, (ﻛَﺘَﺒَﻚ) or (ﻛَﺘَﺒَﻨِﻲ), because it does make sense in Arabic, since a person cannot be a letter or a book that can be written down.

❖ The table below shows the process explained above with some other verbs that might accept the five singular object suffix pronouns:

| Attached to (ﻧﻲ / ـﻨﻲ) | Attached to (ـكِ / كِ) | Attached to (ـكَ/ كَ) | Attached to (ـﻬَﺎ/ ﻫَﺎ) | Attached to (ﻪُ / ـﻪُ) | The Verb & Its Meaning |
|---|---|---|---|---|---|
| ذَكَرَنِي | يَذْكُرُكِ | ذَكَرَكَ | يَذْكُرُهَا | ذَكَرَهُ | ذَكَرَ / يَذْكُرُ to remember, to mention |
| ذَكَرَنِي | يَشْكُرُكِ | شَكَرَكَ | يَشْكُرُهَا | شَكَرَهُ | شَكَرَ / يَشْكُرُ to thank |
| سَمِعَنِي | يَسْمَعُكِ | سَمِعَكَ | يَسْمَعُهَا | سَمِعَهُ | سَمِعَ / يَسْمَعُ to hear |
| عَلَّمَنِي | يُعَلِّمُكِ | عَلَّمَكَ | يُعَلِّمُهَا | عَلَّمَهُ | عَلَّمَ / يُعَلِّمُ to teach |
| أَخَذَنِي | يَأْخُذُكِ | أَخَذَكَ | يَأْخُذُهَا | أَخَذَهُ | أَخَذَ / يَأْخُذُ to take |
| أَمَرَنِي | يَأْمُرُكِ | أَمَرَكَ | يَأْمُرُهَا | أَمَرَهُ | أَمَرَ / يَأْمُرُ to order |
| كَلَّمَنِي | يُكَلِّمُكِ | كَلَّمَكَ | يُكَلِّمُهَا | كَلَّمَهُ | كَلَّمَ / يُكَلِّمُ to talk to |

| | | | | | |
|---|---|---|---|---|---|
| سَأَلَني | يَسْأَلُكِ | سَأَلَكَ | يَسْأَلُهَا | سَأَلَهُ | سَأَلَ / يَسْأَلُ<br>to ask |
| زَارَني | يَزُورُكِ | زَارَكَ | يَزُورُهَا | زَارَهُ | زَارَ / يَزُورُ<br>to ask |

❖ **Using One Imperative Verb Conjugation of Each of the Verbs Above in a Full Sentence:**

١- يَذْكُرُكَ دَائِمًا بِالْخَيْرِ .    He remembers you always for what is good.

٢- نَعَمْ ، أَعْرِفُهُ جَيِّدًا .    Yes, I know him well.

٣- شَكَرَهَا عَلَى الْهَدِيَّةِ .    He thanked her for the gift.

٤- هَلْ تَسْمَعُني جَيِّدًا ؟    Do you hear me well?

٥- مَنْ عَلَّمَكَ اللُّغَةَ الْعَرَبِيَّةَ ؟    Who taught you the Arabic language?

٦- يَأْخُذُهَا إِلَى الْمَدْرَسَةِ كُلَّ يَوْمٍ .    He takes her to school every day.

٧- أَمَرَهُ الشُّرْطِيُّ أَنْ يَرْفَعَ يَدَيْهِ .    The police ordered him to raise his hands.

٨- هَلْ يُكَلِّمُكِ عَنِ الزَّوَاجِ ؟    Does he talk to you about marriage?

٩- سَأَلَني الأُسْتَاذُ سُؤَالاً صَعْبًا .    The professor asked me a difficult question..

١٠- يَزُورُهَا كُلَّ أُسْبُوعٍ .    He visits her every week.

\* \* \*

## ❖ New Vocabulary:

### أَسْمَاء / Nouns

مَنْ = who (relative pronoun)

بِـالْخَيْرِ (بِـ+الْخَيْر) = with good

الشُّرْطِيّ = the police man

الزَّوَاج = the marriage

صَعْبًا = difficult

دَائِمًا = always

الْهَدِيَّة = the gift, the present

يَدَيْه (يَدَ+يْـ+ـه) = his two hands

سُؤَالاً = a question

أُسْبُوعٍ = a week

### أَفْعَال / Verbs

Note: The following verbs' listing will give you the past tense and present tense conjugation of the 3rd person masculine singular and the imperative conjugations of the 2nd person masculine!

ذَكَرَ / يَذْكُرُ / اُذْكُرْ = he remembered / he is remembering / remember!

عَلَّمَ / يُعَلِّمُ / عَلِّمْ = he taught / he is teaching / teach!

أَخَذَ / يَأْخُذُ / خُذْ = he took / he is taking / take!

أَمَرَ / يَأْمُرُ / مُرْ = he ordered / he is ordering / order!

كَلَّمَ / يُكَلِّمُ / كَلِّمْ = he talked to / he is talking to / talk to!

سَأَلَ / يَسْأَلُ / سَلْ = he asked / he is asking / ask!

زَارَ / يَزُورُ / زُرْ = he visited / he is visiting / visit!

رَفَعَ / يَرْفَعُ / اِرْفَعْ = he raised / he is lifting up / raise up! Lift up!

### أَدَوَاتٌ / Particles

أَنْ = to (subjunctive particle with verb)

عَنْ = about

بِـ = with, for

## Remember! / تَذَكَّرْ- تَذَكَّرِي!

1. Verbs of any tense are susceptible to receiving suffix pronouns at the end.

2. These suffix pronouns are exactly the same possessive suffix pronouns that are attached to the end of nouns we have learned earlier.

3. The only exception is the pronoun for the 1st person singular, where we add an extra (نِـ /نْ) between the end of the verb and the (ي / ـي) of the pronoun.

4. The pronouns suffixed to verbs are object pronous, functioning as objects of the verbs they are attached to, since the verbs that receive them must be transitive in nature. They correspond to the English, (**him**, **her**, **you**, & **me**.)

5. The two 3rd person suffix pronouns (ةُ / ـهُ), for masculine, and (ـها), for feminine, may refer either to <u>humans</u> or to <u>non-humans</u>. If they refer to humans, then they are rendered in English as (**him**) and (**her**); if they refer to non-humans, however, they are rendered into English as the neuter (**it**).

6. The suffix pronouns for 2nd persons, both masculine and feminine, (كَ) and (كِ), as well as the 1st person pronoun (نِي) refer only to human beings, and they are rendered into English as (**you**) for the 2nd persons, and as (**me**) for the 1st person.

\* \* \*

## تَدريبَات / Exercises

1. Read the following sentences; identify the verbs and their attached object pronouns by underlining them, and then give each verb's English meanings with the gender of the person: (the first is done for you as an example to follow:

١- <u>كَلَّمَني</u> عَنِ الزَّواجِ .  ⟵  **he talked to me**

٢- سَأَلْتُهُ سُؤالاً صَعْبًا .  ⟵  ..................................

٣- أَعْرِفُها مُنْذُ وَقْتٍ طَويلٍ .  ⟵  ..................................

٥- شَكَرْتُهُ عَلَى الْهَدِيَّةِ . ←  ..............................

٦- نَعَمْ ، أَذْكُرُكَ جَيِّدًا . ←  ..............................

٧- مَنْ عَلَّمَهَا الْعَرَبِيَّةَ ؟ ←  ..............................

٨- أَخَذَنِي إِلَى بَيْتِهِ . ←  ..............................

٩- أَسْمَعُكَ وَأَفْهَمُكَ جَيِّدًا . ←  ..............................

١٠- يَزُورُنِي كُلَّ أُسْبُوعٍ . ←  ..............................

**2. Translate the following sentences into Arabic (orally and in writing):**

1. Do you hear me? = ..............................؟

2. He always remembers you with good. = ..............................

3. She asked him a difficult question. = ..............................

4. I taught her Arabic at the university. = ..............................

5. Does she visit you every week? = ..............................؟

6. He ordered him to raise his hands up. = ..............................

7. My father takes me to school every day! = ..............................

\* \* \*

**3. Translate the following Arabic sentences into English:**

(١) هَلْ تَسْمَعُنِي جَيِّدًا ؟   ..............................?

(٢) سَأَلْتُهَا سُؤَالاً صَعْبًا .   ..............................

(٣) أَذْكُرُكِ دَائِمًا بِالْخَيْرِ .   ..............................

(٤) عَلَّمْتُهَا الْعَرَبِيَّةَ فِي أَمْرِيكَا .   ..............................

(٥) أَشْكُرُكَ عَلَى الْهَدِيَّةِ !   ..............................

202

(٦) أَمَرَهُ الشُّرْطِيُّ أَنْ يَذْهَبَ . ..................................................

(٧) زَارَنِي قَبْلَ أُسْبُوعٍ . ..................................................

(٨) إِلَى أَيْنَ تَأْخُذُنِي ؟ ..................................................?

(٩) هَلْ كَلَّمَكَ عَنِ الزَّوَاجِ ؟ ..................................................?

(١٠) لَا أَفْهَمُكَ جَيِّدًا . ..................................................

\* \* \*

**4.** Fill in the blank cells of the following table with the **appropriate conjugation** of the verb given plus the **appropriate object suffix pronouns** as indicated in the shaded cells on the top of the page; the first is done for you as an example to follow:

| نِي / ـنِي | كِ / ـكِ | كَ / ـكَ | هَا / ـهَا | هُ / ـهُ |
|---|---|---|---|---|
| سَأَلَنِي | سَأَلَكِ | سَأَلَكَ | سَأَلَهَا | سَأَلَهُ |
|  |  |  |  | يَعْرِفُهُ |
|  |  |  | أَعَلِّمُهَا |  |
|  |  | ذَكَرَكَ |  |  |
|  | يَأْمُرُكِ |  |  |  |
| كَلَّمَنِي |  |  |  |  |
|  | أَزُورُكِ |  |  |  |
|  |  | سَمِعَكَ |  |  |
|  |  |  | يَأْخُذُهَا |  |
|  |  |  |  | فَهِمَهُ |

203

## Revision Exercises

> A Note to Teachers: If you are using this book in conjunction with a course you are teaching, you need to know that many of the exercises presented in this section of the book can be used as the basis for making your own tests!

### Section 1

**1. (Translation): Translate into English:**

١- الطَّالِبُ فِي الصَّفِّ .

٢- هَلْ مَعَكَ دَفْتَرٌ وَقَلَمٌ .

٣- كَيْفَ حَالُكَ ؟

٤- دَخَلْتُ مَكْتَبَ الْمُدِيرِ .

٥- الطَّالِبَةُ الْمُجْتَهِدَةُ فِي الْمَكْتَبَةِ .

٦- هَذِهِ حَدِيقَةٌ جَمِيلَةٌ .

٧- يَكْتُبُ التِّلْمِيذُ دَرْسَهُ ؟

٨- أَشْرَبُ فِنْجَانَ الْقَهْوَةِ .

٩- الطَّالِبَانِ الْجَدِيدَانِ مِنْ أَمْرِيكَا .

١٠- هَذَا تِلْمِيذٌ نَشِيطٌ .

* * *

**2. (Using Adjectives):** Fill in the blanks in the following sentences by choosing the appropriate adjective from among those given in the shaded box:

> نَظِيفَةٌ / مُهَذَّبٌ / مُخْلِصُونَ / الصَّالِحَاتُ / الْمَكْسُورُ / الصَّغِيرَةُ / الْجَدِيدَةُ / مُفِيدٌ / مُمْتَازَاتٌ / نَشِيطُونَ

١- هَذَا كِتَابٌ ............... .

٢- السَّيِّدَاتُ ............... مُسْلِمَاتٌ .

٣- هُنَّ بَنَاتٌ ............... .

٤- أَيْنَ السَّيَّارَةُ ............... ؟

٥- هُوَ وَلَدٌ ............... .

٦- هُمْ مُهَنْدِسُونَ ............... .

٧- هَذِهِ غُرْفَةٌ ............... .

٨- أَيْنَ الْكُرْسِيُّ ............... ؟

٩- الْبِنْتُ ............... أُخْتِي .

١٠- الْمُعَلِّمُونَ ............... .

204

3. (Singular-Plural): Change the singular to plural and the plural to singular, as in the first two examples:

١- اَلْمُدَرِّسَاتُ ذَكِيَّاتٌ .      الْمُدَرِّسَةُ ذَكِيَّةٌ .

٢- اَلْمُؤْمِنُ صَادِقٌ .      اَلْمُؤْمِنُونَ صَادِقُونَ .

٣- هُمْ تَلَامِيذُ نَشِيطُونَ .

٤- اَلْمُعَلِّمُ طَيِّبٌ .

٥- السَّيِّدَاتُ عَرَبِيَّاتٌ .

٦- هَلْ هُوَ مُسْلِمٌ ؟

٧- الْمُهَنْدِسُونَ مَاهِرُونَ .

٨- الْوَالِدَةُ رَحِيمَةٌ .

٩- الأَسَاتِذَةُ مَشْهُورُونَ .

١٠- التِّلْمِيذُ نَشِيطٌ .

4. (Correcting Mistakes): There is something wrong with the underlined words in the following sentences; correct the problem in writing and be ready to explain why verbally. The first example is done as a sample to follow:

١- اَلْجَامِعَةُ الْكَبِيرَةُ <u>مَشْهُورٌ</u> .      اَلْجَامِعَةُ الْكَبِيرَةُ <u>مَشْهُورَةٌ</u> .

٢- الْمَسْجِدَانِ <u>الْجَدِيدَتَانِ</u> كَبِيرَانِ .

٣- اَلْكَافِرُونَ <u>خَاسِرَاتٌ</u> .

٤- رَجَعَ الْأُسْتَاذُ مِنَ <u>الْمَكْتَبَةِ</u> .

٥- فَتَحْتُ النَّافِذَةَ <u>الْوَاسِعَ</u> .

205

٦- أَكَلْتُ التُّفَّاحَةُ . .................
٧- تَعْمَلُ الْعَامِلُ فِي السُّوقِ . .................

**5. (Verb Conjugation: Past Tense to Present tense):** Change the underlined verbs from their past tense conjugations to their corresponding present tense conjugations; two are don for you as examples to follow:

١- دَخَلْتُ الْغُرْفَةَ .    أَدْخُلُ الْغُرْفَةَ .

٢- هَلْ ذَهَبْتَ إِلَى السُّوقِ ؟    هَلْ تَذْهَبُ إِلَى السُّوقِ ؟

٣- نَجَحْتَ فِي الْإِمْتِحَانِ . .................

٤- أَخَذَ الرِّسَالَةَ وَقَرَأَهَا . .................

٥- هَلْ عَرَفْتِ الْمُدِيرَ الْجَدِيدَ ؟ .................

٦- عَمِلَتْ فِي جَامِعَةٍ مَشْهُورَةٍ . .................

٧- مَا ذَكَرَ اسْمَ اللهِ . .................

٨- شَرِبْتُ الْحَلِيبَ وَالْعَصِيرَ . .................

**6. (General Drill):** Fill in the blanks in the following sentences by choosing the appropriate word from among those given in the shaded box:

أَعْرِفُ / دَفْتَرِهِ / مَقَالَةً / الْقُرْآنَ / فَهِمْتُ / أَمْ / أَشْكُرُ / الصَّغِيرَةُ / أَخْبَارًا / فِي / تَرْكَبُ / الطَّاوِلَةِ / هَلْ / يَعْمَلُ

١- كَتَبْتُ ............ فِي الْجَرِيدَةِ .   ٢- الرِّسَالَةُ عَلَى ............

٣- يَقْرَأُ ............ فِي الْمَسْجِدِ .   ٤- اَلْبِنْتُ ............ تَأْكُلُ تُفَّاحَةً .

206

٥- .......... الأُسْتَاذُ في مَكْتَبِهِ ؟    ٦- .......... الدَّرْسَ الصَّعْبَ .

٧- .......... اللهِ عَلَى نِعَمِهِ .    ٨- .......... العَامِلُ في الحَدِيقَةِ .

٩- كَتَبَ الوَاجِبَ في .......... .    ١٠- هَلْ أَنْتَ عَرَبِيٌّ .......... أَمْ أَمْرِيكِيٌّ ؟

١١- .......... دَرَّاجَتَهَا الجَدِيدَةَ .    ١٢- أَسْمَعُ .......... هَامَّةً .

١٣- يَلْعَبُ .......... المَلْعَبِ .    ١٤- لا .......... جَوَابَ السُّؤَالِ .

**7. (Prepositions: Meaning and Usage): Fill in the blanks in the following sentences with the appropriate preposition from among those given in the shaded column:**

١- يَذْهَبُ .......... المَدْرَسَةِ كُلَّ يَوْمٍ .

٢- العُصْفُورُ الصَّغِيرُ .......... الشَّجَرَةِ .

٣- .......... أَيْنَ أَنْتِ يَا سَيِّدَةُ ؟

٤- هَلِ الأُسْتَاذُ .......... مَكْتَبِهِ الجَدِيدِ ؟

٥- كَتَبْتُ الرِّسَالَةَ .......... قَلَمِ الرَّصَاصِ .

٦- السَّيَّارَةُ الجَدِيدَةُ .......... المُدِيرِ .

٧- تَحَدَّثَ المُعَلِّمُ .......... أَهَمِّيَّةِ عَمَلِ الوَاجِبِ .

٨- قَلْبُهُ .......... الصَّخْرِ في قَسْوَتِهِ .

| إِلَى |
| بِـ |
| عَلَى |
| عَنْ |
| فِي |
| كَـ |
| لِـ |

**8. (Unscrambling):** Unscramble the following sets of words to make from each a full meaningful sentence, and provide full vocalization:

١- مِنْ / وَ / الصَّيْف / التِّينُ / فَاكِهَة / الْعِنَبُ .

٢- وَ / الْقَمِيصُ / التَّنُّورَةُ / الْخِزَانَة / فِي .

٣- عَلَى / الطِّفْلَةُ / الْكُرْسِيِّ / تَجْلِسُ .

٤- الْمُخْلِصَاتُ / الْمَسْجِدَ / فِي / الْمُؤْمِنَاتُ / الْكَبِيرِ .

٥- الْمُخْتَبَرِ / مِنَ / الطَّالِبُ / قَادِمٌ / الْمُجْتَهِدُ .

٦- الْمُرَاسِلَتَانِ / تُونِسَ / مِنْ / الْأَجْنَبِيَّتَانِ .

٧- لله / خَيْرٍ / الْحَمْدُ / أَنَا / بِـ .

٨- عِنْدَكَ / عَرَبِيٌّ / هَلْ / قَامُوسٌ ؟

٩- لَا / فِي / الطَّالِبُ / يَفْشَلُ / الْإِمْتِحَانِ / الْمُجْتَهِدُ .

## 9. (Interrogative Particles: Meaning and Usage): Fill in the blanks in the following sentences with the appropriate preposition from among those given in the shaded column:

١- ............ حَالُكُمُ الْيَوْمَ ؟
٢- ............ إِلى أَنْتَ ذَاهِبٌ الآنَ ؟
٣- ............ سَمِعْتَ الأَخْبَارَ الْهَامَّةَ ؟
٤- ............ هَذَا الْكِتَابُ الْجَدِيدُ ؟
٥- ............ هَذِه السَّيِّدَةُ الطَّوِيلَةُ ؟
٦- ............ أَنْتَ حَزِينَةٌ يَا أُخْتِي ؟
٧- ............ تَفْعَلُ يَوْمَ الْجُمُعَةِ يَا آدَمُ ؟
٨- ............ مِنْ الطَّائِرَةُ قَادِمَةٌ ؟
٩- ............ قَلَمُكَ أَمْ قَلَمُ الأُسْتَاذِ ؟
١٠- ............ سَافَرْتَ إِلى جَنُوبِ إِفريقْيَا ؟
١١- ............ يَوْمُ امْتِحَانِ اللُّغَةِ الْعَرَبِيَّةِ ؟

| أَ / هَلْ |
| أَيُّ / أَيْنَ |
| كَمْ / كَيْفَ |
| مَتَى / لِمَاذَا |
| مَا / مَاذَا |
| مَنْ |

## 10. (Translation / General): Translate the following English sentences into Arabic and provide full vocalization:

1. This is a new car and that is an old car.    ............................................. .

2. Where is your pen?    ............................................. ؟

3. He is returning from the restaurant.    ............................................. .

4. The boy's bag is on the desk.    ............................................. .

5. The two pupils are absent.    ............................................. .

6. What is the name of the new director?    ............................................. ؟

7. Is she a teacher or a student?    ............................................. ؟

## Section 2

**1. (Plurals):** Give the plurals of the underlined words, and make sure to make any other necessary changes; one is done for you as an example:

١- الطَّبَّاخَةُ الْمَاهِرَةُ فِي الْمَطْبَخِ .        الطَّبَّاخَاتُ الْمَاهِرَاتُ فِي الْمَطْبَخِ .

٢- الْعَامِلُ النَّشِيطُ فِي الْمَصْنَعِ .        ..................................... .

٣- الْمُعَلِّمُ وَالطَّالِبُ صَدِيقَانِ .        ..................................... .

٤- يَقْرَأُ الْمُؤْمِنُ كِتَابَ اللهِ .        ..................................... .

٥- هَلِ الْأُسْتَاذَةُ الْجَدِيدَةُ فِي الْمَعْهَدِ ؟        ..................................... ؟

٦- أَيْنَ الْمُهَنْدِسَةُ الْمَشْهُورَةُ ؟        ..................................... ؟

٧- هُوَ مُدِيرٌ مُمْتَازٌ .        ..................................... .

**2. (General Drill):** Answer the following questions orally in class, and then answer them in writing as a homework assignment:

١- كَيْفَ حَالُكَ ؟        ٢- مَا هَذَا الْكِتَابُ ؟

٣- مِنْ أَيْنَ الطَّائِرَةُ قَادِمَةٌ ؟        ٤- أَيْنَ قَلَمُكَ وَدَفْتَرُكَ ؟

٥- هَلْ عِنْدَكَ سَيَّارَةٌ أَمْ دَرَّاجَةٌ ؟        ٦- مَاذَا تَقْرَأُ الْآنَ ؟

٧- مَنْ هَذَا الرَّجُلُ ؟        ٨- مَتَى تُسَافِرِينَ إِلَى بَلَدِكِ ؟

٩- مَاذَا تُحِبُّ أَنْ تَشْرَبَ ؟        ١٠- هَلْ أَنْتَ عَرَبِيٌّ ؟

**3. (Antonyms – Words Meanings):** Give the words that have opposite meanings to those underlined in the following sentences:

١- اَلْعَامِلُ النَّشِيطُ حَاضِرٌ . ................

٢- اَلْمُؤْمِنُ حَزِينٌ . ................

٣- هَذَا الشَّارِعُ طَوِيلٌ . ................

٤- هَلِ الدَّرْسُ صَعْبٌ ؟ ................

٥- لِمَاذَا أَنْتَ كَسُولٌ ؟ ................

٦- هَذِهِ الْمَرْأَةُ حَزِينَةٌ . ................

٧- أَيْنَ الثَّوْبُ النَّظِيفُ ؟ ................

٨- هَذِهِ مَكْتَبَةٌ جَدِيدَةٌ . ................

٩- هَلِ الْبَابُ مَفْتُوحٌ ؟ ................

١٠- هَذَا بَيْتٌ صَغِيرٌ . ................

**4. (Particles: Meaning and Usage):** Provide the appropriate missing particle to fill in the space in each sentence:

١- هَلْ شَرِبْتَ شَايًا ........ قَهْوَةً ؟  ٢- ........ الطَّائِرَةُ الآنَ ؟

٣- إِلَى ........ أَنْتِ ذَاهِبَةٌ ؟  ٤- ........ صِحَّتِي يَا طَبِيبُ ؟

٥- قَرَأْتُ الْكِتَابَ ........ الْمَقَالَةَ .  ٦- ........ أَخَذَ الْقَامُوسَ مِنْ هُنَا ؟

٧- ........ اسْمُ الْأُسْتَاذَةِ الْجَدِيدَةِ ؟  ٨- اِلْعَبْ ........ الْمَلْعَبِ ........ الْحَدِيقَةِ !

٩- ........ يَبْدَأُ دَرْسُ اللُّغَةِ الْعَرَبِيَّةِ ؟  ١٠- ........ أَيْنَ أَنْتِ يَا سَيِّدَتِي ؟

211

5. (Person-Place Link): Link the person with the place where he or she is likely to be found or to work; the places are given in the shaded box:

اَلسُّوقِ / اَلْمَصْنَعِ / اَلْعِيَادَةِ / اَلْمَطْبَخِ / اَلْمَكْتَبَةِ / اَلْمَدْرَسَةِ / اَلْمَسْجِدِ / اَلْجَامِعَةِ / اَلْبَيْتِ / اَلْمَكْتَبِ

١- اَلْمُدَرِّسَةُ فِي ................. .   ٢- اَلتَّاجِرُ فِي ................. .

٣- اَلْأُسْتَاذُ فِي ................. .   ٤- اَلطَّبَّاخَةُ فِي ................. .

٥- اَلْعَامِلُ فِي ................. .   ٦- اَلْمُسْلِمُ فِي ................. .

٧- اَلْكَاتِبُ فِي ................. .   ٨- اَلطَّبِيبَةُ فِي ................. .

٩- اَلطِّفْلُ فِي ................. .   ١٠- اَلْمُدِيرُ فِي ................. .

6. (Dual): Change the following sentences into dual, following the given example:

اَلْبَابُ الصَّغِيرُ مَفْتُوحٌ .      اَلْبَابَانِ الصَّغِيرَانِ مَفْتُوحَانِ .

١- اَلْعَامِلَةُ نَشِيطَةٌ .

٢- اَلْبَيْتُ الْكَبِيرُ مُغْلَقٌ .

٣- اَلْفَلَّاحُ فَقِيرٌ .

٤- اَلْمُهَنْدِسُ مَوْجُودٌ فِي الشَّرِكَةِ .

٥- اَلْبِنْتُ ذَاهِبَةٌ إِلَى السُّوقِ .

٦- اَلزَّائِرُ الْعَرَبِيُّ فِي الْفُنْدُقِ .

٧- اَلْكِتَابُ الْجَدِيدُ مُمْتَازٌ .

\* \* \*

**7. (Verbs: Present Tense to Past Tense):** Change the underlined present tense verbs to their corresponding past tense, keeping the same person, as in the given example:

| | |
|---|---|
| دَرَسْتُ كِتَابَ اللهِ . | أَدْرُسُ كِتَابَ اللهِ . |

١- هَلْ تَذْهَبُ إلَى النَّادِي ؟ ................................ ؟

٢- يَشْرَحُ الْمُدَرِّسُ الدَّرْسَ . ................................ .

٣- هَلْ تَعْمَلِينَ في هَذِهِ الشَّرِكَةِ ؟ ................................ ؟

٤- أَشْرَبُ فِنْجَانَ الْقَهْوَةِ . ................................ .

٥- لَا أَسْمَعُ صَوْتَ الطَّائِرَةِ . ................................ .

٦- آكُلُ الْخُبْزَ وَالْجُبْنَةَ . ................................ .

٧- هَلْ تَفْهَمِينَ الدَّرْسَ ؟ ................................ ؟

٨- أَنْتَ تَشْكُرُ اللهَ عَلَى نِعَمِهِ . ................................ .

٩- هِيَ تَحْمِلُ طِفْلَهَا عَلَى ظَهْرِهَا . ................................ .

**8. (General):** Choose the correct word from those in brackets to fit in with the rest of the sentence:

١- الْفَلَّاحُونَ (النَّشِيطَانِ / النَّشِيطُونَ) مُحْتَرَمُونَ .

٢- دَخَلْتُ (الشَّرِكَةَ / الشَّرِكَةُ) مِنَ الْبَابِ الْخَلْفِيِّ .

٣- الأُسْتَاذَانِ الزَّائِرَانِ (أَمْرِيكِيُّونَ / أَمْرِيكِيَّانِ) .

٤- (يَأْكُلُ / يَرْكَبُ) السَّيَّارَةَ إِلَى الْعَمَلِ .

٥- (كَيْفَ / هَلْ) حَالُكَ الْيَوْمَ ؟

٦- هَذِهِ أَخْبَارٌ (طَيِّبٌ / طَيِّبَةٌ) .

٧- (أَنَا / أَنْتِ) ذَاهِبٌ إِلَى السُّوقِ .

٨- يَعْمَلُ الطَّبِيبُ في (الْمَطْعَمِ / الْمُسْتَشْفى) .

٩- (كَمْ / مَتَى) مَوْعِدُ وُصُولِ الطَّائِرَةِ ؟

١٠- هَلْ (أَنْتَ / أَنْتُمْ) مِصْرِيُّونَ (وَ / أَمْ) سُودَانِيُّونَ ؟

9. (Translation / General): Translate the following sentences into English verbally:

١- سَافَرْتُ بِالطَّائِرَةِ وَرَجَعْتُ بِالسَّفِينَةِ .

٢- أَذْهَبُ إِلَى الْحَدِيقَةِ الْعَامَّةِ كُلَّ أُسْبُوعٍ .

٣- لَا أَعْرِفُ جَوَابَ هَذَا السُّؤَالِ .

٤- مَا دَرَسَتِ الْبِنْتُ دَرْسَ اللُّغَةِ الْعَرَبِيَّةِ .

٥- مَنْ هَذِهِ السَّيِّدَةُ الطَّوِيلَةُ ؟

٦- اَلْبَابُ مُغْلَقٌ وَالنَّافِذَةُ مَفْتُوحَةٌ .

٧- مَاذَا تَفْعَلُ يَوْمَ الْجُمُعَةِ يَا آدَمُ ؟

٨- أَكْتُبُ رِسَالَةً إِلَى صَدِيقِي الأَمْرِيكِيِّ .

٩- دَرَسَ التِّلْمِيذُ دُرُوسَهُ أَوَّلاً ثُمَّ لَعِبَ فِي الْحَدِيقَةِ .

١٠- اُدْرُسْ وَقْتَ الدَّرْسِ وَالْعَبْ وَقْتَ اللَّعِبِ !

**10. (Translation / General): Translate the following English sentences into Arabic and provide full vocalization (orally and in writing):**

1. The tall man is my friend.    . ......................................................

2. I wrote a letter to my dear mother.    . ......................................................

3. This street is wide and clean.    . ......................................................

4. The boy's pen is on the desk.    . ......................................................

5. He is a very famous calligrapher.    . ......................................................

6. Those are sincere teachers.    . ......................................................

7. Are you (two) new employees?    ؟ ......................................................

8. She is my dear friend.    . ......................................................

9. The little boy is playing in the playground.    . ......................................................

10. Is this your brother or friend?    ؟ ......................................................

**Section 3**

1. (Verb Conjugation and Context Usage): Fill in the blanks in the following with an appropriate verb:

١- (هُوَ) ................ الْمَقالَةَ في الْجَريدَةِ .

٢- (أَنا) ................ الْخُبْزَ في الْمَطْعَمِ .

٣- هَلْ (أَنْتَ) ................ في هَذا الْمَصْنَعِ ؟

٤- (هِيَ) ................ فِنْجانَ الْقَهْوَةِ في الْغُرْفَةِ .

٥- أَنا ................ الْجَريدَةَ وَأَنْتَ ................ الْمَجَلَّةَ .

٦- هَلْ (أَنْتِ) ................ كَيْفَ ................ الْحِصانَ ؟

٧- هَلْ (أَنْتَ) ................ في هَذِهِ الْجامِعَةِ ؟

٨- (أَنا) ................ الأَخْبارَ في التِّلفزيون .

٩- أَيْنَ (هِيَ) ................ ؟ في الْمَكْتَبَةِ أَمْ في الْفَصْلِ ؟

١٠- ................ الطّالِبَةُ في الإمْتِحانِ .

2. (Words Classification): Circle the odd word in each group:

١- السَّفينَةُ – السَّيّارَةُ – الْحافِلَةُ – الْحِمارُ

٢- الْبُرْتُقالَةُ – التُّفّاحَةُ – الْقَهْوَةُ – الْمَوْزَةُ

٣- لَيْلَةٌ – يَوْمٌ – عامٌ – شَهْرٌ – غُرْفَةٌ

٤- الْقَلَمُ – الدَّفْتَرُ – الْمِلْعَقَةُ – الْكِتابُ

٥- كَاتِبٌ – نَجَّارٌ – صِحَافِيٌّ – مُؤَلِّفٌ

٦- الْبَيْتُ – الصَّحْنُ – الْفِنْجَانُ – الإِبْرِيقُ

٧- غُرْفَةٌ – حَمَّامٌ – شَرِكَةٌ – مَطْبَخٌ

٨- قَمِيصٌ – فُسْتَانٌ – ثَوْبٌ – حِمَارٌ

٩- مَعْهَدٌ – جَامِعَةٌ – حُجْرَةٌ – مَدْرَسَةٌ

١٠- كُرْسِيٌّ – طَاوِلَةٌ – بِطِّيخٌ – سَرِيرٌ – خِزَانَةٌ

3. (Forming Questions): Form questions for which the following statements can serve as answers:

١- أَنَا بِخَيْرٍ، الْحَمْدُ لِلَّهِ .

٢- نَعَمْ، هِيَ ذَاهِبَةٌ إِلَى الْمَغْرِبِ .

٣- لَا، اسْمُهَا حَلِيمَةُ .

٤- تَشْرَبُ اللَّبَنَ الْبَارِدَ .

٥- أَنَا قَادِمَةٌ مِنْ لَنْدُنَ .

٦- فِي الإِبْرِيقِ الْكَبِيرِ شَايٌ .

٧- هَذَا مُوَظَّفٌ جَدِيدٌ .

٨- الْمِسْطَرَةُ وَالْمِمْسَحَةُ فِي الدُّرْجِ .

٩- الدَّرْسُ سَهْلٌ .

١٠- هَذِهِ حَدِيقَةُ الْحَيَوَانَاتِ .

4. (Unscramble to Form Meaningful Sentences): Rearrange the following sets of words to make from each a full meaningful sentence:

١- الْغُرْفَة / فِي / هَلْ / سَرِيرٌ ؟
....................................................

٢- مِنَ / الْمُسَافِرُ / يَرْجِعُ / الْيَوْمَ / الْعِرَاقِ
....................................................

٣- جَامِعَة / الطَّالِبُ / الْقَاهِرَة / يَذْهَبُ / إِلَى
....................................................

٤- مِنَ / الْقَلَم / وَ / أَخَذْتُ / الدَّفْتَر / الْحَقِيبَة
....................................................

217

٥- الْمُعَلِّمَةُ / الصَّعْبَ / الدَّرْسَ / شَرَحَت ................................

٦- الْمُؤَلِّفُ / الْقِصَّةَ / في / يَكْتُبُ / الْبَيْت ................................

٧- الْفُنْدُقِ / كَثِيرُونَ / في / زَائِرُونَ ................................

٨- الْغَنِيَّانِ / إلى / التَّاجِرَانِ / ذَهَبَ / السُّوقِ . ................................

5. (Questions & Short Answers): Give a short answer to each question below by using the most appropriate from the words or phrases in the shaded box below:

> الْمُمَرِّضُ / في الْمَطْعَم / في الْفُرْن / الْمُؤَلِّف / في جَنُوبَ إفريقْيَا / الْخَادِمُ / في الْجَامِعَة / في الثَّلَّاجَةِ / صِحَافِيٌّ / السَّائِقُ

١- مَنْ يَعْمَلُ في الْبَيْتِ ؟  ٢- أَيْنَ تَأْكُلُ الطَّعَامَ ؟

٣- أَيْنَ الْخُبْزُ ؟  ٤- مَنْ يَكْتُبُ في الْجَرِيدَة ؟

٥- مَنْ يَعْمَلُ في الْعِيَادَةِ ؟  ٦- أَيْنَ يَدْرُسُ الطَّالِبُ ؟

٧- أَيْنَ اللَّبَنُ ؟  ٨- مَنْ يَرْكَبُ السَّيَّارَةَ ؟

٩- مَنْ يَكْتُبُ الْكِتَابَ ؟  ١٠- أَيْنَ مَدِينَةُ كِيب تاوْن ؟

6. (Linking Grammatical Terms with Specific Words): Link up the appropriate grammatical terms from those in the shaded box with the underlined words in the following sentences:

أَدَاةُ الْإِسْتِفْهَامِ / الْمُثَنَّى / الْفِعْلُ الْمَاضِي / الْمُبْتَدَأُ / الْخَبَرُ / حَرْفُ الْجَرِّ / حَرْفُ الْعَطْفِ / جَمْعُ الْمُذَكَّرِ السَّالِمُ / فَاعِلُ الْفِعْلِ / الْفِعْلُ الْمُضَارِعُ / الْمَفْعُولُ بِهِ / الْإِضَافَةُ

١- الرَّجُلُ الْغَنِيُّ بَخِيلٌ .  
٢- الْخَارِطَةُ عَلَى الْحَائِطِ .  
٣- قَرَأَتْ زَيْنَبُ الْمَسْرَحِيَّةَ .  
٤- الْمَلْعَبَانِ كَبِيرَانِ .  
٥- يَدْرُسُ الطَّالِبُ اللُّغَةَ الْعَرَبِيَّةَ .  
٦- يَفْتَحُ بَابَ الْبَيْتِ .  
٧- هَلِ الْمَرْأَةُ فِي الدُّكَّانِ ؟  
٨- دَخَلَ الْغُرْفَةَ ثُمَّ نَامَ .  
٩- أَمَرَ الْأُسْتَاذُ الطَّالِبَ بِالْخُرُوجِ .  
١٠- الْمُعَلِّمُونَ الْمُمْتَازُونَ فِي الْمَكْتَبِ .

7. (Antonyms): Fill in the blanks by using the antonyms of the underlined words:

١- هَلْ هُوَ نَظِيفٌ أَمْ ................... ؟

٢- الدُّكَّانُ الصَّغِيرُ فِي الْقَرْيَةِ وَالسُّوقُ ................... فِي الْمَدِينَةِ .

٣- الْمَدْرَسَةُ مُغْلَقَةٌ وَالْجَامِعَةُ ................... .

٤- هَذِهِ الْمَرْأَةُ الطَّوِيلَةُ زَوْجَةُ هَذَا الرَّجُلِ ................... .

٥- يَنْجَحُ الطَّالِبُ النَّشِيطُ وَلَا يَنْجَحُ الطَّالِبُ ................... .

٦- يَذْهَبُ إِلَى الْمَدْرَسَةِ صَبَاحًا وَ ................... مِنْهَا .

٧- الْمَرْأَةُ كَرِيمَةٌ لَكِنْ زَوْجُهَا ................... .

219

٨- الأُمُّ حَزِينَةٌ فِي الْبَيْتِ وَالأَبُ ................. فِي الْبُسْتَانِ .

٩- أَخَذَ الْوَلَدُ الْفَقِيرُ قَمِيصًا مِنَ الْوَلَدِ ................. .

١٠- الْمُؤْمِنُ يَعْمَلُ مَعَ ................. فِي نَفْسِ الشَّرِكَةِ .

8. (Singular, Dual & Plural): Fill in the blank cells with the appropriate form of the singular, dual or plural of the given nouns:

| Plural / جَمْعٌ | Dual / مُثَنَّى | Singular / مُفْرَدٌ |
|---|---|---|
|  |  | بِنْتٌ |
|  | مُدَرِّسَانِ |  |
| مُخْلِصَاتٌ |  |  |
|  |  | مُهَنْدِسٌ |
|  | مَدْرَسَتَانِ |  |
| مُسْلِمُونَ |  |  |
|  |  | مُوَظَّفٌ |

9. (Verb Conjugations): Fill in the blank cells with the appropriate conjugation of the past tense, present tense or imperative (command):

| Imperative / الأَمْرُ | Present / الْمُضَارِعُ | Past / الْمَاضِي |
|---|---|---|
|  |  | سَكَنْتَ |
|  | تَكْتُبِينَ |  |
| اِجْلِسْ |  |  |
|  | تَفْهَمُ |  |
|  |  | ذَهَبْتُ |
|  | تَسْمَعُ |  |

220

10. (Translation): Translate the following sentences into English:

١- الرَّجُلُ والْمَرْأَةُ رَاجِعَانِ مِنَ الْمَحْكَمَةِ .

٢- مَا اسْمُكَ ؟ اسْمِي آدَمُ .

٣- هَذَا بُسْتَانٌ كَبِيرٌ وَجَمِيلٌ .

٤- إِلَى أَيْنَ أَنْتِ ذَاهِبَةٌ يَا أُمِّي ؟

٥- مَنِ الطَّالِبُ الْجَدِيدُ فِي الصَّفِّ ؟

٦- الْمُهَاجِرُونَ الصَّالِحُونَ فِي بَيْتِ اللهِ .

٧- فِي مَطْبَخِهَا ثَلَّاجَةٌ جَدِيدَةٌ وَفُرْنٌ قَدِيمٌ .

٨- يَنْجَحُ التِّلْمِيذُ الْمُجْتَهِدُ فِي الْإِمْتِحَانِ .

٩- يَقْرَأُ الطُّلَّابُ الْمَسْرَحِيَّةَ فِي مَكْتَبَةِ الْجَامِعَةِ .

١٠- سَمِعْتُ صَوْتَ الْجَرَسِ ، فَدَخَلْتُ الصَّفَّ مُسْرِعًا .

11. (Translation): Translate the following sentences into Arabic:

1. The pen of the (female) teacher is on the desk.
2. How are the two hardworking farmers?
3. The new (female) nurses are excellent.
4. The students asked me a difficult question.
5. Is she wearing a clean dress or a dirty one?
6. Yes, I went to the city market and bought some fruits.
7. No, that is the new university; the old university is far away from here.
8. Those farmers live in a small village.
9. Where is the bathroom?
10. She remembers her mother always.

## Section 4

1. (Verb Conjugations): Conjugate the stem of the verb given in brackets at the end of the sentence to correspond to its subject; follow the given example:

أَنَا ............ مَقَالَةً فِي الْمَجَلَّةِ . ( كَتَبْ )
↑
كَتَبْتُ

١- أَنْتَ ............ نَصَّ الدَّرْسِ . (فْهَم)

٢- هِيَ ............ فِي الْحَدِيقَةِ . (جَلَس)

٣- أَنْتِ ............ فِي امْتِحَانِ الْجَامِعَةِ . (نْجَح)

٤- أَنَا ............ كِتَابَ اللهِ . (قَرَأ)

٥- هُوَ ............ فِي دِينِ اللهِ . (دْخُل)

٦- هِيَ ............ صَوْتَ الْحِصَانِ . (سَمِع)

٧- أَنَا ............ إِلَى الشَّرْقِ الْأَوْسَطِ . (ذَهَب)

٨- هَلْ أَنْتَ ............ إِلَى بَلَدِكَ بَعْدَ الدِّرَاسَةِ ؟ (رَجَع)

٩- هُوَ لاَ ............ اسْمَ اللهِ . (ذْكُر)

١٠- هَلْ (أَنْتِ) ............ فِي هَذِهِ الْجَامِعَةِ ؟ (دْرُس)

2. (Choosing Words to Suit Contexts): Choose the correct word from those given in parenthesis to fit the context:

١- (كَيْفَ / مَنْ) صِحَّةُ الْوَالِدَةِ الْمَرِيضَةِ ؟

٢- مَنْ (هَذَا / هَذِهِ) الْمُوَظَّفُ الْمُخْلِصُ ؟

٣- أَخَذْتُ الْخُبْزَ (أَمْ / وَ) عَصِيرَ الْبُرْتُقَالِ .

٤- الصُّنْدُوقُ الثَّقِيلُ (مَفْتُوحٌ / مَفْتُوحًا) .

٥- يَشْرَحُ الْأُسْتَاذُ (الدَّرْسُ / الدَّرْسَ) .

٦- (هَلْ / أَيْنَ) خَرِيطَةُ آسْيَا ؟

٧- مِنْ (أَيْنَ / مَا) الطَّائِرَةُ قَادِمَةٌ ؟

٨- هَلْ (عِنْدَكَ / عِنْدِي) طَعَامٌ ؟

٩- أَعْرِفُ (هَذَا / هَذِهِ) الطَّالِبَةَ الْجَدِيدَةَ .

١٠- هَلْ أَنْتِ (قَادِمَةٌ / ذَاهِبَةٌ) مِنْ أَمْرِيكَا ؟

3. (Choosing the Appropriate Interrogative Particle): Choose the correct interrogative particle from those in the shaded box to fill in each blank:

١- ............... مِهْنَةُ وَالِدِكَ ؟

٢- ............... هُوَ فِي مَكْتَبِهِ ؟

٣- ............... أَنْتَ يَا وَلَدُ ؟

٤- إِلَى ............... أَنْتَ ذَاهِبٌ ؟

٥- مِنْ ............... هِيَ قَادِمَةٌ ؟

٦- ............... حَالُ وَالِدِكَ يَا آدَمُ ؟

| |
|---|
| أَيْنَ |
| كَيْفَ |
| هَلْ |
| مَتَى |
| لِمَاذَا |
| مَا |
| مَنْ |

٧– .............. مَوْعِدُ امْتِحَانِ اللُّغَةِ الْعَرَبِيَّةِ ؟

٨– .............. تَذْهَبُ إِلَى السُّوقِ ؟

4. (Choosing the Appropriate Preposition): Choose the correct preposition from those in the shaded box to fill in each blank:

١– الْمِلْعَقَةُ .............. الدُّرْجِ .

٢– رَجَعَ الطَّبِيبُ .............. الْعِيَادَةِ .

٣– الْحَقِيبَةُ .............. الْمَكْتَبِ ؟

٤– .............. أَيْنَ الْأُسْتَاذُ ذَاهِبٌ ؟

٥– .............. أَيْنَ هِيَ قَادِمَةٌ ؟

٦– قَطَعْتُ الْخَشَبَ .............. الْمِنْشَارِ .

٧– هَذِهِ السَّيَّارَةُ .............. مُدِيرِ الْمَدْرَسَةِ .

٨– يَجْلِسُ .............. الْكُرْسِيِّ .

٩– أَخَذْتُ اللَّبَنَ .............. الثَّلَّاجَةِ .

إِلَى / عَلَى / فِي / مِنْ / لِـ / بِـ

* * *

5. (Antonyms): Give the opposite of the underlined word:

١– يَلْعَبُ الْوَلَدُ الصَّغِيرُ فِي الْحَدِيقَةِ .    ٢– الْمُعَلِّمُونَ الْحَاضِرُونَ مَشْهُورُونَ .

٣– الطَّاوِلَةُ الْكَبِيرَةُ فِي الْحَدِيقَةِ .    ٤– الشَّارِعُ ضَيِّقٌ وَقَذِرٌ .

٥– الْبَيْتُ الْجَدِيدُ صَغِيرٌ .    ٦– هُوَ رَجُلٌ فَقِيرٌ لَكِنَّهُ مُتَعَلِّمٌ .

* * *

## 6. (Synonyms): Give the synonymous of the underlined words:

١- طَاوِلَةُ الطَّعَامِ كَبِيرَةٌ .
٢- شَكَرَ التِّلْمِيذُ الْمُدَرِّسَةَ .
٣- فَتَحْتُ شُبَّاكَ الدَّارِ .
٤- هَذَا غُلَامٌ مُهَذَّبٌ .
٥- هَذِهِ حُجْرَةٌ وَاسِعَةٌ .
٦- هُوَ وَالِدٌ كَرِيمٌ .
٧- هِيَ أُمٌّ رَحِيمَةٌ .
٨- اُكْتُبْ فِي كُرَّاسَتِكَ .

* * *

## 7. (Mistake Identification & Correction): Identify the mistake in each of the following sentences, and then correct it:

١- خَرَجَ الْمَرْأَةُ مِنَ الدُّكَّانِ .
٢- الْمُسْلِمُونَ الصَّالِحَانِ فِي الْمَسْجِدِ .
٣- أَسْمَعُ الصَّوْتَ الْحِمَارِ .
٤- هَلِ الطِّفْلَةُ جَمِيلَةٌ وَقَبِيحَةٌ ؟
٥- هُوَ مُتَرْجِمَةٌ مَشْهُورَةٌ .
٦- اجْلِسْ يَا فَاطِمَةَ عَلَى الْكُرْسِيِّ .
٧- مَنْ هَذَا ؟ هَذَا كِتَابٌ .
٨- يَفْهَمُ الدَّرْسَ الصَّعْبَةَ .
٩- فِي الْخِزَانَةُ فُسْتَانٌ وَقَمِيصًا .
١٠- أَخَذَ الْجَرِيدَةَ عَلَى الْمَكْتَبَةِ .

* * *

## 8. (Vocalization): Fully vocalize the following sentences, and then read them with their full vocalization:

١- يعرف الولد ابن المدير .
٢- خرجت من الصف قبل قليل .
٣- من هذا الرجل الطويل ؟
٤- فتحت المعلمة باب الصف .
٥- أعمل في مكتبة الجامعة .
٦- هل تفهمين الدرس جيدا ؟
٧- يسكن الفلاح في قرية صغيرة .
٨- كيف صحة الطفل ؟ هل هو بخير ؟

٩- يكتب الكاتب قصة جديدة . ١٠- هل عندك ورقة وقلم ؟

* * *

9. (Unscramble): Unscramble the following sets of words to make from each a full meaningful sentence; use your notebook to write the final sentence:

١- أَيْنَ / جَاءَ / الصَّحافِيُّ / مِنْ / الزَّائِرُ ؟

٢- السَّبُورَةِ / الدَّرْسَ / تَكْتُبُ / عَلَى .

٣- التَّاجِرَانِ / السُّوقِ / هَلِ / الْمَشْهُورَانِ / فِي ؟

٤- اللهِ / فِي / يَتْلُونَ / الْمَسْجِدِ / كِتَابَ .

٥- حَالُ / الْمَرِيضَةِ / كَيْفَ / السَّيِّدَةِ ؟

٦- وَأَلْعَبُ / أَدْرُسُ / وَقْتَ / اللَّعِبِ / الدَّرْسِ / وَقْتَ .

10. (Translation): Translate the following Arabic sentences into English:

١- الْفُسْتَانُ وَالْقَمِيصُ فِي دُرْجِ الْخِزَانَةِ الْجَدِيدَةِ .

٢- أَشْكُرُ مُدِيرَ مَعْهَدِ اللُّغَةِ الْعَرَبِيَّةِ .

٣- سَمِعْتُ صَوْتَ الْمُدِيرِ فِي مَكْتَبِ الْمُدَرِّسِينَ .

٤- شَرَحَ الْأُسْتَاذُ الْجَدِيدُ الدَّرْسَ الصَّعْبَ عَلَى السَّبُورَةِ .

٥- اِلْعَبْ فِي الْمَلْعَبِ ، وَلَا تَلْعَبْ فِي الشَّارِعِ !

٦- هَلْ بَابُ الْمَكْتَبَةِ مَفْتُوحٌ أَمْ مُغْلَقٌ ؟

٧- نَعَمْ ، سَافَرْتُ إِلَى مِصْرَ وَالسُّودَانِ وَالْمَغْرِبِ وَلِيبِيَا .

٨- هَلْ سَتُسَافِرِينَ بِالطَّائِرَةِ أَوِ السَّيَّارَةِ ؟

٩- سَاعِدِي الْفُقَرَاءَ وَالْمُحْتَاجِينَ !

١٠- أَيْنَ دَرَّاجَتُكِ الْجَدِيدَةُ يَا نُورَا ؟

\* \* \*

11. (Translation): Translate the following English sentences into Arabic:

1.       I entered the classroom after the teacher.

2.       The small boy ate the big apple.

3.       Your old red pen is on the teacher's desk.

4.       Who are you my lady, and where are you from?

5.       Do you know the name of the new professor?

6.       The girl is playing in the garden.

7.       Are the sincere believers in the mosque?

8.       The small village is near by the large city.

9.       Are you going to the airport today?

10.      Where are your pen and your ruler?

\* \* \*

## Section 5

1. (Changing from Singular to Dual): Change the following sentences from singular to dual:

١- الطِّفْلَةُ جَمِيلَةٌ . ..............................

٢- الدَّرْسُ سَهْلٌ . ..............................

٣- هَلِ الْعَامِلَةُ مُخْلِصَةٌ ؟ ..............................  ؟

٤- سَلَّمْتُ عَلَى الْمُعَلِّمِ الْجَدِيدِ . ..............................

٥- هُوَ لاَعِبٌ مَشْهُورٌ . ..............................

\* \* \*

2. (Changing from Singular to Masculine Sound Plural): Change the following sentences from singular to masculine sound plural:

١- الْمُؤْمِنُ مَحْبُوبٌ مِنَ اللهِ . ..............................

٢- الْمُعَلِّمُ مُخْلِصٌ . ..............................

٣- الْمُجْتَهِدُ نَاجِحٌ ؟ ..............................

٤- الْمُسَافِرُ رَاجِعٌ الْيَوْمَ . ..............................

٥- الصَّحَافِيُّ مَشْهُورٌ . ..............................

\* \* \*

228

3. (Changing from Singular to Feminine Sound Plural): Change the following sentences from singular to feminine sound plural:

١- الطَّالِبَةُ جَدِيدَةٌ . ..............................................

٢- الطَّبِيبَةُ عَرَبِيَّةٌ . ..............................................

٣- الْمُجْتَهِدَةُ نَاجِحَةٌ . ..............................................

٤- سَلَّمْتُ عَلَى الأُسْتَاذَةِ الزَّائِرَةِ . ..............................................

٥- الْعَامِلَةُ مُخْلِصَةٌ . ..............................................

\* \* \*

4. (Past Tense Verb Conjugation): Give the correct conjugation of the past tense verb whose stem is given in parenthesis at the end of the sentence:

١- هُوَ ............... الدَّرْسَ الْجَدِيدَ . (دَرَس)

٢- أَنَا ............... السُّؤَالَ جَيِّدًا . (فَهِم)

٣- هِيَ ............... فِي الإِمْتِحَانِ . (نَجَح)

٤- أَنْتَ ............... الْقُرْآنَ قِرَاءَةً جَمِيلَةً . (قَرَأ)

٥- أَنْتِ ............... إِلَى الْمَدْرَسَةِ مُبَكِّرَةً . (ذَهَب)

\* \* \*

5. (Present Tense Verb Conjugation): Give the correct conjugation of the present tense verb whose stem is given in parenthesis at the end of the sentence:

١- أَنَا ............... الأَخْبَارَ كُلَّ يَوْمٍ . (سَمِع)

٢- هُوَ لا ............... السُّؤَالَ جَيِّدًا . (فَهِم)

٣- هِيَ لا ............... الْقَهْوَةَ . (شَرِب)

229

٤- أَنْتَ ............... كُرَةَ الْقَدَمِ جَيِّدًا . (لَعِب)

٥- أَنْتِ ............... رُسُومًا جَمِيلَةً . (رَسْم)

* * *

6. (Imperative (Command) Conjugations): Select the appropriate conjugation from among those given in the shaded box to fill in the spaces of the following sentences:

| |
|---|
| اشْرَبُوا |
| أُخْرُجَا |
| اُكْتُبِي |
| اِلْعَبَنَ |
| اِسْمَعْ |

١- ............... دَرْسَكِ يَا مَرْيَمُ !

٢- ............... كَلَامَ الْأُسْتَاذِ يَا سَمِيرُ !

٣- ............... الْحَلِيبَ يَا تَلَامِيذِي كُلَّ يَوْمٍ !

٤- ............... فِي الْمَلْعَبِ يَا بَنَاتُ !

٥- ............... مِنَ الصَّفِّ يَا مُشَاغِبَانِ !

* * *

7. (Using Prepositions / حُرُوفُ الْجَرِّ): Fill in the blanks with appropriate prepositions:

١- ............... أَيْنَ أَنْتِ مُسَافِرَةٌ ؟

٢- الْمُدِيرُ مَوْجُودٌ ............... الشَّرِكَةِ .

٣- الْمِلْعَقَةُ وَفِنْجَانُ الْقَهْوَةِ ............... الطَّاوِلَةِ .

٤- أَخَذَ الْوَلَدُ قَمِيصًا ............... الْخِزَانَةِ .

٥- هَلْ هُوَ ............... خَيْرٍ ؟

* * *

230

8. (Using Interrogative Particles / أَدَوَاتُ الإسْتِفْهَامِ): Fill in the blanks with appropriate interrogative particles:

١- ................ اسْمُ هَذَا الوَلَدِ الصَّغِيرِ ؟

٢- مِنْ ................ هَذِهِ الزَّائِرَةُ ؟

٣- ................ أَبُوكَ وَ ................ أُمُّكَ ؟

٤- ................ هِيَ خَبَّازَةٌ أَمْ طَبَّاخَةٌ ؟

٥- ................ مَوْعِدُ وُصُولِ الطَّائِرَةِ ؟

\* \* \*

9. (Mistake Identification & Correction): Identify the mistake in each of the following sentences, and then correct it:

١- ذَهَبَةْ مَرْيَمُ إِلَى الْمَعْهَدِ .     ٢- الْمُنَافِقُونَ كَافِرَانِ .

٣- اِسْمَعِي كَلَامَ الْأُسْتَاذِ يَا سَمِيرُ !     ٤- قَرَأْتُ الْكِتَابُ فِي الْمَكْتَبَةُ .

٥- هَلْ هُوَ أُسْتَاذَةٌ فِي الْجَامِعَةِ ؟     ٦- الْمُدَرِّسُ الْجَدِيدَةُ فِي مَكْتَبِهَا .

٧- أَنْتِ تَفْتَحُ النَّافِذَةَ .     ٨- يَشْرَحُ الْمُعَلِّمَةُ الدَّرْسَ الْجَدِيدَ .

٩- أَكَلَ الْبُرْتُقَالَةَ أَوِ التُّفَّاحَةَ .     ١٠- السَّبُّورَةُ جَدِيدٌ .

\* \* \*

231

10. (Using the Arabic Grammatical Terms): From the list in the shaded box, select the Arabic term to describe each underlined word in the following sentences:

> مَفْعُولٌ بِهِ / فَاعِلٌ /
> صِفَةٌ / ضَمِيرٌ /
> حَرْفُ جَرٍّ /
> جَمْعُ مُذَكَّرٍ سَالِمٌ /
> مُبْتَدَأٌ / خَبَرٌ /
> جَمْعُ مُؤَنَّثٍ سَالِمٌ /
> حَرْفُ اسْتِفْهَامٍ /
> فِعْلٌ مَاضٍ / اسْمٌ مُثَنَّى /
> فِعْلٌ مُضَارِعٌ

١- يَأْمُرُ الْمُدِيرُ الطَّالِبَ أَنْ يَخْرُجَ مِنَ الفَصْلِ .

٢- هَذَا حَمَّامٌ نَظِيفٌ .

٣- الأُسْتَاذُ ذَاهِبٌ إِلَى مَكْتَبَةِ الجَامِعَةِ .

٤- هُوَ عَدُوُّ اللهِ .

٥- الْمُؤْمِنُونَ الصَّالِحُونَ ذَاهِبُونَ إِلَى الْمَسْجِدِ .

٦- تَسْمَعُ الْمَرْأَةُ الْمُؤْمِنَةُ نَصَائِحَ زَوْجِهَا .

٧- هَلْ قَبِلَ الأُسْتَاذُ الْهَدِيَّةَ ؟

٨- الطِّفْلَانِ نَائِمَانِ فِي الْحَافِلَةِ .

٩- الطَّالِبَاتُ النَّاجِحَاتُ سَعِيدَاتٌ .

11. (Identifying the Odd Word): Identify the odd word from each of the following groups of words:

١- كُوبٌ – مِلْعَقَةٌ – إِبْرِيقٌ – فِنْجَانٌ .

٢- مَجَلَّةٌ – كِتَابٌ – جَرِيدَةٌ – قَلَمٌ .

٣- كَتَبَ – دَرَسَ – شَكَرَ – قَرَأَ .

٤- نَافِذَةٌ – بَابٌ – جِدَارٌ – سَرِيرٌ .

٥- تَرْجِعُ – تَكْتُبُ – تَذْهَبُ – تَخْرُجُ .

٦- كَبِيرٌ – صَغِيرٌ – عَصِيرٌ – جَمِيلٌ .

232

٧- وَلَدٌ – بِنْتٌ – طِفْلَةٌ – كَلْبٌ .

٨- أَخٌ – أَبٌ – حِمَارٌ – أُمٌّ .

12. (Unscrambling): Unscramble each set of the following words to make from each a full meaningful sentence:

١- رَاجِعٌ / الزَّائِرُ / الشَّرْقِ الأَوْسَطِ / مِن / هَلْ ؟

................................................................؟

٢- الثَّقِيلَ / أَحْمِلُ / إِلَى / الْغُرْفَةِ / الصَّنْدُوقَ .

................................................................ .

٣- الرَّجُلُ / هَلْ / يَسْكُنُ / فِي / أَمْ / الشَّامِ / فِي / مِصْرَ ؟

................................................................؟

٤- الْمَسْجِدِ / الصَّالِحُ / الْمُسْلِمُ / فِي / الْقُرْآنَ / يَقْرَأُ .

................................................................ .

٥- مَشْهُورَةٌ / الْقَاهِرَةِ / هِيَ / فِي / جَامِعَةِ / أُسْتَاذَةٌ .

................................................................ .

\* \* \*

13. (Translation): Translate the following Arabic sentences into English:

١- هَلْ تَذْكُرِينَ صَدِيقَكِ يَا مَرْيَمُ ؟    ٢- هُوَ لاَ يَفْهَمُ الدَّرْسَ الصَّعْبَ .

٣- تَعْمَلُ الْمُمَرِّضَةُ فِي عِيَادَةِ الطَّبِيبِ .    ٤- الْمُعَلِّمَاتُ ذَاهِبَاتٌ إِلَى الْمَكْتَبَةِ .

٥- أَيْنَ كِتَابُكِ وَدَفْتَرُكِ يَا مُنَى ؟    ٦- نَعَمْ ، أَدْرُسُ فِي جَامِعَةٍ أَمْرِيكِيَّةٍ .

٧- مَنْ قَرَأَ كِتَابَ اللهِ فِي بَيْتِهِ ؟    ٨- رَأَيْتُ الْوَلَدَ يَلْعَبُ فِي الشَّارِعِ .

13. (Translation): Translate the following English sentences into Arabic:

1. The student lives in the house of the (female) professor.

2. Do you (feminine) like to sit on the chair or on the sofa?

3. I have an old car and a new bicycle.

4. Are you (masculine) studying at the Arabic language institute?

5. Yes, she came with me to the classroom.

6. The pupils are playing in the play ground.

7. Did you (feminine) take the book and the pen from the drawer?

\* \* \*

14. (Reading & Comprehension Questions): Read the following short text and then answer the questions that follow:

## التِّلْميذُ الذَّكيُّ

ابْنُ أُخْتي تِلْميذٌ في الْمَدْرَسَةِ الإِبْتِدائِيَّةِ ، وَاسْمُهُ آدَمُ . آدَمُ تِلْميذٌ مُجْتَهِدٌ وَذَكِيٌّ . يَصْحُو مِنْ نَوْمِهِ مُبَكِّرًا في الصَّباحِ ، ثُمَّ يَذْهَبُ إِلَى الْمَدْرَسَةِ . في مَدْرَسَتِهِ يَدْرُسُ آدَمُ الدِّينَ وَالْحِسابَ وَالْعُلومَ وَاللُّغَةَ الْعَرَبِيَّةَ . يَدْخُلُ آدَمُ الْفَصْلَ مُبَكِّرًا ، وَيَكْتُبُ الدَّرْسَ الْجَديدَ مِنَ السَّبُّورَةِ . بَعْدَ ذَلِكَ يَقْرَأُ قِصَّةً قَصيرَةً مِنْ كِتابٍ مُفيدٍ . بَعْدَ الدُّروسِ ، يَشْكُرُ الْمُعَلِّمينَ وَالْمُعَلِّماتِ ، وَيَرْجِعُ إِلَى بَيْتِهِ سَعيدًا .

أَسْئِلَةٌ :

١- مَا اسْمُ ابْنِ أُخْتِي ؟

٢- فِي أَيِّ مَدْرَسَةٍ هُوَ تِلْمِيذٌ ؟

٣- هَلْ هُوَ مُجْتَهِدٌ أَمْ كَسُولٌ ؟

٤- هَلْ هُوَ ذَكِيٌّ أَمْ غَبِيٌّ ؟

٥- مَتَى يَصْحُو مِنْ نَوْمِهِ ؟

٦- إِلَى أَيْنَ يَذْهَبُ فِي الصَّبَاحِ ؟

٧- مَاذَا يَدْرُسُ آدَمُ فِي مَدْرَسَتِهِ ؟

٨- مَاذَا يَكْتُبُ آدَمُ مِنَ السَّبُّورَةِ ؟

٩- مَاذَا يَفْعَلُ بَعْدَ ذَلِكَ ؟

١٠- مَاذَا يَفْعَلُ آدَمُ بَعْدَ الدُّرُوسِ ؟

235

# مُلْحَقاتٌ / Appendices

## Appendix 1:

### Greetings, Courtesy Expressions & Class Management Prompts

|  |  |  |  |
|---|---|---|---|
| And may peace be upon you too /(response) | وَعَلَيْكُمُ السَّلامُ | Peace be upon you | السَّلامُ عَلَيْكُمْ |
| Good morning (response) | صَباحَ النُّور | Good morning | صَباحَ الْخَيْر |
| Good evening (response) | مَساءَ النُّور | Good evening | مَساءَ الْخَيْر |
| Hello and welcome | أَهْلاً وَمَرْحَبا | Hello | مَرْحَبا |
| Thanks much | شُكْرًا جَزيلاً | Welcome | أَهْلاً وَسَهْلاً |
| Pardon, Excuse me | عَفْوًا | You're welcome (response) | عَفْوًا |
| How are you? | كَيْفَ الْحال؟ | Happy occasion | فُرْصَةٌ طَيِّبة |
| | | Fine, well | بِخَيْر ، طَيِّب |
| Please, sit down! | تَفَضَّلْ اِجْلِسْ ! | Kindly proceed, Kindly have or sit | تَفَضَّلْ / تَفَضَّلي |
| With peace, with safety | مَعَ السَّلامَة | Goodbye, till we meet again | إلى اللِّقاء |

\* \* \*

|  |  |  |  |
|---|---|---|---|
| Write! | اُكْتُبْ / اُكْتُبِي / اُكْتُبوا | Read! | اِقْرَأْ / اِقْرَئي / اِقْرَؤوا |
| Be silent! | اُسْكُتْ / اُسْكُتي / اُسْكُتوا | Listen! | اِسْتَمِعْ / اِسْتَمِعي / اِسْتَمِعوا |
| Get out! | اُخْرُجْ / اُخْرُجي / اُخْرُجوا | Study! | اُدْرُسْ / اُدْرُسي / اُدْرُسوا |
| Come here! | تَعالَ / تَعالَيْ / تَعالَوْا | Sit down! | اِجْلِسْ / اِجْلِسي / اِجْلِسوا |
| Give me! | هاتِ / هاتي / هاتوا | Take! | خُذْ / خُذي / خُذوا |

# Appendix 2:

## Arabic Grammatical Terminology

| | | | |
|---|---|---|---|
| Conjunction | حَرْفُ عَطْفٍ | The Alphabet | الْحُرُوفُ الْهِجَائِيَّةُ |
| Expression | تَعْبِير | The Definite Article | أَدَاةُ التَّعْرِيفِ |
| Letter / particle | حَرْفٌ | Interrogative particle | أَدَاةُ الْإِسْتِفْهَامِ |
| Particle | أَدَاةٌ | Noun | إِسْمٌ |
| Gender | جِنْسٌ | Preposition | حَرْفُ جَرٍّ |
| Feminine | مُؤَنَّثٌ | Masculine | مُذَكَّرٌ |
| Singular | مُفْرَد | Number | عَدَدٌ |
| Plural | جَمْعٌ | Dual | مُثَنَّى |
| F. Sound Plural | جَمْعُ مُؤَنَّثٍ سَالِمٍ | M. Sound Plural | جَمْعُ مُذَكَّرٍ سَالِمٍ |
| Detached (Subject) Pronoun | ضَمِيرٌ مُنْفَصِلٌ | Pronoun | ضَمِيرٌ |
| Case-ending | إِعْرَابٌ | (Possessive Pronoun) | ضَمِيرٌ مُتَّصِلٌ |
| Accusative | مَنْصُوبٌ | Nominative | مَرْفُوعٌ |
| Tenses | أَزْمِنَةُ الْأَفْعَالِ | Genitive | مَجْرُورٌ |
| Present Tense | الْمُضَارِعُ / الْحَاضِرُ | Past Tense | الْمَاضِي |
| Speaker = 1st person | مُتَكَلِّمٌ | Imperative (command) | الْأَمْرُ |
| Absentee = 3rd person | غَائِبٌ | Addressee = 2nd person | مُخَاطَبٌ |
| Subject | مُبْتَدَأ | Nominal sentence | جُمْلَةٌ إِسْمِيَّةٌ |

| | | | |
|---|---|---|---|
| Predicate | خَبَرٌ | Verbal Sentence | جُمْلَةٌ فِعْلِيَّةٌ |
| Verb | فِعْلٌ | Subject of a verb | فَاعِلٌ |
| Object of a verb | مَفْعُولٌ بِهِ | Indefinite | نَكِرَةٌ |
| Definite | مَعْرِفَةٌ | Adjective | صِفَةٌ / نَعْتٌ |
| Described noun | مَوْصُوفٌ | Possessive expression | الإِضَافَةُ |
| 2nd Term of *Idaafah* | مُضَافٌ | 1st Term of *Idaafah* | مُضَافٌ إِلَيْهِ |

## Appendix 3:

### Pronouns: Subject Pronouns, Possessive Pronouns & Object Pronouns

**Singular Forms**

| Subject Pronouns | English Equivalent | Possessive Pronouns (Attached to Nouns) | English Equivalent | Object Pronouns (Attached to Verbs) | English Equivalent |
|---|---|---|---|---|---|
| هُوَ | He | كِتَابُهُ (ـهُ) | his book | عَرَفَهُ (ـهُ) | He knew him |
| هِيَ | She | كِتَابُهَا (ـهَا) | her book | عَرَفَهُ (ـهَا) | He knew her |
| أَنْتَ | You (masculine) | كِتَابُكَ (ـكَ) | your book | عَرَفَكَ (ـكَ) | He knew you |
| أَنْتِ | You (feminine) | كِتَابُكِ (ـكِ) | your book | عَرَفَكِ (ـكِ) | He knew you |
| أَنَا | I (masculine+feminine) | كِتَابِي (ـي) | my book | عَرَفَنِي (ـنِي) | He knew me |

**Plural Forms**

| | | | | | |
|---|---|---|---|---|---|
| هُمْ | They (masculine) | كِتَابُهُمْ (ـهُمْ) | their book | عَرَفَهُمْ (ـهُمْ) | He knew them |
| هُنَّ | They (feminine) | كِتَابُهُنَّ (ـهُنَّ) | their book | عَرَفَهُنَّ (ـهُنَّ) | He knew them |
| أَنْتُمْ | You (masculine) | كِتَابُكُمْ (ـكُمْ) | your book | عَرَفَكُمْ (ـكُمْ) | He knew you |
| أَنْتُنَّ | You (feminine) | كِتَابُكُنَّ (ـكُنَّ) | your book | عَرَفَكُنَّ (ـكُنَّ) | He knew you |
| نَحْنُ | We (masculine+feminine) | كِتَابُنَا (ـنَا) | our book | عَرَفَنَا (ـنَا) | He knew us |

**Dual Forms** (Specifically two in number)

| | | | | | |
|---|---|---|---|---|---|
| هُمَا | They (masculine) | كِتَابُهُمَا (ـهُمَا) | their book | عَرَفَهُمَا (ـهُمَا) | He knew them |
| هُمَا | They (feminine) | كِتَابُهُمَا (ـهُمَا) | their book | عَرَفَهُمَا (ـهُمَا) | He knew them |
| أَنْتُمَا | We (masculine + feminine) | كِتَابُكُمَا (ـكُمَا) | your book | عَرَفَكُمَا (ـكُمَا) | He knew you |

# Appendix 4:

## PREPOSITIONS and ADVERBS OF PLACE & TIME

| Preposition / Adverb of Place or Time | English Meaning | Used in a Sentence |
|---|---|---|
| إِلَى | to | حَضَرَ الطَّالِبُ إِلَى الْمَدْرَسَةِ . |
| بِـ | with, by | كَتَبَ الْجُمْلَةَ بِالْقَلَمِ . |
| عَلَى | on | الْكِتَابُ عَلَى الطَّاوِلَةِ . |
| عَنْ | about | كَتَبَ كِتَاباً عَنْ تَارِيخِ أَمْرِيكَا . |
| فِي | in, at | الْأُسْتَاذُ فِي الْمَكْتَبِ . |
| كَـ | as, like | الْوَقْتُ كَالسَّيْفِ إِنْ لَمْ تَقْطَعْهُ قَطَعَكَ . |
| لِـ | for, belongs to | هَذَا الْكِتَابُ لِخَالِدٍ . |
| مِنْ | from | الطَّالِبَةُ الْجَدِيدَةُ مِنَ الْكُوَيْتِ . |

| ADVERBS | ADVERBS | ADVERBS |
|---|---|---|
| أَمَامَ | in front of | مَرْيَمُ أَمَامَ بَابِ الْمَتْحَفِ . |
| بَعْدَ | after | حَضَرَ بَعْدَ الظُّهْرِ . |
| تَحْتَ | under, beneath | الْقَلَمُ تَحْتَ الْكِتَابِ . |
| خَلْفَ | behind | الْمَكْتَبَةُ خَلْفَ الْمَتْحَفِ . |
| فَوْقَ | above, on top of | مَكْتَبُ الْمُدِيرِ فَوْقَ مَكْتَبِ السِّكْرِتِيرَة . |
| قَبْلَ | before | حَضَرَتْ قَبْلَ الظُّهْرِ . |
| مَعَ | with | ذَهَبْتُ مَعَ الْأُسْتَاذِ إِلَى الْمَطْعَمِ . |

**Important Note:** *Adverbs of Time* or *Place* function like *Prepositions* in taking the nouns after them as "**objects**". The "**objects**" of *Adverbs* and *Prepositions* are in the "*Genitive Case-Ending*".

\* \* \*

# Appendix 5:

## ARABIC-SPEAKING STATES, NATIONALITIES & CAPITAL CITIES

| State Name | Related Nationality | Capital City | English Equivalent |
|---|---|---|---|
| الْأُرْدُنّ | أُرْدُنِّيّ \ أُرْدُنِّيَّة | عَمَّان | Jordan / Amman |
| الْإِمَارَاتُ الْعَرَبِيَّةُ الْمُتَّحِدَةُ | إِمَارَاتِيّ \ إِمَارَاتِيَّة | أَبُو ظَبْي | United Arab Emirates / Abu Dhabi |
| الْبَحْرَين | بَحْرَينِيّ \ بَحْرَينِيَّة | الْمَنَامَة | Bahrain / Manama |
| الْجَزَائِر | جَزَائِرِيّ \ جَزَائِرِيَّة | الْجَزَائِر | Algeria / Algeria |
| السَّعُودِيَّة | سَعُودِيّ \ سَعُودِيَّة | الرِّيَاض | Saudi Arabia / Riyadh |
| السُّودَان | سُودَانِيّ \ سُودَانِيَّة | الْخَرْطُوم | Sudan / Khartoum |
| الْعِرَاق | عِرَاقِيّ \ عِرَاقِيَّة | بَغْدَاد | Iraq / Baghdad |
| الْكُوَيْت | كُوَيْتِيّ \ كُوَيْتِيَّة | الْكُوَيْت | Kuwait / Kuwait |
| الْمَغْرِب | مَغْرِبِيّ \ مَغْرِبِيَّة | الرِّبَاط | Morocco / Rabat |
| الْيَمَن | يَمَنِيّ \ يَمَنِيَّة | صَنْعَاء | Yemen / San'a |
| تُونِس | تُونِسِيّ \ تُونِسِيَّة | تُونِس | Tunisia / Tunis |
| سُورْيَا | سُورِيّ \ سُورِيَّة | دِمَشْق | Syria / Damascus |
| عُمَان | عُمَانِيّ \ عُمَانِيَّة | مَسْقَط | Oman / Masqat |

| | | | |
|---|---|---|---|
| فِلِسْطين | فِلِسْطينيّ \ فِلِسْطينيّة | الْقُدْس | Palestine / Jerusalem |
| قَطَر | قَطَريّ \ قَطَريّة | الدَّوْحَة | Qatar / Doha |
| لُبْنَان | لُبْنَانيّ \ لُبْنَانيّة | بَيْروت | Lebanon / Beirut |
| لِيبْيَا | لِيبيّ \ لِيبيّة | طَرَابلُس | Libya / Tripoli |
| مِصْر | مِصْريّ \ مِصْريَّة | الْقَاهِرَة | Egypt / Cairo |

\* \* \*

## Appendix 6:

**THE MONTHS OF THE YEAR ACCORDING TO THREE CALENDAR SYSTEMS, THE DAYS OF THE WEEK & THE FOUR SEASONS OF THE YEAR**

| Syriac Origin Calendar Months | Arabized Gregorian Calendar Months | Islamic Calendar Months | Numerical Order |
|---|---|---|---|
| كَانُونُ الثَّاني | يَنَايِر | مُحَرَّم | 1 |
| شُبَاط | فِبْرَايِر | صَفَر | 2 |
| آذَار | مَارْس | رَبِيعُ الأَوَّل | 3 |
| نِيسَان | أَبْرِيل | رَبِيعُ الثَّاني | 4 |
| أَيَّار | مَايُو | جُمَادَى الأُولَى | 5 |
| حُزَيْرَان | يُونْيُو | جُمَادَى الثَّانية | 6 |
| تَمُّوز | يُولْيُو | رَجَب | 7 |

| | | | |
|---|---|---|---|
| آب | أَغُسْطُس | شَعْبَان | 8 |
| أَيْلُول | سِبْتِمْبَر | رَمَضَان | 9 |
| تَشْرِينُ الأَوَّل | أُكْتُوبَر | شَوَّال | 10 |
| تَشْرِينُ الثَّانِي | نُوفِمْبَر | ذُو الْقِعْدَة | 11 |
| كَانُونُ الأَوَّل | دِيسَمْبَر | ذُو الْحِجَّة | 12 |

| | | | |
|---|---|---|---|
| السَّبْتُ Saturday | الأَحَدُ Sunday | الإِثْنَيْن Monday | الثُّلَاثَاءُ Tuesday |
| الأَرْبِعَاءُ Wednesday | الْخَمِيسُ Thursday | الْجُمُعَةُ Friday | |

| | |
|---|---|
| الصَّيْفُ Summer | الْخَرِيفُ Fall, Autumn |
| الشِّتَاءُ Winter | الرَّبِيعُ Spring |

# Appendix 7:

## PAST TENSE (PERFECT) CONJUGATION CHART

| English Equivalent | Subject-Marker Suffix | Verb Form | Corresponding Pronoun |
|---|---|---|---|
| *Singular Forms* | *Singular Forms* | *Singular Forms* | *Singular Forms* |
| He studied. | above last letter (*a*) | دَرَسَ | هُوَ |
| She studied. | ـَتْ (*at*) | دَرَسَتْ | هِيَ |
| You studied. (*masculine*) | ـْتَ (*ta*) | دَرَسْتَ | أَنْتَ |
| You studied. (*feminine*) | ـْتِ (*ti*) | دَرَسْتِ | أَنْتِ |
| I studied. (*masculine & feminine*) | ـْتُ (*tu*) | دَرَسْتُ | أَنَا |
| *Plural Forms* | *Plural Forms* | *Plural Forms* | *Plural Forms* |
| They studied. (*masculine*) | ـُوا (*uu*) | دَرَسُوا | هُمْ |
| They studied. (*feminine*) | ـْنَ (*na*) | دَرَسْنَ | هُنَّ |
| You studied. (*masculine*) | ـْتُمْ (*tum*) | دَرَسْتُمْ | أَنْتُمْ |
| You studied. (*feminine*) | ـْتُنَّ (*tunna*) | دَرَسْتُنَّ | أَنْتُنَّ |
| We studied. (*masculine & feminine*) | ـْنَا (*naa*) | دَرَسْنَا | نَحْنُ |

| Dual Forms | Dual Forms | Dual Forms | Dual Forms |
|---|---|---|---|
| They studied. (two males) | ـَا (aa) | دَرَسَا | هُمَا |
| They studied. (two females) | ـَتَا (ataa) | دَرَسَتَا | هُمَا |
| You studied. (two males or females) | ـْتُمَا (tumaa) | دَرَسْتُمَا | أَنْتُمَا |

# Appendix 8:

### VERB CONJUGATION CHART: PRESENT INDICATIVE *

| Corresponding Pronoun | Mood Marker | Subject Marker Suffix | Subject Marker Prefix | Verb Form |
|---|---|---|---|---|

### Singular Forms

| Corresponding Pronoun | Mood Marker | Subject Marker Suffix | Subject Marker Prefix | Verb Form |
|---|---|---|---|---|
| هُوَ | ـُ above the last radical | | يـَ | يَدْرُسُ |
| هِيَ | ـُ above the last radical | | تـَ | تَدْرُسُ |
| أَنْتَ | ـُ above the last radical | | تـَ | تَدْرُسُ |
| أَنْتِ | نَ | ـِينَ | تـَ | تَدْرُسِينَ |
| أَنَا | ـُ above the last radical | | أَ | أَدْرُسُ |

247

**Plural Forms**

| | | | | |
|---|---|---|---|---|
| هُمْ | نَ | ـُو | يَـ | يَدْرُسُونَ |
| هُنَّ | No mood marker | ـنَ | يَـ | يَدْرُسْنَ |
| أَنْتُمْ | نَ | ـُو | تَـ | تَدْرُسُونَ |
| أَنْتُنَّ | No mood marker | ـنَ | تَـ | تَدْرُسْنَ |
| نَحْنُ | ـُ above the last radical | | نَـ | نَدْرُسُ |

**Dual Forms**

| | | | | |
|---|---|---|---|---|
| هُمَا (Mas.) | نِ | ـا | يَـ | يَدْرُسَانِ |
| هُمَا (Fem.) | نِ | ـا | تَـ | تَدْرُسَانِ |
| أَنْتُمَا (Mas. + Fem.) | نِ | ـا | تَـ | تَدْرُسَانِ |

**Note**: **Present** (**Imperfect**) **Indicative** verbs correspond to English **Simple Present** or to **Progressive Constructions** with "*is / are / am*" and a verb in the "*...ing*" form; such as: *He studies*, *They study*, *She is studying*, *I am studying*.

\* \* \*

# Appendix 9:

## NUMERALS: Cardinal, Ordinal, Multiples of Ten

| Cardinal Numbers | Ordinal Numbers | Multiple of Tens Numbers |
|---|---|---|
| وَاحِد = one | الأَوَّلُ / الأُولَى = the first | |
| إِثْنَان = two | الثَّانِي / الثَّانِيَةُ = the second | عِشْرُونَ / عِشْرِينَ = twenty |
| ثَلاثَة = three | الثَّالِثُ / الثَّالِثَةُ = the third | ثَلاثُونَ / ثَلاثِينَ = thirty |
| أَرْبَعَة = four | الرَّابِعُ / الرَّابِعَةُ = the fourth | أَرْبَعُونَ / أَرْبَعِينَ = forty |
| خَمْسَة = five | الْخَامِسُ / الْخَامِسَةُ = the fifth | خَمْسُونَ / خَمْسِينَ = fifty |
| سِتَّة = six | السَّادِسُ / السَّادِسَةُ = the sixth | سِتُّونَ / سِتِّينَ = sixty |
| سَبْعَة = seven | السَّابِعُ / السَّابِعَةُ = the seventh | سَبْعُونَ / سَبْعِينَ = seventy |
| ثَمَانِيَة = eight | الثَّامِنُ / الثَّامِنَةُ = the eighth | ثَمَانُونَ / ثَمَانِينَ = eighty |
| تِسْعَة = nine | التَّاسِعُ / التَّاسِعَةُ = the ninth | تِسْعُونَ / تِسْعِينَ = ninety |
| عَشَرَة = ten | الْعَاشِرُ / الْعَاشِرَةُ = the tenth | مِئَةٌ = one hundred |
| | | أَلْفٌ = one thousand |

| | | |
|---|---|---|
| | الْحَادِي عَشَرَ / الْحَادِيَة عَشْرَةَ | أَحَدَ عَشَرَ = 11 |
| | الثَّانِي عَشَرَ / الثَّانِيَة عَشْرَةَ | إِثْنَا عَشَرَ = 12 |
| | الثَّالِثَ عَشَرَ / الثَّالِثَة عَشْرَةَ | ثَلَاثَةَ عَشَرَ = 13 |
| | الرَّابِعَ عَشَرَ / الرَّابِعَة عَشْرَةَ | أَرْبَعَةَ عَشَرَ = 14 |
| | الْخَامِسَ عَشَرَ / الْخَامِسَةَ عَشْرَةَ | خَمْسَةَ عَشَرَ = 15 |
| | السَّادِسَ عَشَرَ / السَّادِسَةَ عَشْرَةَ | سِتَّةَ عَشَرَ = 16 |
| | السَّابِعَ عَشَرَ / السَّابِعَةَ عَشْرَةَ | سَبْعَةَ عَشَرَ = 17 |

| | | |
|---|---|---|
| | الثَّامِنَ عَشَرَ / الثَّامِنَةَ عَشْرَةَ | ثَمَانِيَةَ عَشَرَ = 18 |
| | التَّاسِعَ عَشَرَ / التَّاسِعَةَ عَشْرَةَ | تِسْعَةَ عَشَرَ = 19 |
| | الْعِشْرُونَ | عِشْرُونَ = 20 |
| | الْحَادِي وَالْعِشْرُونَ / الْحَادِيَةُ وَالْعِشْرُونَ | وَاحِدٌ وَعِشْرُونَ = 21 |
| | الثَّانِي وَالْعِشْرُونَ / الثَّانِيَةُ وَالْعِشْرُونَ | إِثْنَانِ وَعِشْرُونَ = 22 |
| | الثَّالِثُ وَالْعِشْرُونَ / الثَّالِثَةُ وَالْعِشْرُونَ | ثَلَاثَةٌ وَعِشْرُونَ = 23 |

| | |
|---|---|
| أَرْبَعَةٌ وَعِشْرُونَ    الرَّابِعَةُ وَالْعِشْرُونَ / الرَّابِعُ وَالْعِشْرُونَ | 24 = |
| خَمْسَةٌ وَعِشْرُونَ    الْخَامِسَةُ وَالْعِشْرُونَ / الْخَامِسُ وَالْعِشْرُونَ | 25 = |
| سِتَّةٌ وَعِشْرُونَ    السَّادِسَةُ وَالْعِشْرُونَ / السَّادِسُ وَالْعِشْرُونَ | 26 = |
| سَبْعَةٌ وَعِشْرُونَ    السَّابِعَةُ وَالْعِشْرُونَ / السَّابِعُ وَالْعِشْرُونَ | 27 = |
| ثَمَانِيَةٌ وَعِشْرُونَ    الثَّامِنَةُ وَالْعِشْرُونَ / الثَّامِنُ وَالْعِشْرُونَ | 28 = |
| تِسْعَةٌ وَعِشْرُونَ    التَّاسِعَةُ وَالْعِشْرُونَ / التَّاسِعُ وَالْعِشْرُونَ | 29 = |
| ثَلَاثُونَ       الثَّلَاثُونَ = the thirtieth | 30 = |

# Appendix 10:

## English-Arabic Glossary

| | | | |
|---|---|---|---|
| absent | غَائِبٌ | bag | حَقِيبَةٌ |
| accepted (he) | قَبِلَ | baker | خَبَّازٌ |
| accused | مُتَّهَمٌ | barber | حَلَّاقٌ |
| active | نَشِيطٌ | banana | مَوْزَةٌ |
| airplane | طَائِرَةٌ | bathroom | حَمَّامٌ |
| African | إِفْرِيقِيٌّ | beautiful | جَمِيل |
| airport | مَطَارٌ | bed | سَرِيرٌ |
| American | أَمْرِيكِيّ | believer | مُؤْمِنٌ |
| angry | غَاضِبٌ | bicycle | دَرَّاجَةٌ |
| animal | حَيَوَانٌ | big | كَبِيرٌ |
| ant | نَمْلَةٌ | bird | طَائِرٌ |
| apartment | شَقَّةٌ | book | كِتَابٌ |
| apple | تُفَّاحَةٌ | bottle | زُجَاجَةٌ |
| Arab / Arabic | عَرَبِيٌّ | box | صُنْدُوقٌ |
| article | مَقَالَةٌ | boy | وَلَدٌ |
| asked (he) | سَأَلَ | bread | خُبْزٌ |
| at | عِنْدَ ، فِي | broken | مَكْسُورٌ |
| ate (he) | أَكَلَ | brother | أَخٌ |
| author | مُؤَلِّفٌ | bus | حَافِلَةٌ |
|  |  | busy | مَشْغُولٌ |
| camel | جَمَلٌ | cunning | مَاكِرٌ |
| car | سَيَّارَةٌ | cupboard | خِزَانَةٌ |
| carpenter | نَجَّارٌ | cup | فِنْجَانٌ |
| carried (he) | حَمَلَ | day | يَوْمٌ |

| | | | |
|---|---|---|---|
| cat | هِرٌّ ، قِطٌّ | desk | مَكْتَبٌ |
| center | مَرْكَزٌ | dictionary | قَامُوسٌ |
| chair | كُرْسِيٌّ | difficult | صَعْبٌ |
| chalkboard | سَبُّورَةٌ ، لَوْحٌ | dirty | وَسِخٌ |
| cheap | رَخِيصٌ | disbeliever | كَافِرٌ |
| child | طِفْلٌ | doctor | طَبِيبٌ |
| church | كَنِيسَةٌ | dog | كَلْبٌ |
| city | مَدِينَةٌ | donkey | حِمَارٌ |
| classroom | صَفٌّ ، فَصْلٌ | door | بَابٌ |
| clean | نَظِيفٌ | drank (he) | شَرِبَ |
| clever | ذَكِيٌّ | drawer | دُرْجٌ |
| closed | مُغْلَقٌ | dress | فُسْتَانٌ |
| cold | بَارِدٌ | driver | سَائِقٌ |
| coming | قَادِمٌ | dull | غَبِيٌّ |
| company | شَرِكَةٌ | easy | سَهْلٌ |
| condition | حَالٌ | Egyptian | مِصْرِيٌّ |
| cook | طَبَّاخٌ | emigrant | مُهَاجِرٌ |
| criminal | مُجْرِمٌ | employee | مُوَظَّفٌ |
| cultured person | مُثَقَّفٌ | enemy | عَدُوٌّ |
| engineer | مُهَنْدِسٌ | good | جَيِّدٌ |
| entered (he) | دَخَلَ | going | ذَاهِبٌ |
| evening | مَسَاءٌ | going out | خَارِجٌ |
| examination | إِمْتِحَانٌ ، إِخْتِبَارٌ | governor | حَاكِمٌ |
| excellent | مُمْتَازٌ | grandfather | جَدٌّ |
| factory | مَصْنَعٌ | grandson | حَفِيدٌ |
| failed (he) | فَشِلَ | hall | صَالَةٌ |
| family | أُسْرَةٌ ، عَائِلَةٌ | happy | سَعِيدٌ ، مَسْرُورٌ |

253

| | | | |
|---|---|---|---|
| famous | مَشْهُورٌ | hardworking | مُجْتَهِدٌ |
| farmer | فَلَّاحٌ | he | هُوَ |
| fat | سَمِينٌ | headmaster | مُدِيرٌ |
| father | أَبٌ | health | صِحَّةٌ |
| file | مِلَفٌّ | heard (he) | سَمِعَ |
| fine | طَيِّبٌ ، بِخَيْرٍ | heavy | ثَقِيلٌ |
| food | طَعَامٌ | honest | أَمِينٌ ، شَرِيفٌ |
| fridge | ثَلَّاجَةٌ | horse | حِصَانٌ |
| friend | صَدِيقٌ | hot | حَارٌّ |
| friendly | وَدُودٌ ، أَنِيسٌ | hotel | فُنْدُقٌ |
| from | مِنْ | house | بَيْتٌ ، دَارٌ |
| garden | حَدِيقَةٌ | how? | كَيْفَ ؟ |
| gift | هَدِيَّةٌ | humble | مُتَوَاضِعٌ |
| girl | بِنْتٌ ، فَتَاةٌ | husband | زَوْجٌ |
| glass | كُوبٌ ، كَأْسٌ | hypocrite | مُنَافِقٌ |
| I | أَنَا | letter | رِسَالَةٌ ، خِطَابٌ |
| in | فِي | library | مَكْتَبَةٌ |
| inactive | خَامِلٌ ، كَسُولٌ | Libyan | لِيبِيٌّ |
| industrious | مُجْتَهِدٌ ، مُجِدٌّ | light | خَفِيفٌ |
| inspector | مُفَتِّشٌ | listener | مُسْتَمِعٌ |
| institute | مَعْهَدٌ | lived (he) | سَكَنَ |
| Iraqi | عِرَاقِيٌّ | looked (he) | نَظَرَ |
| island | جَزِيرَةٌ | man | رَجُلٌ |
| journalist | صِحَافِيٌّ | many | كَثِيرٌ |
| juice | عَصِيرٌ | map | خَرِيطَةٌ |
| jug | إِبْرِيقٌ | market | سُوقٌ |

| | | | |
|---|---|---|---|
| just | عَادِلٌ | married | مُتَزَوِّجٌ |
| key | مِفْتَاحٌ | merchant | تَاجِرٌ |
| knew (he) | عَرَفَ | messenger | رَسُولٌ |
| knife | سِكِّينٌ | milk | لَبَنٌ ، حَلِيبٌ |
| Kuwaiti | كُوَيْتِيٌّ | month | شَهْرٌ |
| laboratory | مَعْمَلٌ ، مُخْتَبَرٌ | mosque | مَسْجِدٌ |
| lady | سَيِّدَةٌ | mother | أُمٌّ ، وَالِدَةٌ |
| language | لُغَةٌ | Muslim | مُسْلِمٌ |
| laughing | ضَاحِكٌ | name | إِسْمٌ |
| lecture | مُحَاضَرَةٌ | narrow | ضَيِّقٌ |
| lecturer | مُحَاضِرٌ | new | جَدِيدٌ |
| lesson | دَرْسٌ | news | أَخْبَارٌ |
| news item | خَبَرٌ | present | حَاضِرٌ ، مَوْجُودٌ |
| newspaper | جَرِيدَةٌ | profession | مِهْنَةٌ |
| night | لَيْلَةٌ | professor | أُسْتَاذٌ |
| noble | كَرِيمٌ ، نَبِيلٌ | pupil | تِلْمِيذٌ |
| notebook | دَفْتَرٌ ، كُرَّاسَةٌ | question | سُؤَالٌ |
| nurse | مُمَرِّضٌ | rain | مَطَرٌ |
| obedient | مُطِيعٌ | rainy | مُمْطِرٌ |
| opened (he) | فَتَحَ | read (he) | قَرَأَ |
| on | عَلَى | remembered (he) | ذَكَرَ |
| orange | بُرْتُقَالَةٌ | religion | دِينٌ |
| outstanding | مُتَفَوِّقٌ | religious | دِينِيٌّ ، مُتَدَيِّنٌ |
| parcel | طَرْدٌ | respectful | مُحْتَرَمٌ |
| park | حَدِيقَةٌ عَامَّةٌ | restaurant | مَطْعَمٌ |
| partner | شَرِيكٌ | returned (he) | رَجَعَ |

255

| | | | |
|---|---|---|---|
| pen | قَلَمٌ | returning | رَاجِعٌ |
| photographer | مُصَوِّرٌ | rich | غَنِيٌّ |
| plate | صَحْنٌ | ring | خَاتَمٌ |
| pleasant | لَطِيفٌ | river | نَهْرٌ |
| poet | شَاعِرٌ | rode (he) | رَكِبَ |
| polite | مُهَذَّبٌ | room | غُرْفَةٌ ، حُجْرَةٌ |
| polytheist | مُشْرِكٌ | rubber | مِمْسَحَةٌ |
| poor | فَقِيرٌ | ruler | مِسْطَرَةٌ |
| pot | قِدْرٌ | ruler | حَاكِمٌ |
| sad | حَزِينٌ | speaker | مُتَكَلِّمٌ |
| sat (he) | جَلَسَ | spoon | مِلْعَقَةٌ |
| school | مَدْرَسَةٌ | standing | وَاقِفٌ |
| Saudi | سَعُودِيٌّ | station | مَحَطَّةٌ |
| servant | خَادِمٌ | stingy | بَخِيلٌ |
| she | هِيَ | street | شَارِعٌ |
| shelf | رَفٌّ | strong | قَوِيٌّ |
| shirt | قَمِيصٌ | student | طَالِبٌ |
| shop | دُكَّانٌ | studied (he) | دَرَسَ |
| short | قَصِيرٌ | subject (grammar) | فَاعِلٌ ، مُبْتَدَأٌ |
| sick | مَرِيضٌ | subject | مَوْضُوعٌ |
| sincere | مُخْلِصٌ | succeeded (he) | نَجَحَ |
| sister | أُخْتٌ | successful | نَاجِحٌ |
| sitting | جَالِسٌ | table | طَاوِلَةٌ ، مَائِدَةٌ |
| skilful | مَاهِرٌ | tailor | خَيَّاطٌ |
| skirt | تَنُّورَةٌ | tall | طَوِيلٌ |
| slave | عَبْدٌ | tea | شَايٌ |
| sleeping | نَائِمٌ | teacher | مُدَرِّسٌ ، مُعَلِّمٌ |
| smiling | مُبْتَسِمٌ | test | إِخْتِبَارٌ ، إِمْتِحَانٌ |

| | | | |
|---|---|---|---|
| son | إِبْنٌ | thanked (he) | شَكَرَ |
| sound (noun) | صَوْتٌ | thankful | شَاكِرٌ |
| sound (adjective) | سَلِيمٌ | that | ذَلِكَ / تِلْكَ |
| South Africa | جَنُوبُ إِفْرِيقْيَا | then | ثُمَّ |
| they (m/f) | هُمْ / هُنَّ | well-mannered | مُؤَدَّبٌ |
| thin | نَحِيفٌ | went (he) | ذَهَبَ |
| this (m/f) | هَذا / هَذِه | went out (he) | خَرَجَ |
| to | إِلَى | when…? | مَتَى ….? |
| took (he) | أَخَذَ | who…? | مَنْ ….? |
| towards | إِلَى | why…? | لِمَاذَا ….? |
| translator | مُتَرْجِمٌ | wide | وَاسِعٌ |
| traveler | مُسَافِرٌ | wife | زَوْجَةٌ |
| truthful | صَادِقٌ | window | شُبَّاكٌ |
| Tunisian | تُونِسِيٌّ | woman | امْرَأَةٌ |
| ugly | قَبِيحٌ | word | كَلِمَةٌ |
| uncle (paternal) | عَمٌّ | writer | كَاتِبٌ |
| uncle (maternal) | خَالٌ | year | عَامٌ ، سَنَةٌ |
| understood (he) | فَهِمَ | you (f) | أَنْتِ |
| useful | نَافِعٌ | you (pl. m.) | أَنْتُمْ |
| village | قَرْيَةٌ | you (pl. f.) | أَنْتُنَّ |
| voice | صَوْتٌ | zealous | مُتَحَمِّسٌ |
| waiting | مُنْتَظِرٌ | zero | صِفْرٌ |
| watch | سَاعَةٌ | zoo | حَدِيقَةُ حَيَوَانَاتٍ |
| watermelon | بَطِّيخٌ | | |
| weak | ضَعِيفٌ | | |
| well | حَسَنًا ، بِخَيْرٍ | | |